EMPOWERING EDUCATORS

Insights from Succession Planning
to Classroom Management

EMPOWERING EDUCATORS

Insights from Succession Planning to Classroom Management

Editors

Kazi Enamul Hoque
University of Malaya, Malaysia

Ahmad Zabidi Abdul Razak
University of Malaya, Malaysia

Intan Marfarrina Omar
University of Malaya, Malaysia

World Scientific

NEW JERSEY · LONDON · SINGAPORE · BEIJING · SHANGHAI · TAIPEI · CHENNAI

Published by

World Scientific Publishing Co. Pte. Ltd.
5 Toh Tuck Link, Singapore 596224
USA office: 27 Warren Street, Suite 401-402, Hackensack, NJ 07601
UK office: 57 Shelton Street, Covent Garden, London WC2H 9HE

Library of Congress Cataloging-in-Publication Data
Names: Hoque, Kazi Enamul, editor. | Razak, Ahmad Zabidi Abdul, editor. |
   Omar, Intan Marfarrina, editor.
Title: Empowering educators : insights from succession planning to classroom management /
   Editors Hoque Kazi Enamul, University of Malaya, Malaysia, Ahmad Zabidi Abdul Razak,
   University of Malaya, Malaysia, Intan Marfarrina Omar, University of Malaya, Malaysia.
Description: Hackensack, NJ : World Scientific, [2025] |
   Includes bibliographical references and index.
Identifiers: LCCN 2024044673 | ISBN 9789811294723 (hardcover) |
   ISBN 9789811294730 (ebook) | ISBN 9789811294747 (ebook other)
Subjects: LCSH: School management and organization--Malaysia. | School management
   and organization. | Educational planning--Malaysia. | Educational planning. |
   Classroom management--Malaysia. | Classroom management. |
   Teacher-administrator relationships. | Education--Effect of technological innovations on.
Classification: LCC LB2965.M4 E47 2025 | DDC 371.2009595--dc23/eng/20241018
LC record available at https://lccn.loc.gov/2024044673

British Library Cataloguing-in-Publication Data
A catalogue record for this book is available from the British Library.

Copyright © 2025 by World Scientific Publishing Co. Pte. Ltd.

All rights reserved. This book, or parts thereof, may not be reproduced in any form or by any means, electronic or mechanical, including photocopying, recording or any information storage and retrieval system now known or to be invented, without written permission from the publisher.

For photocopying of material in this volume, please pay a copying fee through the Copyright Clearance Center, Inc., 222 Rosewood Drive, Danvers, MA 01923, USA. In this case permission to photocopy is not required from the publisher.

For any available supplementary material, please visit
https://www.worldscientific.com/worldscibooks/10.1142/13886#t=suppl

Desk Editors: Nambirajan Karuppiah/Pui Yee Lum

Typeset by Stallion Press
Email: enquiries@stallionpress.com

ured journals. His diverse areas of expertise include human resources
© 2025 World Scientific Publishing Company
https://doi.org/10.1142/9789811294730_fmatter

About the Editors

Kazi Enamul Hoque is an associate professor at the Department of Educational Management, Planning, and Policy, Faculty of Education, Universiti Malaya. He has garnered 24 years of teaching experience at various national and international educational institutes. He is the author of six books and 70 full-length research articles in high-impact, peer-reviewed journals. His diverse areas of expertise include human resources in education, leadership, student health, and educational management.

Ahmad Zabidi Abdul Razak is a professor at the Department of Educational Management, Planning, and Policy, Faculty of Education, Universiti Malaya. He is currently the dean, Faculty of Education, Universiti Malaya. He is a former director of the Corporate Performance Centre (CPC), deputy dean of the Research Cluster (Social Advancement and Happiness), deputy dean (Research and Development), Faculty of Education, and head of department (Educational Management, Planning, and Policy), Faculty of Education. He received his bachelor's and master's degrees from Universiti Malaya and his PhD from Massey University, New Zealand. His area of specialization is human resource management in education.

Intan Marfarrina Omar is a senior lecturer at the Department of Educational Management, Planning, and Policy, Faculty of Education, Universiti Malaya. She is actively involved in research and journal writing in the field of industrial and organizational psychology, with a special focus on organizational behavior and educational leadership. In her five years of research experience, she received grants from the Ministry of Higher Education and Universiti Malaya.

About the Contributors

Ahmed Faisal has been working as a principal at a secondary school in the Maldives. He has completed his master's in education management from the Faculty of Education, University of Malaya. He is an expert in the areas of human resource management in education, education management, and educational leadership.

Zihui Fang has done her master's degree in Education Management at the Faculty of Education, University of Malaya. She works with educational human resource management, education management, and educational leadership. With a good academic record and core competences in these areas, she is dedicated to the promotion of research and best practices in education. Beyond academics, it is through her engagement in a wide range of regional social development initiatives, such as community building and educational reforms.

Muhammad Faizal A. Ghani is an Associate Professor in the Department of Educational Management, Administration, and Policy at the Faculty of Education, University of Malaya. His expertise lies in educational leadership, with a focus on educational management, administration, and school finance. He has contributed to academia through 9 books and 200 articles, with his latest book titled *Professional Learning Communities: Theories and Practices*. He has also been invited as a keynote and guest speaker at various international and national conferences, seminars, and workshops.

Ahmed Habeeb has been working as a principal at a secondary school in the Maldives. He has completed his master's in education management from the Faculty of Education, University of Malaya. He is an expert in the areas of human resource management in education, education management, and educational leadership.

Miss Hamdhiyya has been working as a teacher at a secondary school in the Maldives. She has completed her master's in education management from the Faculty of Education, University of Malaya. She is an expert in the areas of human resource management in education, education management, and educational leadership.

Rafiu Jameel has been working as a vice principal at a secondary school in the Maldives. He has completed his master's in education management from the Faculty of Education, University of Malaya. He is an expert in the areas of human resource management in education, education management, and educational leadership.

Shifaz Mohamed has been working as a principal at a secondary school in the Maldives. He has completed his master's in education management from the Faculty of Education, University of Malaya. He is an expert in the areas of human resource management in education, education management, and educational leadership.

Aishath Nadhiya has been working as an assistant principal at a secondary school in the Maldives. She has completed her master's in education management from the Faculty of Education, University of Malaya. She is an expert in the areas of human resource management in education, education management, and educational leadership.

Yang Yang Zhao is a PhD student at the Faculty of Education, University of Malaya. She is an expert in the areas of human resource management in education, education management, and educational leadership.

© 2025 World Scientific Publishing Company
https://doi.org/10.1142/9789811294730_fmatter

Contents

About the Editors		v
About the Contributors		vii
Chapter 1	Teachers' Succession Planning and School Progress *Kazi Enamul Hoque and Zihui Fang*	1
Chapter 2	Teachers' Collective Bargaining and Unionization in Education *Ahmed Habeeb and Ahmad Zabidi bin Abdul Razak*	19
Chapter 3	Best Practices for Vocational Teacher Training *Shifaz Mohamed and Ahmad Zabidi bin Abdul Razak*	35
Chapter 4	Revamping Curriculum Management: Approach for Educators *Miss Hamdhiyya and Kazi Enamul Hoque*	61
Chapter 5	School Management's Roles and Social Justice *Aishath Nadhiya and Kazi Enamul Hoque*	83
Chapter 6	Teachers' Performance Appraisal and Classroom Improvement *Ahmed Faisal and Intan Marfarrina Omar*	99
Chapter 7	Teachers' Motivation and Job Performance *Rafiu Jameel and Intan Marfarrina Omar*	115

Chapter 8	Human Resource Leaders in a Post-COVID-19 Era *Ahmad Zabidi bin Abdul Razak*	127
Chapter 9	Extrinsic Benefits and Teacher Retention *Kazi Enamul Hoque*	135
Chapter 10	Classroom Management and Teachers' Practices *Yang Yang Zhao, Kazi Enamul Hoque, and Intan Marfarrina Omar*	151
Chapter 11	Homework and Teachers' Responsibilities *Yang Yang Zhao, Muhammad Faizal Bin A. Ghani, and Kazi Enamul Hoque*	173

Index   189

© 2025 World Scientific Publishing Company
https://doi.org/10.1142/9789811294730_0001

Chapter 1

Teachers' Succession Planning and School Progress

Kazi Enamul Hoque* and Zihui Fang[†]

Faculty of Education, Universiti Malaya, Kuala Lumpur, Malaysia

*keh2009@um.edu.my

[†]s2037232@siswa.um.edu.my

Abstract

A number of countries are facing a principal succession crisis, reflected in a shortage of qualified principals and a lack of principal succession planning on the one hand and frequent principal turnovers on the other hand. This is detrimental to school progress and has a range of negative consequences. Effective principal succession planning can help principals achieve successful succession and drive school progress. We searched through Web of Science, SCOPUS, and Google Scholar and followed the PRISMA statement to summarize research on the effect of principal succession on school progress. Twenty-two articles were selected for thematic analysis. This chapter summarizes the effect of principal succession on school progress in seven main aspects: (1) student achievement, (2) teacher morale, (3) teacher trust, (4) teacher turnover, (5) school culture, (6) power relationships, and (7) other aspects.

Keywords: Principal's succession planning, school progress, student achievement, teacher trust, school culture.

1. Introduction

Principal succession refers to the systematic process by which the current principal leaves and a new principal arrives (Hargreaves et al., 2003). In recent years, the prevalence of neoliberalism in public sector reform in the United Kingdom and the United States, managerialism, and standardized accountability have made principals external managers of change (Hargreaves & Fink, 2003), and the complexity and unpredictability of principals' work have increased significantly, leading to a decline in the attractiveness of the principalship profession (Thomson et al., 2003). Talented individuals are reluctant to pursue the principalship profession, and many principals who are serving retire early (Reames et al., 2014). At the same time, the "baby boomer" generation of principals is reaching retirement age, and the United Kingdom, the United States, and Canada are facing a principal succession crisis (Mackay, 2006). On the one hand, the principal succession crisis is reflected in the lack of qualified principals and the lack of planning for principal succession, which often involves a stop-gap measure to fill vacancies in a timely manner (Parfitt, 2017). On the other hand, the frequent turnover of principals has led to a significant and negative impact on the sustainability of school development (Miller, 2013). Some scholars have referred to this as "revolving door principalship" (Macmillan, 2000). This crisis has led stakeholders to systematically review the policy structure and procedures for principalship succession, conduct systematic research, and link principalship succession to school sustainability based on extensive empirical research (Hargreaves & Goodson, 2006).

Principal succession has a significant impact on school development. As the study of leadership succession advanced, principal succession began to be studied in the 1970s, and over the course of about 50 years, it has become an important element in principal leadership research. For many scholars, strong administrative leadership is a central and necessary characteristic of a good school. When an influential position in a school faces replacement, there can be a ripple effect throughout the school, which in turn can have broad and far-reaching consequences. Thus, principal succession research is important to schooling practice and school progress. However, existing research on principal succession is limited (Aravena, 2020), and there are no studies that specifically address the effect of principal succession planning. Therefore, the purpose of this paper is to fill this gap by summarizing in detail the effect of principal succession planning on school progress.

2. Methodology

This study followed PRISMA guidelines to conduct a systematic review. This approach was chosen because it ensures the quality of the review and allows replication of the review methodology (Shamseer *et al.*, 2015). Moreover, the research procedure as shown in Figure 1 was followed in this chapter.

3. Data Collection

To ensure the high quality of the searched articles to enhance the credibility of this literature review, large comprehensive electronic databases and core journals were prioritized. Two major databases were identified for the search in this study — Web of Science and SCOPUS. Since Google Scholar contains more comprehensive articles and covers a very wide range of research areas (Saadatdoost *et al.*, 2015), this study also used Google Scholar as an important addition to the literature sources.

Two basic concepts were considered for the search keywords: ("principal succession"/"principal turnover"/"principal rotation") and ("school progress"/"school improvement"/"school growth"). Synonyms, alternative spellings, and related terms were considered in identifying keywords for each concept. The different keywords were combined in the two different databases, namely, Web of Science and SCOPUS, and Google

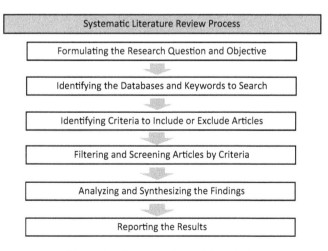

Figure 1. The procedures of this study.

Scholar when conducting the search. The screening criteria for the articles in this study are shown in Table 1.

Since PRISMA has the advantage of allowing replication of review methods and facilitating the transparency of the research process (Shamseer *et al.*, 2015), the process of selecting articles for this study was based on the PRISMA statement for reporting systematic reviews and meta-analysis. The specific screening process is shown in Figure 2.

Table 1. Article screening criteria.

Inclusion criteria	Exclusion criteria
English language	Non-English languages
Empirical studies	Essentially non-empirical studies such as viewpoints, editorials, opinions, or books
Core journal articles in the field of education	Non-journal articles such as academic conference proceedings
Focus on the effect of principal succession on school progress	Focus on other school leaders/personnel or other research fields

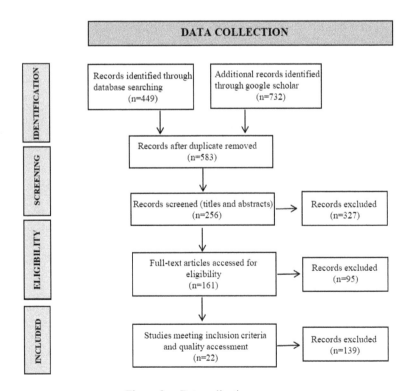

Figure 2. Data collection process.

4. Data Analysis

Since the purpose of this paper is to systematically review the extrinsic incentives that impact teacher retention, this study used a widely used software for qualitative data analysis: ATLAS.ti. This software was chosen for data analysis because it has the following advantages: It is easy to learn and has an intuitive interface; it has strong data analysis capabilities and a beautiful presentation of results, which can be very helpful in improving the scientific and normative aspects of qualitative research (Guidry, 2002); and the software helps to build networks and relationships, and users can combine and decompose them according to themes, categories, and visualize relevant questions to gain deeper insights (Ngalande & Mkwinda, 2014).

The details of using the software for data analysis are as follows: First, install software ATLAS.ti.22.0.0 and create a project named "the Effects of cipal Succession Planning on School Progress." Second, place the selected high-quality papers in a folder and add this folder to ATLAS.ti. Third, code or write memos and comments separately for each article in the folder. When coding, distill the main idea of the selected content or paragraph in concise language as much as possible and group these codes into different categories. These categories are the effect of principal succession on school progress, such as student achievement, teacher morale, teacher trust, teacher turnover, school culture, power relationships, and other aspects. Fourth, explore the links between the different categories and generalize the links into different themes. Finally, write a report based on the established themes and the results of the analysis.

5. Results

In selecting the articles to be reviewed, firstly, a total of 1181 articles were identified by keywords. Second, 598 duplicate articles were eliminated, leaving 583 articles. Third, 327 articles that were not related to the topic were eliminated by reading the article titles and abstracts, leaving 256 articles. Fourth, 95 articles were not eligible as access to the full text was unavailable, leaving 161 articles. Finally, the articles related to the topic were further finely screened, resulting in a total of 22 high-quality sample papers for this research.

The effect of principals' succession on school progress in the 22 journal articles is reflected in the following aspects: student achievement, teacher morale, teacher trust, teacher turnover, school culture, power

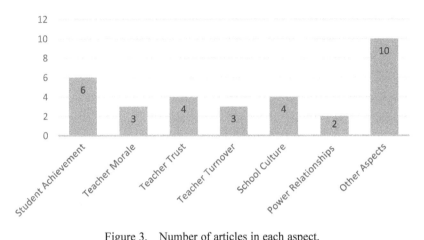

Figure 3. Number of articles in each aspect.

relations and structure, and other aspects. The number of articles in each aspect is shown in Figure 3.

The effect of principal succession, turnover, or rotation on school progress has both positive and negative aspects. Table 2 summarizes the effects and specific findings regarding principal succession, turnover, or rotation. To review, the following are the main aspects of these effects:

5.1. *Effect 1-student achievement*

The impact of principal succession, turnover, or rotation on student achievement is controversial. Principals were shown to be second only to classroom teaching in terms of affecting student learning in school (Leithwood *et al.*, 2004). However, some scholars think that principal turnover causes a drop in student achievement (Béteille *et al.*, 2012; Henry & Harbatkin, 2019). Mascall *et al.* believe that principal turnover is not related to student achievement (Mascall *et al.*, 2011). Other scholars have argued that the effect of principal turnover on student achievement is time-limited. For example, Rowan and Denk's five-year follow-up study of 149 schools with principal turnover found that principals affected school performance in the second year of succession, that the frequency

Table 2. The effects of principal succession and specific findings.

Effects	Findings	Sources
Student achievement	Principals' influence on student achievement is second only to classroom instruction, and the succession of outstanding principals is beneficial to student academic achievement.	Leithwood et al. (2004)
Student achievement	The frequency of principal succession is inversely related to student achievement.	Rowan & Denk (1984)
Student achievement	Within five years of a new principal's succession, student achievement continued to decline in the first two years and increased during the final three years. There was little change in average student academic achievement after that.	Miller (2013)
School culture, student achievement, classroom teaching	Principal turnover is closely associated with the organizational culture of schools and classroom teaching, and is not related to student achievement.	Mascall et al. (2011)
Student achievement, teacher turnover	Principal turnover is linked to the decline in student achievement and the increase in teacher turnover.	Henry & Harbatkin (2019)
Teacher retention rate, student achievement	The frequency of principal turnover will lead to a low teacher retention rate and poor student performance in terms of achievement, especially in schools with severe poverty, low performance, and inexperienced teachers.	Béteille et al. (2012)
Teacher turnover	Principal turnover will affect teachers leaving the school.	Bartanen et al. (2019)
Teacher morale	New principals create a teaching and learning environment with stability, safety, and security that can lead to high teacher morale.	Northfield et al. (2011)
School culture, teacher morale	Principal succession may cause changes in school culture and positively or negatively affect teacher morale.	Meyer et al. (2009).

(*Continued*)

Table 2. (*Continued*)

Effects	Findings	Sources
Teacher trust	Teachers' trust in a succeeding principal depends on the principal's ability to accomplish tasks and interpersonal skills. Succeeding principals need to be intentional about their efforts to earn the trust of their staff, rather than relying on the authority of their leadership position to earn trust. A prerequisite for a succeeding principal to build trust is to support teachers and other staff in achieving organizational goals and doing their best to improve student achievement and attainment.	Northfield (2014)
Teacher trust	Principals and teachers build trust at four progressive levels: role trust, practice trust, integrative trust, and correlative trust.	Macmillan *et al.* (2004)
Teacher trust	In order to ease the potential anxiety that comes with principal succession, succeeding principals should look for ways to build trust with teachers as soon as possible. New principals should be proactive in engaging teachers at the outset.	Macmillan *et al.* (2011)
Teacher trust	Principal turnover is one of the factors that affect trust between principals and teachers.	Lee (2015)
Power relationships	Principal turnover is a devastating occurrence that can change channels of communication, reorganize power relationships, influence decisions-making, and upset the balance of activities within the school.	Miskel & Cosgrove (1985)

Table 2. (*Continued*)

Effects	Findings	Sources
Teacher morale, school culture, power structure, and operating style of the school	Outstanding principals can quickly change teacher morale, influence school culture and power structures and the way the school operates, and help the school take on a new look in a relatively short period of time.	Hargreaves *et al.* (2003)
School culture	Rapid principal turnover can negatively impact school culture.	Mascall & Leithwood (2010)
Principal burnout, principal professional development	Succession can also benefit principals by helping them prevent burnout, creating opportunities to develop new skills and experience new challenges, and providing the opportunity to collaborate with many teachers to promote professional development.	Lortz (1985)
Principals' work ability	By working in different schools, principals gain a wealth of experience in interacting with people and dealing with problems, developing leadership skills, broadening their horizons, and applying creative approaches to analyze and solve problems.	Lortz (1985)
Teacher professional development	The opportunity for teachers to work with different principals also promotes their professional development.	Lortz (1985)
Prevention of power monopoly	Succession helps change the network of relationships in school and prevents the power monopoly.	Lortz (1985)
Revolving door syndrome	Frequent turnover of principals can create a revolving door syndrome, leading to staff agreeing to reform initiatives but refusing to make a commitment to them.	Yildirim & Kaya (2019)

(*Continued*)

Table 2. (*Continued*)

Effects	Findings	Sources
Instability of school	Principal turnover may lead to instability in the school environment, thereby reducing the expected benefits of replacing the principal. The instability caused by poor succession planning may undermine the efforts made by the school and limit the long-term growth of the school.	Fink & Brayman (2004)
Chaos and disorder among teachers, students, and communities	Principal succession may disrupt the established home–school identity, disrupt the well-established relationships between the previous principal and students, disrupt the systems and procedures in place at the school, and lead to chaos and disorder among teachers, students, and communities.	Lindsey (1979)
School effectiveness	Rotating high-performing principals to other schools and replacing them with low-performing principals can often diminish the previous effectiveness of the school and render successful schools mediocre.	Hargreaves (2005)
Teaching quality	Principal turnover may negatively affect the teaching quality in low-socioeconomic-status schools.	Pietsch *et al.* (2020)

of succession was inversely related to student achievement, and that schools with more low-socioeconomic-status students had higher academic gains than schools with fewer low-socioeconomic-status students, but the effect decreased over time (Rowan & Denk, 1984). Miller found that within five years of a new principal's succession, student achievement continued to decline in the first two years and then increased in the third year; after that, there was little change in average student academic achievement. Thus, the increase in student achievement with principal turnover may simply be a reflection of a mean regression rather than based on the positive effects of principal turnover (Miller, 2013).

5.2. *Effect 2 — Teacher morale*

Principal succession implies a change in the principal–teacher relationship, and the effect on schools is directly reflected in improved teacher morale and trust-building. Principals are a decisive factor in bringing in and retaining excellent teachers, and research has found that principal succession significantly affects teacher morale and teacher trust (Meyer *et al.*, 2011).

Principal succession may have positive or negative effects on teacher and organizational morale. Northfield *et al.* found that the creation of a stable, safe, and secure teaching and learning environment by a new principal can lead to high teacher morale (Northfield *et al.*, 2011). Outstanding principals can quickly change teacher morale (Hargreaves *et al.*, 2003). Findings from Meyer *et al.* suggest that three factors influence teacher morale during the period of principal succession: informal leadership, staff experience, and how well the succeeding principal is recognized (Meyer *et al.*, 2009). In order to motivate teachers' morale, succeeding principals need to be more involved in teachers' activities and listen to their opinions.

5.3. *Effect 3 — Teacher trust*

The process of building trust is complicated and dynamic. Trust is considered the "organizational lubricant" that influences all aspects of students' lives (Brezicha & Fuller, 2019). Trust is critical in producing positive discourse between principals and teachers (Arar, 2019).

The rate of principal turnover is one of the factors affecting teachers' trust in principals (Lee, 2015). The building of trust between succeeding principals and teachers often involves a long period of "gaming." The succeeding principal's leadership style and management style often cause discomfort among teachers. In order to mitigate the potential discomfort that comes with principal succession, the succeeding principal should explore ways to build trust with teachers as soon as possible. The new principal should break down the walls at the beginning (i.e. the door to the principal's office) and integrate with teachers from the outset

(Macmillan et al., 2011). For successive principals, trust depends on one's ability to accomplish tasks and interpersonal skills (Northfield, 2014). Macmillan et al. argued that principals and staff build trust in a progressive manner from four levels: role trust, practice trust, integrative trust, and correlative trust (Macmillan et al., 2004).

5.4. Effect 4 — Teacher turnover

Most studies believe that principal succession or turnover leads to lower teacher retention and higher turnover. For example, Bartanen et al. found that principal turnover can affect teacher turnover (Bartanen et al., 2019). Some other researchers have also linked principal turnover to the increase in teacher turnover (Henry & Harbatkin, 2019). Frequent turnover of school leaders can lead to lower teacher retention, especially in schools with severe poverty, low performance, and inexperienced teachers (Béteille et al., 2012).

5.5. Effect 5 — School culture

Outstanding new principals can influence school culture (Hargreaves et al., 2003). Principal succession is likely to result in changes in school culture (Meyer et al., 2009). Mascall et al. found that principal turnover is closely related to school culture (Mascall et al., 2011). Rapid principal turnover can have a negative impact on school culture (Mascall & Leithwood 2010).

5.6. Effect 6 — Power relationships

Outstanding new principals can influence the power structure and the way a school operates, helping the school take on a new look in a relatively short period of time (Hargreaves et al., 2003). However, Miskel & Cosgrove (1985) considered principal turnover as a disruptive event that changes communication channels, reshapes power relationships, influences decision-making, and breaks the balance of activities within the school.

5.7. Effect 7 — Other aspects

5.7.1. The positive effects of principal succession on school progress

Succession can benefit principals by helping them prevent burnout, creating opportunities to develop new skills and experience new challenges, providing them the opportunity to collaborate with many teachers to promote professional development, and helping them overcome boredom or complacency, especially later in their careers. By working in different schools, principals can gain a wealth of experience in interacting with people and dealing with problems, developing their leadership skills, broadening their horizons, and using creative approaches to analyze problem (Lortz, 1985). Also, the opportunity for teachers to work with different principals can contribute to their professional growth. If the school is composed of students from diverse ethnic, religious, and socioeconomic backgrounds, then successive principals have the opportunity to expand their understanding of cultures and value systems and make decisions that benefit the school district. Succession also changes the network of relationships in the school and prevents the principal from monopolizing power (Lortz, 1985).

5.7.2. The negative effects of principal succession on school progress

The frequent turnover of principals can lead to a revolving door syndrome, resulting in staff agreeing to reform initiatives but refusing to make a commitment toward reform (Yildirim & Kaya, 2019). Maintaining organizational stability is an important factor in the healthy functioning of education systems and schools, and principal turnover may lead to instability in the school environment, thereby reducing the expected benefits of the turnover. Particularly for schools undergoing improvement, there needs to be a certain level of stability in the organization to sustain the development of the school over a period of time. Instability induced by poor succession planning may undermine the efforts made by the school and limit its long-term growth. Without longer-term leadership stability or continuity, it is unlikely that schools and districts will institutionalize improvement efforts over time (Fink & Brayman, 2004). In addition, principal succession may upset established home–school identities, damage the well-established relationships between the previous principal and students, disrupt the systems and procedures in place in the school, and lead to chaos and disorganization among teachers, students, and communities (Lindsey, 1979). Frequent leader turnover can also lead to schools progressing under one principal, but regressing under another. Rotating highly effective principals to other schools and replacing them with less experienced leaders can often erode the previous effectiveness of the school and render successful schools mediocre (Hargreaves, 2005). Principal turnover may also negatively affect the quality of instruction in low-socioeconomic-status schools (Pietsch et al., 2020). Scholars also view principal turnover as a devastating occurrence that can change channels of communication, reorganize power relationships, influence decisions-making, and upset the balance of activities within the school (Miskel & Cosgrove, 1985).

6. Discussion

This chapter aims to review the effects of principal succession, turnover, or rotation on school progress as analyzed in core journals in the field of education. The effects are two-sided, as principal succession, rotation, or turnover can have positive and negative effects on schools. These effects are reflected in the following aspects: student achievement, teacher morale, teacher trust, teacher turnover, school culture, power relationships, and other aspects.

The effect of principal succession, rotation, or turnover on student achievement is controversial. There are four main arguments: (1) principal succession is beneficial to student achievement; (2) principal succession leads to a decline in student achievement; (3) principal succession is not related to student achievement; and (4) the effect of principals on student achievement is time-limited. The reasons for the different findings may be that student achievement is influenced by various other factors such as socioeconomic status, parental education (Farooq et al., 2011), teacher experience (Gerritsen et al., 2017), teaching quality (Quint et al., 2007), and school facilities (Hopland, 2013).

This chapter is limited in its study of the effects of principal succession because there are only a few studies that focus on principal succession.

Furthermore, this chapter focuses more on principal succession because of the extremely limited research on principal succession planning. This chapter limits the publication period to 2010–2021 in order to screen more articles for review, which also leads to the possible lack of cutting-edge and innovative nature of this literature review. In addition, due to time and conditions, only three electronic databases — Web of Science and Scopus — and Google Scholar were selected for the search, and other electronic databases on the topic of principal succession as well as paper journals were not systematically and exhaustively compiled. This may have made this study less comprehensive and detailed. In addition, the search for keywords may have missed other synonymous expressions, resulting in incomplete articles being extracted. With the increasing trend of principal turnover and the limited research on it (Aravena, 2020), there is an urgent need for future research to focus more on ipal succession and principal succession planning.

7. Conclusion

This chapter uses a systematic approach to review the impact of principal succession on school progress in elementary and secondary schools. This chapter identifies both positive and negative impacts of principal succession on school progress in terms of student achievement, teacher morale, teacher trust, teacher turnover, school culture, power relationships, and other aspects. This review not only fills a research gap in this area but also enables schools to understand the effects of principal succession and identify the necessity for principal succession planning, thereby reducing the negative impacts of principal succession, turnover, or rotation and promoting school stability and sustainability. In addition, this review will also provide a guideline to help new principals with effective job planning and support them in achieving a successful succession.

References

Arar, K. (2019). Arab principals' and teachers' perceptions of trust and regulation and their contribution to school processes. *Leadership and Policy in Schools*, *18*(4), 648–663.

Aravena, F. (2020). Principal succession in schools: A literature review (2003–2019). *Educational Management Administration & Leadership*, 1741143220940331.

Bartanen, B., Grissom, J.A., & Rogers, L.K. (2019). The impacts of principal turnover. *Educational Evaluation and Policy Analysis, 41*(3), 350–374.

Béteille, T., Kalogrides, D., & Loeb, S. (2012). Stepping stones: Principal career paths and school outcomes. *Social Science Research, 41*(4), 904–919.

Brezicha, K.F. & Fuller, E.J. (2019). Building teachers' trust in principals: Exploring the effects of the match between teacher and principal race/ethnicity and gender and feelings of trust. *Journal of School Leadership, 29*(1), 25–53.

Farooq, M.S., Chaudhry, A.H., Shafiq, M., & Berhanu, G. (2011). Factors affecting students' quality of academic performance: A case of secondary school level. *Journal of Quality and Technology Management, 7*(2), 1–14.

Fink, D. & Brayman, C. (2004). Principals' succession and educational change. *Journal of Educational Administration, 42*(4), 431–449.

Gerritsen, S., Plug, E., & Webbink, D. (2017). Teacher quality and student achievement: Evidence from a sample of Dutch twins. *Journal of Applied Econometrics, 32*(3), 643–660.

Guidry, J.A. (2002). LibQual+™ spring 2001 comments: A qualitative analysis using Atlas. ti. *Performance Measurement and Metrics, 3*(2), 100–107.

Hargreaves, A. (2005 June). Leadership succession. In *The Educational Forum* (Vol. 69, No. 2, pp. 163–173). Taylor & Francis Group.

Hargreaves, A. & Fink, D. (2003). Sustaining leadership. *Phi Delta Kappan, 84*(9), 693–700.

Hargreaves, A. & Goodson, I. (2006). Educational change over time? The sustainability and nonsustainability of three decades of secondary school change and continuity. *Educational Administration Quarterly, 42*(1), 3–41.

Hargreaves, A., Moore, S., Fink, D., Brayman, C., & White, R. (2003). *Succeeding Leaders. A Study of Principal Rotation and Succession.* Toronto, Ontario, Canada: Ontario Principals' Council.

Henry, G.T. & Harbatkin, E. (2019). Turnover at the top: Estimating the effects of principal turnover on student, teacher, and school outcomes. *Education Working Paper No. 19–95.*

Hopland, A.O. (2013). School facilities and student achievement in industrial countries: Evidence from the TIMSS. *International Education Studies, 6*(3), 162–171.

Lee, L.C. (2015). School performance trajectories and the challenges for principal succession. *Journal of Educational Administration, 53*(2), 262–286.

Leithwood, K., Seashore, K., Anderson, S., & Wahlstrom, K. (2004). Review of research: How leadership influences student learning.

Lindsey, J.F. (1979). The principal scramble: Any district can play. *Thrust for Educational Leadership, 9*(1), 29–30.

Lortz, K.M. (1985). An analysis of the rotation of elementary principals in Iowa (professional growth, transfer, systematic, management succession). (Doctoral dissertation, The University of Iowa).

Mackay, K. (2006). Ask for a super-human school leader? Receive a succession crisis. *Teacher*, *168*, 48–49.

Macmillan, R. (2000). Leadership succession, cultures of teaching and educational change. *The Sharp Edge of Educational Change: Teaching, Leading and the Realities of Reform*, pp. 52–71, London: Routledge.

Macmillan, R.B., Meyer, M.J., & Northfield, S. (2004). Trust and its role in principal succession: A preliminary examination of a continuum of trust. *Leadership and Policy in Schools*, *3*(4), 275–294.

Macmillan, R.B., Meyer, M.J., Northfield, S., & Foley, M. (2011). The school district and the development of trust in new principals: Policies and actions that influence succession. In *Principals in Succession* (pp. 27–39). Dordrecht: Springer.

Mascall, B. & Leithwood, K. (2010). Investing in leadership: The district's role in managing principal turnover. *Leadership and Policy in Schools*, *9*(4), 367–383.

Mascall, B., Moore, S., Jantzi, D., Walker, K., & Sacks, R. (2011). Survive and thrive: Leadership distribution as a strategy for frequent principal turnover. In *Principals in Succession* (pp. 89–108). Dordrecht: Springer.

Meyer, M.J., Macmillan, R.B., & Northfield, S. (2009). Principal succession and its impact on teacher morale. *International Journal of Leadership in Education*, *12*(2), 171–185.

Meyer, M., Macmillan, R., & Northfield, S. (2011). Principal succession and the micropolitics of educators in schools: Some incidental results from a larger study. *Canadian Journal of Educational Administration and Policy*, (117), 1–26.

Miller, A. (2013). Principal turnover and student achievement. *Economics of Education Review*, *36*, 60–72.

Miskel, C. & Cosgrove, D. (1985). Leader succession in school settings. *Review of Educational Research*, *55*(1), 87–105.

Ngalande, R.C. & Mkwinda, E. (2014). Benefits and challenges of using ATLAS. ti. Digital Repository of Technische Universität Berlin, http://nbn-resolving.de/urn:nbn:de:kobv:83-opus4-44224.

Northfield, S. (2014). Multi-dimensional trust: How beginning principals build trust with their staff during leader succession. *International Journal of Leadership in Education*, *17*(4), 410–441.

Northfield, S., Macmillan, R., & Meyer, M.J. (2011). Trust during transition: Strategic leadership and trust development during principal succession. In *Principals in Succession* (pp. 109–137). Dordrecht: Springer.

Parfitt, C.M. (2017). Creating a succession-planning instrument for educational leadership. *Education Leadership Review*, *18*(1), 21–36.

Pietsch, M., Tulowitzki, P., & Hartig, J. (2020). Examining the effect of principal turnover on teaching quality: A study on organizational change with repeated classroom observations. *School Effectiveness and School Improvement, 31*(3), 333–355.

Quint, J.C., Akey, T.M., Rappaport, S., & Willner, C.J. (2007). Instructional leadership, teaching quality and student achievement. New York: MDRC.

Reames, E.H., Kochan, F.K., & Zhu, L. (2014). Factors influencing principals' retirement decisions: A southern US perspective. *Educational Management Administration & Leadership, 42*(1), 40–60.

Rowan, B. & Denk, C.E. (1984). Management succession, school socioeconomic context, and basic skills achievement. *American Educational Research Journal, 21*(3), 517–537.

Saadatdoost, R., Sim, A.T.H., Jafarkarimi, H., & Mei Hee, J. (2015). Exploring MOOC from education and Information systems perspectives: A short literature review. *Educational Review, 67*(4), 505–518.

Shamseer, L., Moher, D., Clarke, M., Ghersi, D., Liberati, A., Petticrew, M., & Stewart, L.A. (2015). Preferred reporting items for systematic review and meta-analysis protocols (PRISMA-P) 2015: Elaboration and explanation. *BMJ*, 349:g7647, 1–25.

Thomson, P., Blackmore, J., Sachs, J., & Tregenza, K. (2003). High stakes principalship — Sleepless nights, heart attacks and sudden death accountabilities: Reading media representations of the United States principal shortage. *Australian Journal of Education, 47*(2), 118–132.

Yildirim, M.C. & Kaya, A. (2019). The contributions of school principals as constructivist leaders to their schools' organizational change. *Asian Journal of Education and Training, 5*(1), 1–7.

© 2025 World Scientific Publishing Company
https://doi.org/10.1142/9789811294730_0002

Chapter 2

Teachers' Collective Bargaining and Unionization in Education

Ahmed Habeeb* and Ahmad Zabidi bin Abdul Razak†

Faculty of Education, University of Malaya, Kuala Lumpur, Malaysia

*shifax@gmail.com

†zabidi@um.edu.my

Abstract

In the field of education, collective bargaining and unionization play a critical role in shaping working conditions and compensation for teachers. This chapter explores the history of collective bargaining in education and the role of unions in shaping the future of the field. The authors argue that unions play a key role in negotiating fair contracts for education employees. The benefits of unionization include job security, a voice in the workplace, community and solidarity among workers, promoting high standards in education, and contributing to the overall improvement of society. Collective bargaining provides a platform for employees to negotiate better working conditions, promotes stability in the workplace, promotes equality and fairness, contributes to the overall health of the economy, and promotes innovation and efficiency. However, there are barriers to effective collective bargaining such as limited bargaining power, lack of legal recognition and protection, and employer resistance. Recommendations to overcome these barriers include providing legal recognition and protection for collective bargaining, ensuring the right to strike without fear of retaliation, addressing employer resistance, addressing the power imbalance, considering the economic climate, promoting political neutrality, promoting transparency and accountability, and supporting union membership. By addressing these barriers and promoting unionization in education, we can create a more equitable and just workplace for educators and support staff.

Keywords: Collective bargaining, unionization, negotiation, right-to-work, grievance procedures.

1. Introduction

Collective bargaining and unionization are important concepts in the field of education. Collective bargaining refers to the negotiation process between an employer (in this case, the school district or education institution) and a union representing the employees (teachers, support staff, etc.) to reach an agreement on working conditions, wages, benefits, and other employment-related issues.

Unionization, on the other hand, refers to the formation of a labor union by workers in a particular industry, including education, for the purpose of advocating for their rights, improving working conditions, and negotiating fair compensation. Unionized teachers and support staff have a collective voice and can work together to achieve their common goals.

In the field of education, collective bargaining and unionization play a critical role in shaping the working conditions and compensation for teachers, support staff, and other employees. By negotiating with school district administrators and governing boards, unions have the ability to negotiate contracts that improve the working conditions, wages, and benefits of education employees. Additionally, unions provide a platform for teachers to advocate for the rights of students and the quality of education they receive.

In this chapter, we have explored the history of collective bargaining and unionization in education, the current state of labor relations in the field, and the impact that collective bargaining and unionization have on teachers, students, and the education system as a whole. We have also examined the challenges that unions face in negotiating fair contracts and the role that collective bargaining and unionization play in shaping the future of education. Through an examination of the key issues and players involved, this chapter provides a comprehensive overview of the complex and dynamic landscape of collective bargaining and unionization in education.

2. Collective Bargaining

Collective bargaining in educational settings provides a fair and structured framework for improving student learning, promoting a positive atmosphere in public schools, and ensuring that employees are paid professionally. When management and educators agree on compensation, benefits, and working conditions, it benefits both parties; successful collective bargaining interactions are a regular process in the best educational environments. These interactions are often conducted monthly by a collaborative union committee.

On January 4, 2013, the Maldives ratified the International Labor Organization's (ILO) eight fundamental conventions, which cover four categories of fundamental rights and principles in the workplace, including the right to collective bargaining and freedom of association, the elimination of forced labor, child labor, and employment discrimination. The ILO aims to raise awareness of industrial relations principles in various industries, including tourism, government, and construction.

The field of labor economics, which examines job satisfaction differences between union and non-union members, has received significant attention (Garcia-Serrano, 2009). Employee surveys often show that union members have lower job satisfaction compared to non-members (Bryson et al., 2010).

Effective management in educational institutions requires delegation of responsibilities, establishment of a chain of command, and provision of a safe and suitable environment. Although it may inspire and motivate actions, carrying the responsibility does not essentially entail them (Shaturaev, 2021). Quality leadership is crucial during collective bargaining, as the worldwide economy is rapidly growing, and most countries understand the importance of a highly qualified workforce. Meeting the demand for high-quality education is challenging, and schools are shifting from maintenance to performance (Lu, 2016).

The main goal of collective bargaining is to establish a solid and stable partnership between the school and its staff. A positive attitude toward collective bargaining is necessary to achieve long-term organizational goals (Michael, 1982). Educational control involves influencing others in educational settings to achieve desired outcomes and actions, and those who carry a designated responsibility have an effect on others and are therefore leading (Shaturaev, 2021).

Educational management and administration should be centrally concerned with the processes that maintain existing services and develop new policies (Bush, 2007; Bolam, 2004). The fairness of management practices is a crucial mechanism through which unions can improve well-being by influencing perceived fairness and developmental content (O'Brady & Doellgast, 2021). Collective bargaining under unionization ensures better working conditions and a secure work environment without the fear of reprisal (based on the literature review). Working together to negotiate an agreement with management protects the things that matter, such as health care, fair raises, security, and stability in schedules.

3. Unionization

There is an increasing body of research that advocates for teachers' unions as the most dominant influence in the public education sector in terms of their ability to impact school budgets, organization, and student learning outcomes (Brunner et al., 2020). Trade unionism, or the organized labor movement, originated in the 19th century in the United States, Great Britain, and Europe. Although small worker associations appeared in Britain in the 18th century, they remained sporadic due to opposition from proprietors and government groups. American unions adopted collective bargaining as a means to improve financial conditions for workers, while British unions favored political activism which eventually led to the formation of the Labour Party (Duignan, 2019).

The first teachers' association, the Society of Associated Teachers of New York, was established in 1874 (Donley, 1976). However, there was debate over the purpose and role of teacher associations, with the federal government having its own stance on public employee unions and teachers struggling with their philosophical approach toward unionism and collective bargaining. In the past, it was believed that the government and its departments should be independent and protected from external pressures, but President Franklin Roosevelt in 1935 believed that public employees should have a voice in decision-making (Rogers, 1988).

As public schools grew larger and more complicated, the position of superintendent of schools was created to manage daily operations, while middle management jobs such as principals became important (Kennedy, 1984; Argyle, 1980). However, this further limited teachers' involvement in decision-making. In the early 1960s, teachers became more aware of the need to participate actively in decisions affecting their education, and collective bargaining became widely accepted as a means for teachers to have more power in their districts (Adams, 1970; Rogers, 1988).

Albert Shanker (1975) believed that a developed and mature labor–management partnership through collective bargaining would enhance education and resolve many disputes. The declining buying power of teachers since the Second World War and the influence of private sector labor unions also contributed to the growth of teacher collective bargaining (Rogers, 1988). However, in many advanced economies, the proportion of workers covered by collective agreements has decreased or remained stable in recent decades, and in many developing countries, only a small portion of the workforce is covered (Susan et al., 2011).

Effective school leadership is crucial, but principals often face challenges in managing schools effectively (Oduol, 2019). This research provides an overview of literature and practices, theories, and analysis of management related to finding solutions to these challenges.

According to the ILO, "All negotiations which take place between an employer, a group of employers or one or more employers' organizations, on the one hand, and one or more workers' organizations, on the other, for:

(a) determining working conditions and terms of employment; and/or
(b) regulating relations between employers and workers; and/or
(c) regulating relations between employers or their organizations and a workers' organization or workers' organizations." (Article 2).

4. Elements of Collective Bargaining and Unionization

Collective bargaining and unionization in education are processes by which educators, including teachers, support staff, and administrators, negotiate with their employer over the terms and conditions of their employment. The purpose of these processes is to provide educators with a voice in the workplace and to ensure that they have a representative who can negotiate on their behalf. Collective bargaining and unionization in education comprise several key elements, including representation, a collective bargaining agreement (CBA), the bargaining unit, negotiations, grievance procedures, and strikes (ILO, 2015).

Representation is the cornerstone of collective bargaining and unionization in education. When educators join a union, they are effectively gaining a voice in the workplace and a representative who can negotiate on their behalf. For example, a group of high school teachers may join a teachers' union to have a say in decisions related to their working conditions, such as class sizes, schedules, and support services. The role of unions in representing educators is critical to the success of collective bargaining and unionization in education (Casey *et al.*, 2018).

A CBA is a written document that outlines the terms and conditions of employment, including wages, benefits, working hours, and other working conditions. The CBA is the result of negotiations between the union and the employer and is designed to provide clarity on the terms and conditions of employment. For example, a CBA between a school district and a teachers' union may specify that teachers will receive a salary increase of 3% per year and receive a certain number of sick days and personal days each year (ILO, 2023).

The bargaining unit is the group of employees who are covered by the CBA. In education, the bargaining unit typically includes teachers, support staff, and administrators. For example, a bargaining unit in a school district may include all teachers, school librarians, and instructional coaches. The bargaining unit is an important element of collective bargaining and unionization in education as it determines which employees are covered by the CBA and who will benefit from the terms and conditions outlined in the agreement (Sonia *et al.*, 2020).

Negotiations are the heart of collective bargaining and unionization in education. During negotiations, the union and the employer discuss the terms and conditions of employment with the goal of reaching a mutually agreed upon CBA. For example, during negotiations, the school district and the teachers' union may discuss the school district's budget, teacher salaries, and class sizes, with the goal of reaching an agreement that benefits both parties. Negotiations are an essential part of the collective bargaining and unionization processes as they provide the opportunity for both parties to discuss their needs and reach a mutually agreeable solution (Susan *et al.*, 2011).

Grievance procedures are a critical element of collective bargaining and unionization in education. A grievance procedure is a process for resolving disputes between the union and the employer over the interpretation and application of the CBA. For example, if teachers feel that their working conditions are not in line with the CBA, they may file a grievance through the union, which will then negotiate with the school district to resolve the issue. Grievance procedures provide a mechanism for resolving disputes and ensure that the terms and conditions outlined in the CBA are being followed (ILO, 2023).

Strikes are a collective action taken by union members to protest and demand changes in working conditions. For example, if a school district and a teachers' union are unable to reach an agreement during negotiations, the teachers may go on strike to protest and demand changes. Strikes are a powerful tool for educators in their efforts to negotiate better working conditions and are an important element of collective bargaining and unionization in education (Rabiu & Kamal, 2006).

Some countries have "right-to-work" legislation that prevent firms from recruiting required personnel. "Right-to-work" laws are laws that limit the power of unions in collective bargaining by making it more difficult for employees to unionize (Gondhalekar & Kessler, 2021). These laws restrict the ability of unions to require that employees pay union dues as a condition of employment. This means that even if a majority of employees in a workplace have voted to unionize, individual employees may choose not to pay union dues or fees, reducing the resources available to the union to negotiate on their behalf.

According to right-to-work laws, unions are still required to represent all employees in the bargaining unit, regardless of whether they are union members or not. This can make it more difficult for unions to advocate effectively for their members, as they may have limited resources to do so. Additionally, right-to-work laws can also limit the ability of unions to take collective action, such as striking, as they may not have the support of all employees in the bargaining unit (Jeffrey & Casey, 1991). In contrast, in countries without right-to-work laws, employees who benefit from collective bargaining agreements negotiated by their union are typically required to pay union dues or fees as a condition of employment. This provides unions with a stable source of funding, which allows them to negotiate effectively on behalf of their members (Gondhalekar & Kessler, 2021).

In the field of education, right-to-work laws can have a significant impact on the ability of educators, including teachers, support staff, and administrators, to unionize and negotiate for better working conditions. In states with strong right-to-work laws, educators may find it more difficult to form unions and negotiate with their employers over wages, benefits, working hours, and other working conditions. On the other hand, in states without right-to-work laws, educators are more likely to have the resources and support they need to negotiate effectively on their own behalf (Paul, 2021).

5. Benefits of Collective Bargaining

Collective bargaining is the process of negotiation between an employer and a group of employees, typically represented by a union, to determine the terms and conditions of their employment. The importance and benefits of collective bargaining are numerous and cannot be overstated (Solomon, 2019).

One of the key benefits of collective bargaining is that it provides a platform for employees to negotiate better working conditions, such as higher wages, better benefits, improved job security, and a safer workplace. Without the ability to collectively bargain, individual employees would have little bargaining power and would be at the mercy of their employers. Collective bargaining gives employees a voice and empowers them to negotiate for better working conditions, making the workplace fairer for everyone (Fourie, 2018).

According to Rabiu & Kamal (2006), collective bargaining promotes stability in the workplace. Collective bargaining agreements provide a clear understanding of the rights and responsibilities of both employees and employers, reducing the likelihood of conflicts and disputes. The agreements also set clear rules and procedures for resolving disputes, reducing the risk of strikes and other disruptive actions. This stability is beneficial for both employees and employers, as it helps to create a more productive and harmonious workplace. Collective bargaining also helps to promote equality and fairness in the workplace. By negotiating as a group, employees can ensure that their rights and interests are taken into account and that they are not treated unfairly by their employers. Collective bargaining helps to prevent discrimination and ensure that all employees are treated equally, regardless of their race, gender, age, or any other characteristic (Doellgast & Benassi, 2020).

Collective bargaining also contributes to the overall health of the economy. When employees have a voice in their workplace and are able to negotiate for better wages and benefits, they are more likely to be satisfied with their jobs and stay with their employers for longer. This increased job stability benefits the economy as a whole, as it reduces the cost of employee turnover and helps to maintain a stable and skilled workforce. Collective bargaining also promotes innovation and efficiency in the workplace. By working together, employees and employers can identify ways to improve the workplace and increase productivity. The collective bargaining process provides a forum for employees to raise concerns and suggest new ideas, and for employers to listen and respond to those ideas. This promotes a culture of innovation and continuous improvement, making the workplace more efficient and effective. Therefore, collective bargaining cannot be overstated. It provides a platform for employees to negotiate better working conditions, promotes stability in the workplace, promotes equality and fairness, contributes to the overall health of the economy, and promotes innovation and efficiency. It is an essential tool for ensuring that employees have a voice in their workplace and that their rights and interests are taken into account.

6. Benefits of Collective Unionization

Unionization has become an increasingly important issue in the education sector as educators and support staff seek to secure better working conditions, salaries, and benefits. Unionization refers to the process of forming a union, or a group of workers who come together to negotiate with their employer about their employment conditions, salaries, and benefits. Collective bargaining is the negotiation between the union and the employer to draft a contract that outlines the terms and conditions of employment for the workers. The significance of unionization in collective bargaining in education is immense, as it provides a means for educators and support staff to assert their voice in the workplace and advocate for their rights and interests.

The significant benefit of unionization in education is that it provides a sense of security for educators and support staff. Through union negotiations, contracts can be established that guarantee fair salaries, benefits, and employment conditions for union members. This is particularly crucial in the education sector, where the workload can be demanding and the pay is often lower compared to other professions. By forming a union, educators and support staff can ensure they are paid a fair wage for their work and protected from arbitrary or unjust treatment by their employer.

Unionization in education also allows educators and support staff to have a voice in the workplace. Unions offer a platform for workers to represent their rights and interests and engage in discussions with their employers about relevant issues. This is particularly important in the education sector, as decisions regarding the workload of teaching and support staff, salaries, and benefits can significantly impact the quality of education and the well-being of educators and support staff. By having a voice in the workplace, educators and support staff can contribute to shaping policies and practices that affect their employment conditions and the quality of education for students. In addition to these advantages, unionization in education also promotes a sense of community and solidarity among educators and support staff (Susan, 2005). Unions bring together workers from diverse backgrounds and experiences, providing them with the opportunity to collaborate and achieve common goals. This sense of community can offer support and encouragement for educators and support staff as they face workplace challenges and can strengthen the workforce. By working together, educators and support staff can effectively advocate for their rights and interests and promote the well-being of the education sector.

Moreover, unionization in education can also play a role in maintaining and promoting high standards in the education sector. Unions can negotiate contracts that include provisions for professional development and training and advocate for policies that support the continuous improvement of the quality of education. This is crucial for both educators and support staff, as well as for students, as it ensures that the education sector is providing the highest-quality education possible. The creation of unions in the education sector can also help to promote the value of education and the important role that educators and support staff play in shaping the future of students (Borseth, 2022).

In addition to the benefits outlined, unionization in education also has wider implications for society. A strong education sector, with well-supported and fairly compensated educators and support staff, is essential for the development of a well-educated and informed society. By advocating for better employment conditions and salaries, unions in the education sector can contribute to the improvement of society as a whole. Furthermore, the creation of unions in the education sector can also serve as a model for other sectors and encourage the growth of organized labor in other industries.

It is important to note that the creation of unions in the education sector is not without challenges. There can be resistance from employers, who may view unions as a threat to their authority and control. Educators and support staff may also face challenges in organizing and forming a union, particularly in environments where the laws and regulations surrounding unionization are unfavorable.

7. Constraints and Barriers in Collective Bargaining

Collective bargaining, the process of negotiating the terms and conditions of employment between an employer and a union representing the employees, is a crucial component of labor relations in many industries, including education. Despite its importance, there are several challenges that can limit its effectiveness.

One of the major challenges is a lack of legal recognition for collective bargaining in some countries, making it difficult for unions to engage in meaningful negotiations with employers (Rabiu & Kamal, 2006). This can also result in retaliation from employers for advocating for their members and workers having no recourse if their rights are violated. The right to strike, another critical component of collective bargaining, is also restricted in many countries, making it difficult for workers to use their collective power to negotiate for better wages, benefits, and working conditions.

Employer resistance is another challenge, with some employers viewing unions as a threat to their authority or not wanting to pay higher wages and benefits negotiated by unions. Employers may use tactics such as intimidating workers, promoting anti-union sentiment, or engaging in illegal practices to resist unions. The power imbalance between the employer and workers, exacerbated by a lack of legal protections, weak enforcement mechanisms, and limited resources available to unions, can also hinder the effectiveness of collective bargaining (Fei, 2018).

Broader economic conditions, such as high unemployment, weak consumer demand, and low wage growth, can also impact the effectiveness of collective bargaining, as employers may be less willing to agree to the demands of unions and workers may have less bargaining power. Political interference can also influence the outcome of negotiations between employers and unions, making it difficult for unions to negotiate fair and equitable outcomes for workers (Fei, 2018).

Lack of transparency and accountability in negotiations between employers and unions can also hinder collective bargaining, with negotiations often conducted behind closed doors and limited opportunities for workers to participate in the negotiation process. The decline in union membership in many countries also makes it more challenging for unions to exert bargaining power and negotiate for fair outcomes (Fei, 2018).

8. Recommendations for Overcoming Barriers

Collective bargaining is a critical process that allows workers to negotiate with employers for better wages, benefits, and working conditions. However, there are several barriers that can prevent collective bargaining from being effective. To overcome these barriers, the following recommendations can be made.

Governments should provide legal recognition and protection for collective bargaining and ensure that unions have the right to negotiate with employers on behalf of their members. This will give workers a stronger voice and ensure that their rights are protected. Additionally, governments should ensure that workers have the right to strike without fear of retaliation. This is a critical component of collective bargaining and will give workers the ability to take collective action when necessary.

Governments should take steps to address employer resistance to collective bargaining and unionization efforts. This may include enforcing labor laws, penalizing employers who engage in anti-union practices, and promoting a positive view of unions. Additionally, governments should work to address the power imbalance between employers and workers and ensure that workers have access to strong and effective unions. This may include strengthening legal protections for workers, improving enforcement mechanisms for labor laws, and providing resources to unions.

When negotiating collective bargaining agreements, it is important to consider the broader economic context, including the level of unemployment, consumer demand, and wage growth. This will help ensure that agreements are fair and equitable for workers. Additionally, governments should avoid interfering in negotiations between employers and unions and promote a politically neutral environment for collective bargaining. This will help ensure that unions can negotiate for fair and equitable outcomes without political interference. Finally, negotiations between employers and unions should be transparent and accountable, with opportunities for workers to participate in the process and hold their representatives accountable. Governments should support union membership and encourage workers to join unions, giving workers a stronger voice in the workplace and access to strong and effective bargaining power.

9. Conclusion

Unionization and collective bargaining in education are important for improving working conditions and benefits for educators and support staff. The benefits of unionization include job security, a voice in the workplace, community and solidarity among workers, promoting high standards in education, and contributing to the overall improvement of society. Collective bargaining provides a platform for employees to negotiate better working conditions, promotes stability in the workplace, promotes equality and fairness, contributes to the overall health of the economy, and promotes innovation and efficiency. However, there are barriers to effective collective bargaining such as limited bargaining power, lack of legal recognition and protection, and employer resistance. Recommendations to overcome these barriers include providing legal recognition and protection for collective bargaining, ensuring the right to strike without fear of retaliation, addressing employer resistance, addressing the power imbalance, considering the economic climate, promoting political neutrality, promoting transparency and accountability, and supporting union membership. By addressing these barriers and promoting unionization in education, we can create a more equitable and just workplace for educators and support staff.

References

Adams, C.F. (1970), "Alienation and Negotiation Process", U.S. Department of Health, Education and Welfare National Institute of Education. http://www.eric.ed.gov/PDFS/ED117846.pdf (EriĢim Tarihi: 20.05.2021).
Argyle, M. (1980). *The Social Psychology of Work*. Penguin Books.
Bolam. (2004). Leadership preparation and development — A perspective from the United Kingdom.
Borseth, C. (2022). Teachers' union's collective bargaining agreements and their impact on school functions. *Bethel University. Spark Repository*. Retrieved from https://spark.bethel.edu/etd/813.

Brunner, E., Hyman, J., & Ju, A. (2020). School finance reforms, teachers' unions, and the allocation of school resources. *Review of Economics and Statistics, 102*(2), 473–489.

Bryson, J., Berry, F.S., & Yang, K. (2010). The state of public strategic management research: A selective literature review and set of future directions. *The American Review of Public Administration, XX*(X), 127.

Bush, T. (2007). Educational leadership and management: Theory, policy, and practice. *South African Journal of Education, 27*(3), 391–406. Retrieved from tony.bush@ntlworld.com.

Casey, E.G., William, K., & Ben, P. (2018). Exploring the politics of collective bargaining and unions in education. *Educational Policy*, 1–9. doi:10.1177/0895904817752882.

Doellgast, V. & Benassi, C. (2020). Collective bargaining. In *Handbook of Research on Employee Voice.* Virginia Doellgast: Edward Elgar Publishing.

Donley, M. (1976). The American teacher: From obedient servant to militant professional. *Phi Delta Kappan, 1*, 112–117.

Duignan, B. (2019, September 24). *Britannica.* Retrieved from trade union: https://www.britannica.com/topic/trade-union.

Fei, W. (2018). Social justice leadership — Theory and practice: A case of Ontario. *Educational Administration Quarterly, 54*(3), 470–498. doi:10.1177/0013161X18761341.

Fourie, E. (2018). The impact of school principals on implementing effective teaching and learning practices. *International Journal of Educational Management*, 1–25. https://doi.org/10.1108/IJEM-08-2017-0197.

Gondhalekar, V. & Kessler, L. (2021). Right-to-work laws: A brief review. *SSRN*, 32. doi:10.2139/ssrn.3887029.

García-Serrano, C. (2009). Job satisfaction, union membership and collective bargaining. *European Journal of Industrial Relations, 15*(1), 91–111.

ILO. (2015). *Collective Bargaining.* Geneva: International Labour Organization. Retrieved from https://www.ilo.org/travail/info/instructionmaterials/WCMS_425004/lang--en/index.htm.

ILO. (2023). Questions and answers. International Labour Organization (ILO). Retrieved from https://www.ilo.org/empent/areas/business-helpdesk/faqs/lang--en/index.htm.

Jeffrey, S. & Casey, I. (1991). Excludability and the effects of free riders: Right-to-work laws and local public sector unionization. *Public Finance Quarterly, 19*, 293–315.

Kennedy, J. (1984). When collective bargaining first came to education: A superintendents viewpoint. *Government Union Review, 1*(1), 4–26.

Lu, Y. L. & Lin, Y. C. (2016). How to identify effective schools in the new period: use the fuzzy correlation coefficient of distributed leadership and school effectiveness. *International Journal of Intelligent Technologies and Applied Statistics, 9*(4), 347–359.

Michael, D. (1982). *Collective Bargaining, Teachers and Job Satisfaction.* Drake University.

O'Brady, S. & Doellgast, V. (2021). Collective voice and worker well-being: Union influence on performance monitoring and emotional exhaustion in call centers. Industrial relations. *A Journal of Economy and Society, 60*(3), 307–337. doi:10.1111/irel.12286.

Oduol, T. (2019). Ethical dilemmas in education: A case study of challenges faced by secondary school leaders in Kenya. *Journal of Educational Administration, 57*(6), 601–614. https://doi.org/10.1108/JEA-05-2017-0060.

Paul, B. (2021, February 11). Boycewire.com. Retrieved from BoyceWire https://boycewire.com/collective-bargaining-definition-types-and-examples/.

Rabiu, S.S. & Kamal, H.H. (2006). The right to collective bargaining in Malaysia in the context of ILO standards. *Asian Journal of Comparative Law,* (1), 1–20. doi:10.1017/S219460780000079X.

Rogers, R. (1988). San Joaquin county teachers' perceptions of collective bargaining. University of the Pacific Theses and Dissertations. Retrieved from https://scholarlycommons.pacific.edu/uop_etds/3418.

Shaturaev, J. (2021). Scientific horizon in the context of social crisis. The difference between educational management and educational leadership and the importance of the educational responsibility. *Academic Research in Educational Sciences, 3*(8), 126–137.

Sonia, M., Erica, G.F., Gail, T.F., & Brad, J. (2020). Collective dimensions of leadership: Connecting theory and method. *Human Relations, 73*(4), 441–463. doi: 10.1177/0018726719899714.

Solomon, M.K. (2019). Influence of leadership as a determinant of collective bargaining agreement on performance of state corporations in Kenya. *International Journal of Human Resource and Procurement, 8*(1), 47–57. Retrieved from http://www.ijsse.org.

Susan, H., Tayo, F., & Thomas, A.K. (2011). Collective bargaining for the 21st century. *Journal of Industrial Relations, 53*(2), 225–247. doi:10.1177/0022185610397144.

Susan, M.J. (2005). The effects of collective bargaining on teacher quality. Collective Bargaining in Education: Negotiating Change in Today's Schools, pp. 111–140. Retrieved from https://www.researchgate.net/profile/Susan-Johnson-37/publication/267417829_The_Effects_of_Collective_Bargaining_on_Teacher_Quality/links/56b3ea2e08ae636a540d20e1/The-Effects-of-Collective-Bargaining-on-Teacher-Quality.pdf.

© 2025 World Scientific Publishing Company
https://doi.org/10.1142/9789811294730_0003

Chapter 3

Best Practices for Vocational Teacher Training

Shifaz Mohamed[*,‡] and Ahmad Zabidi bin Abdul Razak[†,§]

Faculty of Education, University of Malaya, Kuala Lumpur, Malaysia

†*Department of Educational Management, Planning and Policy Faculty of Education, University of Malaya, Kuala Lumpur, Malaysia*

‡*shifax@gmail.com*

§*zabidi@um.edu.my*

Abstract

The SDGs of the UN and the Education 2030 framework of the OECD emphasize the importance of vocational education in promoting life-long learning and preparing students for the future workforce. Research shows that generic or employability skills, also known as "soft skills," are the most in-demand skills in the current labor market. However, many countries are struggling to fulfill the requirements of industries, even though skilled education-based TVET programs are incorporated within their education systems. The availability of skilled and qualified trainers or teachers is a major challenge for these countries. This chapter proposes a model for preparing vocational teachers to provide the necessary knowledge and skills, focusing on best practices in curriculum, teaching and learning strategies, assessments, and outcomes. This study emphasizes the importance of a future-focused curriculum framework that incorporates the needs and experiences of students, aligns with educational policies and societal expectations, and takes into consideration the institutional and societal context in which the school operates. The role of the vocational teacher is to guide students in acquiring and organizing the syllabus and using effective learning methods, with a focus on competence-based assessment. The outcome of good vocational teacher training is human capital development, which builds intelligence, work energy, optimism, trustworthiness, and commitment.

Keywords: Vocational education, teacher training, competency, professional development, modern methods.

1. Introduction

The Sustainable Development Goals (SDGs) of the United Nations (UN) and the Education 2030 framework of the Organization for Economic Co-operation and Development (OECD) both emphasized the importance of vocational education in promoting lifelong learning and preparing students for the future workforce (UNESCO, 2016; OECD, 2018; Taysum, 2019). According to numerous research studies, certain types of generic skills, also known as employability skills, are the most in-demand skills in today's labor market (Pang et al., 2018; Nusrat & Sultana, 2019). In addition, these generic skills are referred to as "soft skills," which encompass a wide range of non-academic abilities that involve group interaction and aspects of personality (Abdullah et al., 2019). Furthermore, labor force requires young people to be equipped with these employable skills to become a resilient member of the workforce (Willison et al., 2017).

The school learning process is thought to enhance a pupil's intellectual potential, solve social needs, increase employability so that they can contribute to the economy, and promote a firm social and political system (Fatade et al., 2017). However, linking the gap between education and employment is recognized as a barrier in most countries. Many countries across the globe, especially OECD countries, are dealing with challenges to fulfill the requirements of industries, even though skilled education-based programs or Technical Vocational Education and Training (TVET) programs are incorporated within the system (Gill, 2018). Besides, these countries need to focus on affordable, high-quality TVET access, the acquisition of technical and vocational skills for employment, respectable work, entrepreneurship, the eradication of gender disparity, and ensuring access for the most vulnerable. The availability of skilled and qualified trainers or teachers is a major challenge for these countries (Affero *et al.*, 2018; Chinedu *et al.*, 2018a; Dewey, 1916; Jailani Yunos *et al.*, 2019). In this chapter, we will delve into the ways that vocational teachers can be better prepared to provide the knowledge and skills needed for success in the labor force. By exploring best practices in curriculum, teaching and learning strategies, assessments, and outcomes, a model is recommended along with the challenges in vocational teacher training.

2. Good Curriculum for Good Outcomes

A curriculum is the foundation of education, defining how a system of education should operate and how people should be brought up in society (Beauchamp, 1975; Yaşar & Aslan, 2021). Dewey (1916) acknowledged the definitions of the standardized curriculum but insisted that the curriculum should begin with the child and added that the teacher needs to create a connection between the material with the student. Consequently, Dewey (1916) defined the curriculum as a set of pre-planned experiences (Yaşar & Aslan, 2021). Curriculum theory, as a sub-theory of educational theory, is concerned with the creation of knowledge in professional education and serves a wider purpose than curriculum practices (Beauchamp, Curriculum Theory, 1975).

Different scholars have different perspectives on curriculum theory. According to Beauchamp (1982), curriculum theory is a body of linked claims or propositions that give meaning to the concept of curriculum, its creation, implementation, and evaluation. Kridel (2010) described it as an interdisciplinary study that examines the curriculum's historical, gendered, political, racial, ethnic, global, post-modern, autobiographical, and religious components. Macdonald (1971) viewed it as one of the least understood notions in education theory while McCutcheon (1982) saw it as a collection of approaches for analyzing, interpreting, and comprehending educational phenomena. Mordhorst and Jenert (2022) used Kelly (2009) as the source to define curriculum theory, stating that curriculum theory is concerned with how to incorporate broad educational objectives into a program that offers opportunities for learning and supports students in achieving those goals as effectively as feasible.

According to John Dewey, an influential educational reformer in the 20th century, curriculum theory is deeply involved in the three contextual layers in which schools are situated and operate: the institutional context, which includes educational policies, school types, streams or programs, school subjects, grade levels, and assessment and examination requirements; the societal context, which includes social structures or conditions and social expectations on education (school and classroom cultures, teacher and student characteristics, teacher–student interactions, classroom activities, outside-classroom activities, etc.); and the national and international context, which is also part of the societal context (Dewey, 1916; Deng, 2016). Overall, curriculum theory is seen as a fundamental framework for the learning environment from which teachers should create instruction plans for particular classroom populations (Beauchamp, 1975; Beauchamp, 1982; Yaşar & Aslan, 2021; Mordhorst & Jenert, 2022).

Often, the implementation of any vocational education and training (VET) curriculum occurs in the complementary physical and social contexts of educational institutions and enterprises, each with its own purposes, objectives, processes, and practices (Choy & Wärvik, 2019). Furthermore, Choy and Wärvik (2019) stated that for learning to be properly integrated as students build their occupational competence to become effective members of the workforce and society, they must engage in this duality and reconcile the experiences they have received in each location. According to McConnell *et al.* (2009), a person with more education and training is able to contribute a greater quantity of valuable and productive work than someone with less education and training (Wuttaphan, 2017).

Teachers constantly refine their pedagogy and tailor their lessons to the abilities and talents of their pupils (Panth & Maclean, 2020). The logical and optimal use of technology (in line with the teachers' institutional mission and curriculum) is referred to as pedagogical/curricular competence, whereas didactic/methodological competence enhances learning experiences by integrating ICT into other educational activities in a motivating way (Vilppola *et al.*, 2022). A future-focused curricular framework for education and training is required so that students may confidently prepare for and adapt to new needs and know how to reskill and upskill in order to stay current and effective (Panth & Maclean, 2020; Kamaluddin *et al.*, 2021). In addition, the curricula for TVET should include three main competencies: personal traits to deal with the environment within the TVET system; teaching, learning, and training to understand pedagogy, subject knowledge, and required skills in the VET curriculum; and technical and innovative skill to cater to the diverse needs of occupational areas within the labor force (Affero *et al.*, 2018).

Based on the literature, it is evident that curriculum theory is the study of how to incorporate educational objectives into a program that offers opportunities for learning effectively. According to scholars, it serves as the fundamental framework for the learning environment from which teachers should create instruction plans. John Dewey, an influential educational reformer in the 20th century, believed that curriculum theory is deeply involved in the three contextual layers in which schools operate — the institutional context, societal context, and the national and international context. The curriculum should provide opportunities for learning that support students in achieving their goals effectively and provide a foundation for teachers to create instruction plans for their specific classroom populations. A future-focused curriculum framework is necessary for students to adapt to new needs and reskill effectively. The TVET curriculum should include three main competencies: personal traits; teaching, learning, and training; and technical and innovative skill. Therefore, to enhance the curriculum for vocational teacher education, it is important to incorporate the needs and experiences of the students, align with educational policies and societal expectations, and take into consideration the institutional and societal context in which the school operates. In addition, vocational teacher training programs and the TVET curriculum should be explored to the greatest extent possible to enhance pedagogical abilities and get acquainted with innovative strategies to meet the diverse needs of pupils.

3. Teaching and Learning in VET Teacher Training

Effective and independent learning requires students to be aware of their own learning strategies, strengths and weaknesses, as well as the teacher's role to guide them in acquiring, organizing, and accessing the syllabus, using effective learning methods and procedures, and familiarizing themselves with relevant theories and concepts (Tóth, 2012). The constructivist theory, where students build their own knowledge from experience, is supported by today's theories of learning and has been emphasized in recent research on Career and Technical Education (Marques, 2017). The constructivist theory was first advocated by Jean Piaget (1896–1980), Lev Semyonovich Vygotsky (1896–1943), John Dewey (1859–1952), and Jerome Seymour Bruner (1915–2016) (Obi et al., 2019).

Piaget believed that children acquire knowledge by creating mental models of their surroundings (Piaget, 1976; Brau, 2018; Shapiro, 2020; McLeod, 2022). Vygotsky emphasized the importance of social interaction for cognitive development and learning in the context of relationships (Obi *et al.*, 2019). Dewey believed that learning occurs when a person actively participates in the learning setting, and education is most effective when it is based on action knowledge (Dewey, 1916; Shapiro, 2020). Bruner's theory states that learning occurs when students construct their own knowledge by applying prior knowledge or experiences to novel situations (Bruner, 2009; Obi *et al.*, 2019; Shapiro, 2020). He also emphasized that the theory of instruction should cover four key areas: learners' willingness to learn, making the content make sense to them, the most efficient steps that can be taken, and the types of rewards and punishments that will be given (Bruner, 2009).

The level of teacher competency has an impact on the quality of education; it has become a key factor in raising teacher proficiency, particularly for vocational educators (Minghat *et al.*, 2020). It only makes logical sense that if teaching and learning are to be successful in these shifting paradigms, a highly educated, committed, and effective teaching workforce is required (Guthrie *et al.*, 2009). Today, teaching and learning need to be integrated, which requires intellectualization with a world of work: At the personal level, it alludes to mental operations that transfer and link information learned in many locations (Choy & Wärvik, 2019).

TVET reforms depend heavily on teacher qualifications and education (Choy & Warvik, 2019). To meet the various needs of students and their learning preferences, teachers must offer a range of adaptable teaching strategies (Ali *et al.*, 2020). Several scholars cited that there are numerous teaching strategies available in the context of teaching and learning TVET, which include project-based learning, career-based learning, distance learning, e-learning, and other active learning techniques (Guthrie *et al.*, 2009; Chinedu *et al.*, 2018a, 2018b; Choy & Warvik, 2019; Ali *et al.*, 2020).

Thus, VET teachers are required to have continuous professional development to master their knowledge, abilities, and teacher characteristics (Ahmad & Rochimah, 2022). Efu (2020) viewed continuous professional development as personal development that includes both formal and informal growth. Some countries like Indonesia define VET teacher professional development as a sustained effort to advance knowledge, attitudes, and abilities to advance professionalism (Ahmad & Rochimah,

2022). Since teacher-centered, lecture-based, and rarely interactive approaches dominate in teacher preparation, the necessity for continued professional development is essential (Habler & Haseloff, 2022). Moreover, several literature reviews also revealed a determination to support these ideas and frequent references to interactive learning (Chinedu et al., 2018a; Choy & Warvik, 2019; Habler & Haseloff, 2022).

The theory of constructivism posits that students build their own knowledge from experience, which is supported by current theories of learning. The constructivist viewpoint is also emphasized in recent research on career and technical education. The theory of constructivism was first advocated by individuals such as Jean Piaget, Lev Vygotsky, John Dewey, and Jerome Bruner, who believed that learning occurs when students construct their own knowledge by applying prior knowledge or experiences to novel learning situations. The vocational teacher's role in this process is to guide students in acquiring, organizing, and accessing the syllabus, using effective learning methods and procedures, and getting familiar with relevant theories and concepts. Thus, teaching and learning theories are essential in every teaching and learning program. Integration in teaching and learning refers to doing interactive activities with students, employing the proper tools in teaching, communicating in a strategic manner to give vocational significance to varied practices in the workplace. Therefore, teaching and learning are integral parts of vocation teacher training programs. Effective teaching and learning strategies in vocational teacher training will lead to better learning outcomes and also empower teachers to continue learning and improving after the completion of their training.

4. Importance of Assessment for VET Teacher Training

Assessment is a crucial element in the process of vocational teacher training. The theories of assessment are closely related to the concept of social learning theory or sociocultural learning theory which emphasizes the importance of culture and interaction in the development of cognitive abilities. According to Vygotsky (1978), meaningful learning occurs when people are taught to use the tools of their culture, and learning is improved when the teacher and the learner share a similar perspective. Teachers are expected to foster an environment where students can be motivated to think and act in real-world situations beyond their current level of ability. Furthermore, the theory gives a more suitable grand explanation to comprehend learning progression (Shepard & Penuel, 2018).

The National Research Council (2001) states that every assessment is built upon three interrelated components: a theory of what students know and how they acquire competence in a subject area (cognition); tasks or circumstances used to gather data regarding student performance (observation); and a process for drawing conclusions from those observations (interpretation). In order to avoid compromising the validity of the conclusions reached from the assessment, these three components need to be expressly connected and created as a cohesive whole. Formative and summative tasks should be included in classroom assessments because they are both essential to instruction and learning. Formative tasks are those that are specifically created to be used as a tool for guiding lesson planning and summative tasks are those that are created to determine student grades.

Assessment of learning (AOL) is similar to the traditional idea of summative assessment, where student achievement is measured at the conclusion of a learning cycle (e.g. term tests, culminating projects, and essays) (DeLuca & Klinger, 2010). On the other hand, formative assessment is the process of analyzing, assessing, or rating students' work or performance with the goal of forming and enhancing students' competence. In the classroom setting, instructors make decisions on whether to repeat work, give further practice, or move on to the next stage for certain students based on their assessments of students' knowledge or comprehension (Tunstall & Gipps, 1996).

The nature, context, and style of the assessment can greatly impact a student's performance, which is why it is important to distinguish between competence, which is the fundamental capacity to function, and performance, which is the demonstration of that capacity in a specific setting or situation. CBA, which focuses on the ability to use a skill, is a more effective approach as it takes into account the evolving needs of students, teachers, and society. It also places a strong emphasis on the potential future activities and opportunities of graduates (Gipps, 1994; Butova, 2015; Ana *et al.*, 2019).

Typically, TVET programs use checklists, peer evaluation, teacher observations, presentations, and assessment rubrics to evaluate students' knowledge and skills (Schrode, 2017). This involves summative, formative, and competency-based evaluation, which is already explained in previous section. Current policies and practices, as mentioned by Li *et al.* (2019), in vocational teacher training programs, current regulations and practices encourage TVET innovation in curriculum, management, and instructional assessment techniques (Junmin Li *et al.*)

Formative assessment to enhance teaching and learning is clearly distinguishable from large-scale testing to track changes, hold schools accountable, evaluate instructors and training programs, or guide selection and placement decisions (Shepard & Penuel, 2018; Shepard, 2019). To guarantee an equal assessment for all students, policymakers stressed the significance of a strong alignment and tightening of the various components of the curriculum chain, including the choice of content, organization, and assessment, as well as the steering chain from the state to the local authorities and schools, in order to ensure an equal assessment for all students (Nordin & Sundberg, 2018). In addition, the standards-based education movement has increased the demand for teachers who are proficient in student assessment and evaluation (DeLuca & Klinger, 2010). However, most of the studies on the development of assessment literacy have largely concentrated on teachers' assessment attitudes (primarily in-service), giving little thought to pre-service assessment programs (DeLuca & Klinger, 2010; Minghat *et al.*, 2020).

According to Ana *et al.* (2019), the CBA planning process includes comprehending the standards or benchmarks required for the assessment, identifying the evidence needed for the assessment, choosing the appropriate methodologies for obtaining evidence, and formulating the assessment conclusion. The literature suggests that once the assessment tools, procedures, and evidence identification are in place, the assessors can begin CBA arrangement with the essential phases as outlined in the Figure 1.

Sociocultural theory stresses culture and interaction in cognitive development. Every assessment has three interrelated parts: cognition; observation; and drawing inferences from evidences. Teachers need to be well aware of the types of assessments and the late assessment strategies used in vocational studies. Students' assessment techniques need to be incorporated into vocation teacher preparation programs as the success of the vocational system heavily relies on teachers' assessment attitudes. Distinguishing competence from performance is important because assessment and evaluation strategies affect student performance. CBA planning entails understanding the benchmarks, finding the evidence

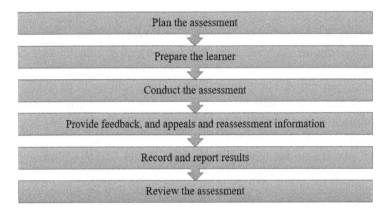

Figure 1. Steps in planning and conducting an assessment (Department of Training and Workforce Development, 2016).

needed, determining the best data-gathering methods, and making a conclusion. Hence, CBA is the most appropriate method in vocational education, as it involves a systematic planning process that helps ensure valid and reliable assessments.

5. Outcomes of Quality VET Training

The outcome of the development of vocational teacher training is human capital development (Fitz-enz, 2000), which refers to the skills and qualities that an employee brings to their work, such as intelligence, rewarding work energy, a usually optimistic attitude, trustworthiness, and commitment. Furthermore, Fitz-enz (2000) observed that aptitude, originality, inventiveness, and what are referred to as "street smarts" are all aspects of one's capacity to learn (how to get things done). On the other hand, Becker (1964) believed that each individual has a unique set of skills or abilities that they may develop or add to with training and education.

In the context of training and personal development, the Social Cognitive Learning Theory (SCLT) is referred to, which has been widely used to study self-regulation and is based on the idea that people learn through observation and human cognitive processes (Schunk, 2012). According to this idea, the entire human experience is produced by a dynamic interaction between behavior, cognition, and environment (Resurreccion, 2012). Career choices and routes are influenced by prior interactions and experiences (Bandura, 1999). Furthermore, people are also influenced by their environment; so, one's choice of surroundings determines one's future personality (Nabavi, 2012). One's self-efficacy is increased when one sees others work to complete a task, which provides inspiration that one can complete it as well by putting in the necessary effort and cultivating a conducive environment (Bandura, 1999; Theodore, 2020).

John Holland's idea of vocational choice offers a framework for delineating individuals' professional happiness (Nauta, 2010; Ayriza et al., 2020). Holland has developed precise guidelines for how six personality types — Realistic, Investigative, Artistic, Social, Enterprising, and Conventional influence achievement, tenure, and satisfaction, as well as how personality affects work and other environments (Holland, 1959; Nauta, 2010; Maldonado et al., 2020). According to Holland, people should make decisions about career environment based on their needs, values, and personality attributes (Ayriza et al., 2020).

The TVET curriculum and teacher education standards need to be customized as every country has unique features in occupational requirements in industries. Students' personality types and opinions about their academic program have an impact on their satisfaction levels (Affero et al., 2020). For example, TVET educator standards in ASEAN countries have three major components — personal and social, pedagogical and teaching methodologies, and technical (German Agency for International Cooperation, 2017) — which is not same as the components in Malaysian TVET educator standards (Affero et al., 2018). According to Schrode (2017), continuous qualitative surveys and quantitative data need to be collected based on teachers' pedagogical practices, teaching quality, and graduate satisfaction to revise TVET standards and curriculum so that TVET institutions can cater to the industrial needs of their country.

Employability of students is an evident of effectiveness of the TVET system. Teachers play key role in this practice of employability by utilizing their training and experiences. In the context of employability, providing career guidance and counseling is critical (Chinedu et al., 2018). Quality teachers are critical to achieving targets (Ali et al., 2020). Students must be made aware of their fundamental personal needs, aptitudes, resources, and potential; as a result, they must be made aware of both their strengths and weaknesses (Ana et al., 2019). Students also need to be given relevant, useful knowledge that will help solve difficulties that they face while studying and in the future in the labor market. Hence, there is a serious need for improvement in teaching methods and approaches for the creation of employability skills in students.

Good vocational teacher training produces results that contribute to human capital development. Vocational teacher education develops human capital traits such as intelligence, work energy, optimism, trustworthiness, and dedication. The founder of human capital theory argued that everyone has unique skills that may be developed via training. Human capital theorists recommend vocational teacher preparation that includes knowledge, skills, and capacities to sustain productive results. Social cognitive learning theory details how an individual's personal attributes, behavioral features, and response to those traits affect social structure parts of replicating an observed behavior and the outside world, including results or repercussions and act-based characteristics. Career choice and environment influence a person's personality and self-efficacy. John Holland's idea of vocational choice offers a framework for understanding individuals' professional happiness and how personality affects work and achievement. The employability of students is utilized to benchmark the success of the vocational system. Teachers are the key stakeholders in TVET provision so vocational teacher programs need to be monitored and updated based on feedback from the evaluation process. Students need to be made aware of their personal needs, aptitudes, and potential and given relevant knowledge to help solve difficulties they may face in the future.

6. Global Practices of TVET Teacher Training

According to Bohne *et al.* (2017), the industries, economies, and social conditions of highly developed countries like Germany are intended to be purposefully shaped through vocational programs. This is supported by the findings of Ismail *et al.* (2016), Grosch (2017), the German Agency for International Cooperation (2019), and Choy & Wärvik (2019), who argue that the success of the Technical and Vocational Education and Training (TVET) system as a whole, and the education and training of learners, depends heavily on TVET employees, especially TVET teachers, making them a crucial component of the TVET system globally. In countries like Australia and Sweden, as noted by Choy & Wärvik (2019), vocational teachers have dual responsibilities of preparing students to fulfill the demanding vocational standards of a profession while also providing them with specialized cultural skills that will assist them in transitioning into their new careers and overcoming market entry barriers and promoting the social inclusion of students who tend to be on the boundaries. To achieve this, teachers are encouraged to identify innovative pedagogical approaches as interventions that respond to and support students' backgrounds. Furthermore, Choy & Wärvik (2019) suggested integrating the TVET teacher education curriculum with the TVET curriculum, as referenced by several other scholars.

In addition to preparing their pupils for a changing world, TVET teachers also need to prepare themselves as noted by Grosch (2017). He cites the example of the educational systems of all ASEAN countries which are currently being synchronized to be competency- and outcomes-based, incorporating relevant competency standards and assessment into their educational systems (Affero *et al.*, 2016; Grosch, 2017; German Agency for International Cooperation, 2019). Teachers must be able to actively support and mold this process in addition to taking part in it (Grosch, 2017).

The success of TVET systems depends heavily on TVET teachers, who play a crucial role in preparing students to meet vocational standards and acquire specialized cultural skills. In developed countries like Germany, Australia, and Sweden, TVET teachers are also tasked with promoting social inclusion among students from disadvantaged backgrounds by identifying innovative pedagogical approaches. To prepare themselves for these responsibilities, TVET teachers must be able to actively support and participate in the ongoing process of aligning educational systems with competency- and outcomes-based standards and assessments.

7. Best Practices of TVET and Vocational Teacher Training

The International Vocational Education Training (IVET) teacher profession is governed by national IVET laws or by a national standard or qualifications system in all European nations (Misra, 2011). According to Pearson, the majority of the member states provided both pre-service and in-service training (CBI & Pearson, 2019). Teachers who enroll in school-based Continuous Vocational Education Training (CVET) receive pre-service trainings. A wide range of CVET teachers are offered ongoing training at universities, training facilities, and other locations (e.g. France, Italy, the UK). To encourage and enforce industry workers to become teachers, Europe's nations need to implement appealing recruitment and training policies (Misra, 2011). Continuous professional development and recruiting incentives are two major obstacles (Ali et al., 2020). Finland's VET system offers evidence that these problems are solvable. People with great practical expertise and self-esteem are drawn to careers in vocational teacher education (Misra, 2011). Furthermore, Misra (2011) cited another study (Lasonen & Gordon 2008) that there are more candidates than there are spots available in vocational teacher training colleges each academic year.

The Singapore Institute of Technical Education (ITE) has centered its efforts on five key elements to build a world-class TVET system: (a) industry-relevant and responsive curriculum, (b) learner-centered and discipline-specific pedagogies, (c) credible and reliable assessment and certification system, (d) engaging and authentic learning environment, and (e) enthusiastic and qualified faculty (Tan & Seet, 2020). Dual-system education programs integrate school-based (theoretical instruction) and work-based (practical instruction) instruction. This is meant to bridge the skills gap and ensure that students acquire the information and skills necessary to boost their employability (Dernbach, 2020). Educational reforms in Brunei Darussalam aligned TVET courses and curricula with corporate needs. Under a new method, industry experience has been emphasized in the appointment of TVET teachers. Brunei is making further steps to create a dual education system by increasing the number of apprenticeship programs (UNESCO, 2021).

Job satisfaction, mentoring, and assistance from the vocational institute all contribute to teachers remaining in the profession (Pazim et al., 2021). Permanent contracts for teachers increase both in-school and systemic retention rates (Doherty, 2020). According to Deever et al. (2020), knowing teachers are doing a good job, having enough time to perform work obligations, and administrative/principal support were the three most important criteria that affected the motivation to stay in the teaching profession.

In best practices of vocational teacher training, it is evident that both pre-service training and in-service training are provided to teachers. The trainings include both pedagogical practices and industrial exposure. Furthermore, vocational systems across the globe encourage industrial experts to become vocational teachers to strengthen the exposure provided to the students. The best vocational system continuously consults all stakeholders of vocational studies to improve vocational teacher training programs.

8. Challenges of TVET Teacher Training

Today, TVET can no longer be seen as the exclusive domain of educational institutions; rather, the private and public sectors must take part in the TVET reform initiative in order to continuously improve the knowledge and skill sets of TVET students with qualified TVET trainers in order to keep up with the quickly evolving and increasingly competitive economic conditions (Adams & Cheah, 2022). Major changes are required to improve work effectiveness and process efficiency to survive and develop excellence: One aspect involves human resources or strategies utilized by TVET institutions to train or educate teachers (Ali *et al.*, 2020). A study conducted by Universiti Tun Hussein Onn Malaysia and Federal University of Technology, Minna discovered that teachers who have not obtained TVET teacher education are assigned to teach vocational education and recommended that vocational teacher education programs be reoriented to use best practices for sustainability in vocational education (Chinedu *et al.*, 2018). In addition, the following issues were identified in the professional development of vocational teachers: (1) training or workshop activities are not conducted on a regular basis; (2) training has little impact on teacher competence as often the trainer's competence is not in accordance with the field of expertise; (3) training is conducted on weekdays so teachers find it challenging to take part in the activities; and (4) teachers have some administrative duties (Ahmad & Rochimah, 2022; Murwaningsih & Fauziah, 2022).

A study conducted by the Karlsruhe Institute of Technology in Germany identified a deficiency in certain competencies across ASEAN countries, including the application of modern Technical and Vocational Education and Training (TVET) methods, competency-based assessment, and student-centered teaching-learning approaches (Grosch, 2017). Teachers' understanding of students' build employability skills and their ability to help improve the skills are essential for high-quality education and have the potential to enhance their teaching techniques (Okolie *et al.*,

2020). However, teachers could lack perspective regarding the labor market abilities worth focusing on for job entry, and this is where career education experts/advisors play a vital part in the framework (Ahmad & Rochimah, 2022).

TVET is now widely acknowledged as an essential element that fosters the development of high-quality human capital for the Fourth Industrial Revolution and is no longer connected with preparing employees for low-wage occupations (Adams & Cheah, 2022). Hence, to deal with the transition in the economy from a labor-intensive to a capital-intensive era, this industrialization age requires more skilled, technically proficient, and scientifically educated employees. However, there are difficulties in finding qualified teachers with teaching experience in the field of vocational education (Antera, 2022). However, there are professional experts who lack certificates and teaching experience (Deever *et al.*, 2020). Similarly, there are qualified teachers who are capable of instructing the curriculum but lack the necessary industrial competencies.

According to a joint committee of the ILO and UNESCO, TVET professionals are in short supply everywhere (Rawkins, 2019). Over 90% of African countries reported teacher shortages and high attrition rates in the TVET sector (Symeonidis, 2015). This has been described as a "pervasive phenomenon" in the growing economies of East Asia and Southeast Asia (Rawkins, 2019) based on a study by Euler (2015). Among four major concerns, the joint committee highlighted that the lack of research on successful TVET teachers and the variability of TVET providers and actors within each country are two factors that hold back systems in terms of recruitment and pre-service training. Consequently, pre-service training and recruitment efforts usually lack clear, cohesive procedures and inadequately prepare trainees for the systems.

In rapidly changing, competitive economic conditions, the private and public sectors must participate in TVET reform in order to maintain TVET teacher training. In developing countries, TVET teacher education needs sustainability. In addition, continuous professional development activities, expertise in industrial knowledge, and training flexibility must be in place in TVET provision. Modern TVET methods and concepts like competency-based assessment and student-centered teaching–learning need to be incorporated into teacher training programs to strengthen TVET provision in ASEAN countries. Teachers in vocational subjects must also be exempt from extraneous responsibilities, as they should be occupied with internship arrangements, career counseling, and the employability of their students.

9. Recommendation

Today, TVET has become an important aspect in fostering the development of quality human capital for the Fourth Industrial Revolution. The public and private sectors need to join hands to improve the knowledge and skill sets of students through qualified vocational teachers in order to cope with rapidly changing and competitive economic conditions. Scholars have identified TVET teachers' training and their continuous professional development as major issues in the field. Furthermore, it has been identified that vocational teachers across Asia lack certain competencies, such as modern TVET methods and concepts, CBA approaches, and student-centered teaching and learning methods. In addition, teachers also need to be equipped with the essentials of high-quality TVET provision, which are the understanding and the ability to help students build employability skills. Over 90% of African countries have a shortage of qualified TVET professionals and teachers, and the TVET sector has a high attrition rate.

UNESCO and the ILO have outlined the need for research on successful vocational teachers and the variability of TVET providers as the two major factors that are causing problems in terms of recruitment and preservice training. TVET teacher training needs modern methods and concepts to ensure continuous industrial training and to provide flexibility to adapt to the rapidly changing economy. TVET teachers should also be free from extraneous responsibilities and occupied with tasks such as career counseling, internship arrangements, and the employability of their students. Considering the best practices, challenges, and needs identified from the literature about vocational teacher training, the model shown in Figure 2 is proposed for vocational teacher training.

The concept of TVET teacher training is an input–output process (Schrode, 2017). Students, teaching resources, and learning processes serve as the system's initial inputs. The teaching and learning process then channels the system's outputs out into the community (in terms of the employability of graduates, quality teaching, and socioeconomic benefits). The process starts with the TVET curriculum, which consists of both student curriculum and teacher training standards. Based on this embedding, formative, summative, and competency-based teaching and learning methodologies are used, producing targeted program outcomes.

To be relevant, a TVET system must be able to predict and match skills with training demands at all levels, as well as adapt to a dynamic

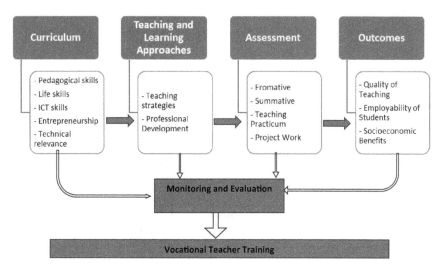

Figure 2. Conceptual model adapted using model of Schrode (2017).

environment. Typically, for a labor market to function properly, robust employment, educational, and skills policies, as well as the related support structures, are required. The effectiveness of the strategies utilized to train the system has a huge impact on the TVET system. The practices of vocational teacher training depend on the curriculum, the technical expertise provided to the teachers, and the employability of the students. By considering these variables, best practices of vocational teacher training can be established and implemented.

10. Conclusion

In conclusion, vocational teacher training is a key aspect of maintaining the competitiveness of rapidly changing economies and preparing students for the 4th I.R. It is crucial for TVET institutions to prioritize the training of teachers to meet these needs due to the increasing demand for skilled and technically proficient employees. Both the private and public sectors must be involved in the TVET reform initiative to ensure continuous improvement of TVET education. Modern TVET methods and concepts, such as competency-based assessment and student-centered teaching and learning, must be incorporated into vocational teacher training programs. Furthermore, the importance of continuous professional development and industrial expertise in vocational education cannot be overstated. Shortages of TVET professionals and high attrition rates have been reported globally, making pre-service training and recruitment efforts even more critical. Hence, a sustainable model for TVET teacher training that incorporates all the best practices discussed in this chapter is imperative for providing high-quality vocational education and meeting the demands of the evolving economic landscape.

References

Abdullah, Z., Hoque, K.E., Ramlan, N.H., & Shafee, S. (2019). Designing the structural model of TVET lecturers' professionalism and generic skills based on an empirical study in Malaysia. *Sage Open*, 1–18. https://doi.org/10.1177/2158244019861456.

Adams, D. & Cheah, S.K. (2022). Technical and vocational education and training in Malaysia reflections, recognition, and renaissance. In D.D. Adams (ed.), *Education in Malaysia* (pp. 183–194). Oxfordshire, England: Routledge.

Affero, I., Hassan, R., Hussin, H., & Hanafiah, M. (2018). The development of tvet educator competencies for quality Educator. *Journal of Technical Education and Training*, *10*(2), 38–48. https://doi.org/10.30880/jtet.2018.10.02.004.

Affero, I., Hassan, R., & Kamal, M.A. (2020). The relationship between personality types, academic program preferences, and student satisfaction in TVET. *Journal of Technical Education and Training*, *12*(1), 45–58.

Ahmad, M. & Rochimah, H. (2022). Professional development and interpersonal communication: Influence on vocational teachers teaching performance. *Jurnal Pendidikan Vokasi*, *12*(1), 12–20. https://doi.org/doi.org/10.21831/jpv.v12i1.44218.

Ali, M., Koehler, T., & Triyono, B. (2020). Evaluation of Indonesian technical and vocational education in addressing the gap in job skills required by industry. In *2020 Third International Conference on Vocational Education and Electrical Engineering (ICVEE)* (pp. 157–167). Surabaya: National YunLin University of Technology. https://doi.org/10.1109/ICVEE50212.2020.9243222.

Ana, A., Widiaty, I., Murniati, D.E., Deauansavanh, Saripudin, S., & Grosch, M. (2019). Applicability of competency-based assessment for TVET interns: Comparing between Indonesia and Laos. *Journal of Technical Education and Training*, *11*(2), 45–56.

Antera, S. (2022). Being a vocational teacher in Sweden: Navigating the regime of competence for vocational teachers. *International Journal for Research in Vocational Education and Training*, *9*(2), 269–293. https://doi.org/doi.org/10.13152/IJRVET.9.2.6.

Ayriza, Y., Suryana, D., & Margaretha, M. (2020). The application of Holland's theory in career guidance: Personality types and career satisfaction. *Journal of Career Education and Development*, *34*(2), 145–157. https://doi.org/10.1016/j.jced.2020.04.003.

Bandura, A. (1999). Handbook of personality. In D. L. A. Pervin & O. P. John (eds.), *The Coherence of Personality* (2nd edn., pp. 154–196). New York: Guilford Publications.

Bandura, A. (1999). Social cognitive theory: An agentic perspective. *Asian Journal of Social Psychology*, *2*(1), 21–41. https://doi.org/10.1111/1467-839X.00024.

Beauchamp, G.A. (1975). *Curriculum Theory*. Wilmette, IL: Kagg Press.

Beauchamp, G.A. (1982). *Curriculum Theory: A Framework for Learning and Teaching*. Harper & Row.

Beauchamp, G.A. (1982). *Curriculum Theory: Meaning, Development, and Use*. Wilmette, IL: Kagg Press.

Bohne, C., Eicker, F., & Haseloff, G. (2017). Vocational education and training in Germany: Shaping industries and economies through targeted programs. *International Journal of Vocational Education and Training Research*, *8*(2), 101–113. https://doi.org/10.1080/XXXX.

Brau, A. (2018). The development of cognitive structures in children: Understanding Piaget's theory. *Journal of Developmental Psychology*, *29*(4), 209–222. https://doi.org/10.1080/08981928.2018.1481512.

Bruner, J.S. (2009). *The Process of Education* (expanded edition). Harvard University Press.

Butova, Y.G. (2015). The history of development of competency-based education. *Asian Social Science*, *11*(3), 240–244.

CBI & Pearson. (2019). *Education and Learning for the Modern World: CBI/Pearson Education and Skills Survey Report 2019*. London: Confederation of British Industry (CBI) and Pearson.

Chinedu, C.C., Mohamed, A., & Ajah, A.O. (2018a). A case analysis of the visibility of sustainability in a TVE teacher training program: Evidence from the program curriculum of an HEI. *Traektoriâ Nauki = Path of Science*, *4*(1), 5001–5011. https://doi.org/10.22178/pos.30-7.

Chinedu, C.C., Mohamed, A., & Ajah, A. (2018b). A systematic review on education for sustainable development: Enhancing TVE teacher training program. *Journal of Technical Education and Training*, *10*(1). https://doi.org/10.30880/jtet.2018.10.01.009.

Chinedu, C.C., Olabiyi, O.S., & Kamin, Y. (2018). Strategies for improving the employability of technical and vocational education and training graduates in Nigeria. *Education + Training*, *60*(7/8), 735–749.

Chinedu, C.C., Olabiyi, O.S., & Kamin, Y. (2018). Reorienting vocational teacher education: The need for best practices in vocational education for sustainability. *Journal of Technical Education and Training*, *12*(1), 33–45.

Choy, S., & Wärvik, G.B. (2019). Integration of learning in educational institutions and workplaces: A dual perspective on vocational education and training. *Journal of Vocational Education & Training, 71*(4), 515–533.

Deever, D.A., Grubaugh, S., Levitt, G., & Gonzales, G. (2020). Why new career & technical education teachers leave, why new ones stay and how principals affect attrition and retention rates. *Journal of Education and Human Development, 9*(2), 1–12. https://doi.org/10.15640/jehd.v9n2a1.

DeLuca, C. & Klinger, D.A. (2010). Assessment literacy development: Identifying gaps in teacher candidates' learning. *Assessment in Education: Principles, Policy & Practice, 17*(4), 419–438. https://doi.org/10.1080/0969594x.2010.516643.

Department of Training and Workforce Development. (2016). *Assessment in the VET Sector.* West Perth, Western Australia, Australia.

Department of Training and Workforce Development. (2016). *Steps in Planning and Conducting an Assessment.* Government of Western Australia. Retrieved from https://www.dtwd.wa.gov.au.

Dernbach, A. (2020). Bridging the skills gap: Enhancing employability through vocational education and training. *Journal of Education and Workforce Development, 25*(2), 118–130.

Dewey, J. (1916). *Democracy and Education: An Introduction to the Philosophy of Education.* New York: Free Press. https://doi.org/www.ilt.columbia.edu/publications/dewey.html.

Doherty, J. (2020). A systematic review of literature on teacher attrition and school-related factors that affect it. *Teacher Education Advancement Network Journal, 12*(1), 75–84.

Efu, S.I. (2020). An evaluative inquiry into continuing professional development: Understanding faculty perceptions. *Teacher Development, 24*(5), 688–708.

Fatade, A.O., Udeani, U.N., Ogunleye, A., Olabiyi, O.S., & Awofala, A.O. (2017). School Administrators' perceptions of the employability of preservice science, technology, and mathematics teachers through teaching practice in Nigeria. *International Journal of Research in Education and Science, 3*(1), 42–55.

Fitz-enz, J. (2000). *The ROI Human Capital: Measuring the Economic Value of Employee Performance.* American Management Association.

German Agency for International Cooperation (GIZ). (2017). *TVET Educator Standards in ASEAN: Development and Implementation.* Bonn: GIZ.

German Agency for International Cooperation (GIZ). (2019). *Advancing Vocational Education and Training: Frameworks and Initiatives in Germany.* Bonn: GIZ.

Gill, R. (2018). Building employability skills for higher education students: An Australian example. *Journal of Teaching and Learning for Graduate Employability, 9*(1), 84–92.

Gipps, C. (1994). *Beyond Testing: Towards a Theory of Educational Assessment.* Routledge.

Grosch, M. (2017). Developing a competency standard for TVET teacher education in ASEAN countries. *Jurnal Pendidikan Teknologi dan Kejuruan, 23*(3), 270–286.

Guthrie, H., Harris, R., Simons, M., & Karmel, T. (2009). Teaching for technical and vocational education and training. In D.L. Saha & A. Dworkin (eds.), *International Handbook of Research on Teachers and Teaching* (pp. 851–863). Boston, MA: Springer.

Habler, B. & Haseloff, G. (2022). TVET research in SSA: Recommendations for thematic priorities. *Africa Journal of Technical and Vocational Education & Training, 7*(1), 3–27. https://doi.org/10.53832/opendeved.0268.

Holland, J.L. (1959). A theory of vocational choice. *Journal of Counseling Psychology, 6*(1), 1–11.

Ismail, A., Hassan, R., Masek, A., Hamzah, N., Ismail, I.M., & Subramaniam, T.S. (2016, December). Implementation of vocational training into TVET's teacher program for national core standard. In 2016 IEEE 8th International Conference on Engineering Education (ICEED) (pp. 28–31). IEEE.

Ismail, A., Hassan, R., & Kamal, M.A. (2016). The role of vocational education and training in enhancing industrial development: A comparative analysis of Malaysia and Germany. *Journal of Technical Education and Training, 8*(2), 23–35.

Jailani Yunos, J., Ismail, Z., & Ahmad, T.B.T. (2019). The challenges in ensuring skilled and qualified trainers for technical and vocational education and training (TVET) in Malaysia. *Journal of Technical Education and Training, 11*(3), 113–123.

Kamaluddin, M.A., Hoque, K.E., Razak, A.Z., & Yaacob, M.M. (2021). Examining the effectiveness of lifelong learning programme on the learners: A way forward to policy. *Malaysian Online Journal of Educational Management, 9*(2), 46–62.

Kridel, C. (Ed.). (2010). *Encyclopedia of Curriculum Studies*. Sage Publications.

Lasonen, J., & Gordon, L. (2008). The supply and demand of vocational teachers: Challenges in vocational teacher education. *Journal of Vocational Education and Training, 60*(4), 329–344.

Li, J., Wang, X., & Zhao, J. (2019). Innovations in vocational teacher training programs: Curriculum, management, and instructional assessment. *Journal of Technical and Vocational Education, 41*(2), 123–138.

Macdonald, J.B. (1971). Curriculum theory. *Journal of Educational Research, 64*(5), 195–200.

Maldonado, G., Rothwell, W., & Rothwell, A. (2020). Personality, career choice, and job satisfaction: Revisiting Holland's theory. *International Journal of Career Development, 17*(3), 201–213. https://doi.org/10.1108/IJCD-2020-0412.

Marques, M. (2017). Constructivist approaches in career and technical education: Bridging theory and practice. *Journal of Career and Technical Education, 32*(1), 45–58. https://doi.org/10.1016/j.jcte.2017.05.004.

McCutcheon, G. (1982). What is curriculum theory? A critique of the current thinking. *Educational Theory*, *32*(2), 121–130.

McLeod, S. (2022). Piaget's theory of cognitive development. Simply Psychology. Retrieved from https://www.simplypsychology.org/piaget.html.

Minghat, A.D., Mustakim, S.S., Ana, A., Kassymova, G.K., & Suparman. (2020). Measuring technical and vocational education and training (TVET) teacher's technical competency and the development of programme-specific-directory. *International Journal for Psychological Rehabilitation*, 3730–3735. https://doi.org/10.37200/IJPR/V24I8/PR280387.

Misra, P.K. (2011). VET teachers in Europe: Policies, practices and challenges. *Journal of Vocational Education & Training, 63*(1), 27–45. https://doi.org/10.1080/13636820.2011.552732.

Mordhorst, C., & Jenert, T. (2022). Curriculum theory as a lens for understanding educational development. *Higher Education Research & Development*, *41*(5), 1213–1228.

Murwaningsih, M., & Fauziah, H. (2022). Issues in the professional development of vocational teachers: Challenges and recommendations. *Journal of Vocational Education and Professional Development*, *15*(3), 110–123.

Nabavi, R.T. (2012). Bandura's social learning theory and social cognitive learning theory. *Theory of Developmental Psychology*, *1*(1), 1–8.

Nauta, M.M. (2010). The development, evolution, and status of Holland's theory of vocational personalities: Reflections and future directions. *Journal of Counseling Psychology*, *57*(1), 11–22.

Nordin, A. & Sundberg, D. (2018). Exploring curriculum change using discursive institutionalism — A conceptual framework. *Journal of Curriculum Studies, 50*(6), 820–835. https://doi.org/10.1080/00220272.2018.1482961.

Nusrat, M., & Sultana, S. (2019). Employability skills for entry-level positions: A study on perceptions of employers and graduates. *International Journal of Business and Management Research*, *7*(2), 56–65.

Obi, E., Ofoegbu, G.I., & Okeke, T.E. (2019). Constructivist learning strategies in modern education: Applying prior knowledge to new contexts. *International Journal of Educational Research*, *56*(2), 87–99.

OECD. (2018). *The Future of Education and Skills: Education 2030*. Paris: Organisation for Economic Co-operation and Development. Retrieved from https://www.oecd.org/education/2030.

Okolie, U.C., Elom, E.N., Igwe, P.A., Binuomote, M.O., & Igu, N. (2020). How TVET teachers foster employability skills: Insights from developing countries. *International Journal of Training Research*, 1–20. https://doi.org/10.1080/14480220.2020.1860301.

Pang, E., Wong, M., Leung, C.H., & Coombes, J. (2018). Competencies for fresh graduates' success at work: Perspectives of employers. *Industry and Higher Education*, *32*(1), 46–57.

Panth, S., & Maclean, R. (2020). Refined pedagogy and lesson tailoring for diverse learner abilities in vocational education. *International Journal of Vocational and Technical Education, 12*(3), 123–134.

Pazim, K.H., Mahmud, R., Fabeil, N.F., Nordin, M.N., & Langgat, J. (2021). Special education teachers job satisfaction in Malaysia: A review. *Turkish Journal of Computer and Mathematics Education, 12*(11), 5329–5332.

Piaget, J. (1976). *Piaget's Theory of Cognitive and Affective Development: Foundations of Constructivism* (3rd ed.). New York: Longman.

Rawkins, C. (2019). *A Global Overview of TVET Teaching and Training: Current Issues, Trends and Recommendations.* International Labour Organization and United Nations Educational, Scientific and Cultural Organization.

Resurreccion, P.F. (2012). The interplay of behavior, cognition, and environment in learning. *Journal of Educational Psychology, 30*(3), 110–125.

Schrode, N. (2017). The "three branch model" of further education of in-company vocational educators: Linking in-company learning projects, external training in further education and universitylearning. In D.F. Eicker, G. Haseloff, & B. Lennartz (eds.), *Vocational Education and Training in Sub-Saharan Africa: Current Situation and Development* (pp. 183–210). W. Bertelsmann Verlag GmbH & Co.KG.

Schunk, D.H. (2012). *Learning Theories: An Educational Perspective* (6th ed.). Pearson.

Shapiro, L. (2020). The development of cognitive models in children: A modern perspective. *Cognitive Development Studies, 42*(1), 110–120.

Shepard, L.A., Penuel, W.R., & Pellegrino, J.W. (2018). Using learning and motivation theories to coherently link formative assessment, grading practices, and large-scale assessment. *Educational Measurement: Issues and Practice, 37*(1), 21–34.

Shepard, L.A. (2019). Classroom assessment to support teaching and learning. *The ANNALS of the American Academy of Political and Social Science, 683*(1), 183–200.

Symeonidis, S. (2015). Teacher shortages and attrition in African TVET systems: A regional overview. *African Journal of Vocational Education, 7*(4), 100–112.

Tan, J., & Seet, W. (2020). Building a world-class TVET system: The Singapore Institute of Technical Education's approach to curriculum, pedagogy, and faculty development. *International Journal of Vocational Education and Training, 10*(3), 225–240.

Taysum, A. (2019). *Education Policy as a Roadmap to Achieving the Sustainable Development Goals: Effecting a Paradigm Shift for Peace and Prosperity Through New Partnerships.* Emerald Publishing Limited.

Theodore, K. (2020). The influence of self-efficacy and environment on task completion: A practical approach. *Journal of Behavioral Studies*, *45*(2), 78–93.

Tóth, Z. (2012). Effective learning strategies in higher education: A guide for students and teachers. *Higher Education Review*, *44*(3), 75–89.

Tunstall, P., & Gipps, C. (1996). Teacher feedback to young children in formative assessment: A typology. *British Educational Research Journal*, *22*(4), 389–404.

Uler, D. (2015). Teacher shortages and attrition in vocational education and training: A global challenge. *International Journal of Vocational Education and Training*, *22*(1), 45–58.

UNESCO. (2016). *Strategy for Technical and Vocational Education and Training (TVET) (2016–2021)*. Paris: United Nations Educational, Scientific and Cultural Organization. Retrieved from https://unesdoc.unesco.org.

UNESCO. (2021). National Education for All 2015 review report: Brunei Darussalam, World Education Forum, Incheon, Republic of Korea. UNESCO, Paris.

UNICEF. (2019). Maldives country report. *South Asia Youth Skills and Solution Forum* (pp. 1–4). Mumbai: UNICEF.

Vilppola, J., Lämsä, J., Vähäsantanen, K., & Hämäläinen, R. (2022). Teacher trainees' experiences of the components of ICT competencies and key factors in ICT competence development in work-based vocational teacher training in Finland. *International Journal for Research in Vocational Education and Training*, *9*(2), 146–166. https://doi.org/10.13152/IJRVET.9.2.1.

Vygotsky, L.S. (1978). *Mind in Society: The Development of Higher Psychological Processes*. Harvard University Press.

Willison, D., Thomson, L.A., Connell, P., & Scott, F.J. (2017). Empowering students by enhancing their employability skills. *Journal of Further and Higher Education*, 1–17. https://doi.org/10.1080/0309877X.2017.1394989.

Wuttaphan, N. (2017). Human capital theory: The theory of human resource development, implications, and future. *Life Sciences and Environment Journal*, *18*(2), 240–253.

Yaşar, Ş., & Aslan, M. (2021). The role of curriculum in shaping societal values: A comparative perspective. *International Journal of Educational Development*, *81*, 102–119.

© 2025 World Scientific Publishing Company
https://doi.org/10.1142/9789811294730_0004

Chapter 4

Revamping Curriculum Management: Approach for Educators

Miss Hamdhiyya[*] and Kazi Enamul Hoque[†]

Faculty of Education, Universiti Malaya, Kuala Lumpur, Malaysia

[*]s2160503@siswa.um.edu.my

[†]keh2009@um.edu.my

Abstract

Curriculum management is a complicated procedure that includes planning, creating, executing, and assessing the student learning experience, which includes setting learning goals, choosing suitable teaching materials, devising assessment processes, and assessing the efficacy of the learners. In order for curricular modifications to be effective, educational managers must not only comprehend and interpret policy but also take into account their own views, values, practices, and interests. This chapter aims to advocate for a collaborative approach to curriculum management in which education managers take an active and important role in creating the curriculum to fulfill the requirements of both students and society. For this purpose, the authors identified a few barriers and described what school managers needed to consider while designing and revamping the curriculum. In order to understand the curriculum, some strategies have been highlighted that educators should follow in the curriculum design process. The chapter concludes with the recommendation for school managers to take a proactive approach and involve teachers in decision-making processes for curricular modifications.

Keywords: Curriculum management, collaborative approach, barriers to curriculum management, curricular modification.

1. Introduction

As the world undergoes fast and unprecedented change, the significance of education in determining the future has grown. Curriculum, which serves as the cornerstone of education and determines students' learning experiences, is at the forefront of this change (Nieveen & Kuiper, 2021). Due to the fast changes in technology, social and economic structures, and global dynamics, there is an increasing need to revise conventional curriculum management practices (Nieveen & Kuiper, 2021).

Curriculum management is a complicated procedure that includes planning, creating, executing, and assessing the student learning experience (Miles, 2021). It includes setting learning goals, choosing suitable teaching materials, devising assessment processes, and assessing the efficacy of the curriculum (Nordin & Sundberg, 2018). In recent years, it has become more apparent that educators must take a more active role in curriculum management. This shift in focus has been influenced by the expanding diversity of student populations, the increasing relevance of digital literacy, and the necessity for lifelong learning (Nordin & Sundberg, 2018).

To revamp curriculum management, educators must build and implement contemporary, engaging, and inclusive curricula (Miles, 2021). This requires an in-depth comprehension of the different needs of students, the most current technology developments, and the shifting dynamics of the global economy (Tapala et al., 2021). Educators must also develop critical thinking, problem-solving, and creativity in a school environment that accommodates different learning styles (Tapala et al., 2021). In addition, they must work with administrators, parents, and the community to ensure that the curriculum meets the needs of all kids. This requires continuous review and input to guarantee the curriculum's continued relevance and effectiveness throughout time. Additionally, educators must be ready to adapt and adjust the curriculum in response to changes in the learning environment and the needs of the student population.

For the success of education in the twenty-first century, the involvement of educators in curriculum management is vital (Lähdemäki, 2019). To create a relevant, engaging, and inclusive learning environment, educators must be proactive, imaginative, and collaborative Educators can build a future in which all students realize their full potential and make major contributions to society via their efforts (Lähdemäki, 2019). This chapter discusses the significant role educators play in curriculum management and how they may improve the quality and effectiveness of education. This chapter emphasizes the challenges that educators encounter when managing the curriculum and presents practical solutions and best practices that can be utilized to reform curriculum management and improve student learning results. Ultimately, this chapter advocates for a collaborative approach to curriculum management in which educators take an active and important role in creating the curriculum to fulfill the requirements of both students and society.

2. Barriers to Curriculum Management

In this section, the focus is on examining the current body of literature relating to the challenges of curriculum management. The difficulties in administering the curriculum stem from a lack of knowledge, which is exacerbated by insufficient resources, an excessive workload, and conflicting roles among leaders and members of the senior management team (SMT) (Cheung & Man Wong, 2011; Cooper, 2017; Donaldson, 2014; Edwards-Groves *et al.*, 2019; Kimpston & Rogers, 1986; Memon, 1997; Nordin & Sundberg, 2018; Tapala *et al.*, 2021; Tong, 2010).

2.1. Resistance to change

For curricular modifications to be effective, instructors must not only comprehend and interpret policy but also take into account their own views, values, practices, and interests. Unfortunately, governments frequently fail to consider these crucial aspects (Nsibande, 2002; Glatthom, 2000). It is not unusual for instructors to resist change, which may be due to a variety of reasons, including uncertainty, low motivation, lack of clarity, ambiguity, insufficient resources and support, and a desire to retain established methods (Carl, 1995).

Principals have a crucial role in ensuring successful curriculum management, but encounter a number of obstacles, including cultural traditions, material resources, and social structures (Marianne et al., 2003). Due to the historic discrimination and bureaucratic processes, some principals may oppose ceding decision-making authority during periods of curricular reform (Wallace & Huckman, 1999; Marianne et al., 2003; Zakunzima, 2005). Now that schools are more democratically run, principals have to share authority with their SMT (Zakunzima, 2005). By doing so, they may develop a curriculum that is more effective and inclusive, taking into consideration the different needs and viewpoints of both instructors and students.

2.2. Workload

According to Cardno (2003), school management in the modern era requires a high level of responsibility; however, many leaders avoid this responsibility. Scholars believe that principals have a vast array of responsibilities and that the job has become increasingly difficult and constrained over the years (Cheung & Man Wong, 2011; Harding et al., 1976; Memon, 1997; Tong, 2010). In certain instances, administrative activities such as financial and property administration take precedence over curriculum management, which can make it impossible to provide students with a quality education. Frequently, the bulk of middle managers' time is spent on paperwork, interruptions, managing school problems, and dealing with employees, students, and parents, making it difficult for them to dedicate sufficient time to curriculum oversight (Mafora & Phorabatho, 2013). Due to these variables, the efficient administration of curriculum may face several obstacles (Harding et al., 1976; Memon, 1997; Tong, 2010). It is vital to resolve these obstacles in order to properly administer the curriculum and produce beneficial educational outcomes.

2.3. Lack of training and knowledge

The process of managing and reforming curriculum is a challenging task that requires leaders to remain up to date with frequent changes in curriculum policies and their implementation (Mafora & Phorabatho, 2013). According to Fasso et al. (2016), leaders in schools play a crucial role in comprehending educational policies and curricular policy texts. Curriculum management demands a combination of knowledge, abilities, and attitudes. However, Cardno (2003) asserted that most leaders lack the necessary skills and knowledge to successfully oversee the curriculum, which limits their ability to provide strategic leadership essential for effective curriculum administration. In a recent study, Tapala *et al.* (2021) discovered that principals' training did not equip them to maintain the curriculum change process, resulting in ineffective teaching and learning.

Principals require expertise in curricular management, as teachers often require help and assistance in dealing with complex curriculum areas (Edwards-Groves *et al.*, 2019). If school leaders lack the requisite skills and expertise, it might be difficult to offer teachers appropriate direction and support the curriculum reform process. Mohamed (2017) conducted a study which showed that the NCF was not implemented according to the policy's stipulations, primarily due to a lack of training. Therefore, it is critical to provide school leaders with the required skills, knowledge, and attitudes for successful curriculum management in order to promote effective teaching and learning. In this way, educators can make sure that pupils get a good education that will help them in the future.

2.4. *Lack of resources*

Due to a lack of resources, effective curriculum management in Maldives schools is difficult to achieve (Shiyama & Shafeeqa, 2017b). Physical, human, and financial resources are required to provide successful curriculum administration (Tapala *et al.*, 2021). A key problem that educators confront when implementing curriculum effectively is a shortage of resources. According to Tapala *et al.* (2021), instructors are frequently forced to teach in overcrowded classes due to a teacher shortage, making it impossible to maintain an appropriate student–teacher ratio. Furthermore, some schools lack the financial resources to purchase instructional aids, furniture, and other physical resources that are essential to improve teaching and learning. These resource constraints make lesson planning difficult for instructors and impede effective curriculum management.

Several studies have highlighted that a key barrier to successful curriculum management is a shortage of resources (Cheung & Man Wong, 2011; Cooper, 2017; Edwards-Groves *et al.*, 2019; Geduld & Sathorar, 2016; Rudhumbu, 2015; Tapala *et al.*, 2021; Traver-Mart *et al.*, 2021). A lack of resources limits the amount of work that can be completed, affecting the quality of curriculum delivery. To summarize, a lack of resources poses a significant obstacle to the effective administration of the curriculum and educators must discover ways to overcome these constraints in order to ensure that students receive the greatest possible education.

2.5. *Role conflict*

Effective curriculum management in schools requires a clear understanding of roles by all stakeholders, according to Cooper (2017). However, Marsh (2003) suggested that the multifaceted nature of principals' positions makes it difficult for them to manage curriculum administration efficiently. Gleeson *et al.* (2020) claimed that department heads make most of the curriculum decisions, which may lead to conflict with school leaders and deputies. This, combined with their other responsibilities, creates further challenges for curriculum management (Mafora & Phorabatho, 2013). Due to past management practices, the responsibility for certain tasks may be ambiguous, leading to confusion (Alkahtani, 2017; Van Wyk, 2020). Failure to manage these conflicting responsibilities could have a negative impact on the entire school community (Donaldson, 2014; Edwards-Groves *et al.*, 2019; Geduld & Sathorar, 2016; Rudhumbu, 2015; Tapala *et al.*, 2021; Tong, 2010).

3. Understanding the Curriculum

In the realm of education, the term "curriculum" refers to a plan for learning, encompassing standards for both student learning and teacher instruction. Depending on the context, it can refer to a wide variety of resources, including teaching methods, class size, learning hours, and assessment processes. Ultimately, the curriculum is an organized set of activities and subjects that contribute to students' development throughout the school day. To understand various practices such as curriculum management, design, and evaluation, it is essential to have a clear understanding of what "curriculum" means (Cooper, 2017; Mikser *et al.*, 2016; Stoll *et al.*, 2006).

3.1. *Curriculum management*

A majority of researchers consider that curriculum management is the most important task in education. This encompasses academic leadership, instructional leadership, and administration of the core business of the school, which includes teaching and learning activities. In addition, it includes the collection, organization, and support of the official curriculum within the classroom's limits (Tapala et al., 2021; Cardno, 2003). Content management requires effective leadership skills such as encouraging, inspiring, and assisting instructors in acquiring the essential curriculum (Hughson, 2022; Tapala et al., 2021; Traver-Mart et al., 2021).

3.2. Curriculum reform

Curriculum reforms strive to evaluate and revise the "content" of knowledge, as well as learning-related concerns (Gilbert, 2010). Recognizing that educational institutions must adapt to the needs of the modern world, governments throughout the world are implementing reforms in their educational systems (Donaldson, 2014; Geduld & Sathorar, 2016; Miles, 2021; Tapala et al., 2021). The need to give students 21st-century skills and attitudes, as well as the possible influence of a particular curriculum on their learning outcomes, is driving the interest in curriculum adjustment, which is being implemented at varying speeds and via a variety of approaches.

However, curricular changes are difficult to accomplish because they need modifications to several facets that may contradict the deeply held beliefs and subjective realities of individuals and institutions (Fullan, 2015, as cited in Cheung & Man Wong, 2011). Fullan argued that for an educational reform to be effective, at least three aspects must change: materials, instructional methods, and attitudes. Viennet & Pont (2017) investigated the causes of the obstacles to implementing educational reforms, such as a shift in leadership toward greater decentralization, increased knowledge and participation by more stakeholders in the creation of education policy, and an increased emphasis on education outcomes. Launching and sustaining the curriculum involve several challenges, including high expenditure, the sensitivity of the results, and the risk aversion of stakeholders (Memon, 1997). In addition, new teaching and management strategies must be investigated in order to teach and administer the new curriculum in a classroom. As various nations have learned, the leadership style or attitude of school leaders and managers has a significant impact on the curriculum's successful implementation (Cheung & Man Wong, 2011).

3.3. Leadership approaches to curriculum management

The implementation of leadership in curriculum management depends on the senior management team's (SMT) ability to effectively execute their leadership responsibilities. Mafora & Phorabatho (2013) emphasized the importance of visionary leadership in directing the curriculum management of an SMT, which involves developing and interpreting the school's purpose and vision in line with curriculum standards. This, in turn, can motivate both teachers and students to achieve high levels of success. According to Thurlow (2000, as cited in Tapala *et al.*, 2021), strong leadership and the adoption of effective leadership strategies are necessary for efficient curriculum delivery and management. Similarly, dynamic leadership that promotes a commitment to excellent curriculum management can have a positive impact on teacher morale and motivation (West Bumham, 1992, as cited in Van Wyk, 2020).

However, it is important to note that school leaders as curriculum implementers may impact negatively on teachers' curriculum engagement (Cardno, 2003; Evans, 1998, as referenced in Traver-Mart *et al.*, 2021). In the past, bureaucratic school curriculum management methods have hindered teachers' engagement in curriculum creation and implementation, particularly in disadvantaged areas (Shiyama & Shafeeqa, 2017a). To promote successful curriculum administration, SMTs should use leadership practices that recognize teachers' efforts and establish cooperative, supportive, and facilitative relationships with teachers (Boone, 2015). Coleman *et al.* (2003), as well as Mikser *et al.* (2016), have highlighted the importance of interpersonal contact between senior leaders and workers in promoting effective curriculum management decision-making. Participatory leadership styles, such as collegial models, have also been suggested for effective curriculum decision-making, as they improve relationships with the top management team and provide teachers with the freedom to choose academic content that facilitates effective learning (Craig, 1989, as cited in Rudhumbu, 2015). This is achieved through teacher-to-teacher dialogue and curriculum-related consensus (Donaldson, 2020; Memon, 1997; Rudhumbu, 2015; Tong, 2010; Preedy, 1989).

To further aid SMTs in effective curriculum management, Thurlow (2000, as cited in Tapala *et al.*, 2021) proposed three frameworks. First, school managers must select a set of guiding principles to control curriculum management, based on the school's policies and practices for curriculum management decision-making. Second, there must be clarity of roles and responsibilities for all curriculum management staff, ensuring each team member has a shared understanding of their role and is supported in it. Finally, curriculum leaders must adopt approaches that promote curriculum management, as they serve as the foundation for effective curriculum management and can motivate instructors to actively identify and address curriculum challenges (Coleman *et al.*, 2003; Tapala *et al.*, 2021).

4. Principal's Role in Implementing the Curriculum

Leaders in educational institutions cannot effectively administer the curriculum without first until they firmly understand that their specific function occupies within the bigger picture. The data should ultimately contribute to more efficient curriculum management, resulting in improved education for everyone (Donaldson, 2014).

4.1. Creating a positive learning environment

Successful implementation of a new curriculum depends on the educational environment in which it will be implemented (Mafora & Phorabatho, 2013). In an optimal environment, educators should focus on objectives, synergistic communication, decentralized power, efficient use of resources, cohesiveness, and flexibility, as well as a positive attitude toward curriculum implementation (Cooper, 2017). The principal is responsible for modifying the learning environment to reflect these qualities (Cooper, 2017; Harding *et al.*, 1976). To establish such an environment, administrators must first embrace the curriculum change and demonstrate their commitment to it, rather than seeing it as a directive from above (Gleeson *et al.*, 2020). In addition, administrators should engage teachers in decision-making processes and provide them with the appropriate resources. This may enhance and sustain teacher morale and commitment to change (Alkahtani, 2017).

4.2. Planning

In curriculum management, planning is the most critical component. Craig (1989, as cited in Rudhumbu, 2015) argued that planning should begin with a clear articulation of goals or a vision that generates commitment and passion. Similarly, Smit & Cronje (1999, as quoted in Alkahtani,

2017) defined planning as a management activity aimed at ensuring that all stakeholders understand the organization's purpose, mission, goals, and strategies. For successful implementation of new curricula, principals must determine and provide the necessary resources (Gleeson *et al.*, 2020; Mafora & Phorabatho, 2013; Van Wyk, 2020). This requires leaders to contextualize the planning process and ensure that the proposed activities address the unique circumstances of their schools. If the implementation strategies do not consider the specific school context, curriculum improvements are likely to fail. Jansen (1998, as cited in Geduld & Sathorar, 2016) asserted that the failure of a well-designed curriculum is due to the lack of a specialized approach that addresses the unique context of under-resourced schools. Therefore, it is crucial to adopt a tailored approach that aligns with the school's context to plan and implement curricula effectively.

4.3. *Providing adequate resources*

In order to ensure that teaching and learning are aligned with the school's objectives, it is the responsibility of school administrators to coordinate school activities (Ministry of Education, 2015). This includes allocating topics and class grades to teachers based on their qualifications and areas of competence. Failure to assign appropriate responsibilities to teachers can negatively impact their confidence and morale, leading to resistance (Mafora & Phorabatho, 2013; Van Wyk, 2020).

Moreover, it is the principal's duty to find, purchase, and distribute the necessary resources (Ministry of Education, 2015). This entails evaluating the cost of effectively implementing the new educational program and ensuring that planned activities are within the budgeted amount. According to the Ministry of Education (2015), schools should allocate funds specifically for curriculum reform or modification. Without sufficient and adequate resources, curriculum goals are unlikely to be achieved (Alkahtani, 2017). A lack of resources has been identified as one of the most significant barriers to curriculum implementation by various scholars (Alkahtani, 2017; Cheung & Man Wong, 2011; Cooper, 2017; Donaldson, 2020; Gleeson *et al.*, 2020; Rudhumbu, 2015; Tapala *et al.*, 2021; Tong, 2010; Van Wyk, 2020). Hence, school leaders must ensure that adequate resources are organized to support curriculum implementation. School administrators bear the responsibility for coordinating school activities to ensure that teaching and learning align with the school's objectives. Additionally, they must allocate responsibilities to teachers based on their qualifications and competence and provide adequate resources to support curriculum implementation. Failure to fulfill these responsibilities may hinder the achievement of the school's objectives.

4.4. *Monitoring*

Monitoring teaching and learning activities is a critical aspect of curriculum management that contributes to the professional development of instructors (Edwards, 2012; Memon, 1997). However, it is important for principals to ensure that the monitoring process does not make teachers feel like they are being scrutinized in the classroom (Mafora & Phorabatho, 2013). Instead, they should emphasize that the goal of monitoring is to support teachers in delivering high-quality instruction to facilitate learning (Edwards, 2012; Keesing-Styles *et al.*, 2014; Mafora & Phorabatho, 2013). Encouraging teachers to experiment with new approaches, evaluating their practices, and enhancing their judgment should be a part of a principal's leadership style. This necessitates that school leaders have an in-depth understanding of educational theories, possess strong teaching abilities, and are well versed in both general and specific subject matter (Donaldson, 2020; Fasso *et al.*, 2016; Rudhumbu, 2015; Van Wyk, 2020). By creating a supportive environment that encourages experimentation and self-reflection, principals can cultivate a community of teachers who are continually improving their teaching abilities to enhance the quality of education for their students.

4.5. *Continuous professional development*

The nature of education is one that is continually evolving; thus, educators must continuously advance their knowledge and skills (Lahdemaki, 2019; Tapala *et al.*, 2021). School leaders play a crucial role in fostering an environment favorable to staff growth. To do so, they must acknowledge their teachers' strengths and shortcomings and give the appropriate support and tools (Geduld & Sathorar, 2016). This assistance may take numerous forms, including seminars, conferences, in-service training, advanced research, and product creation (Cooper, 2017; Donaldson, 2014; Geduld & Sathorar, 2016; Lahdemaki, 2019; Pietarinen *et al.*, 2017). The ultimate objective of teacher development should be to generate teachers who are capable of self-evaluation and self-correction, as opposed to just producing teachers who adhere to a specified teaching method (Tapala *et al.*, 2021).

Edwards-Groves *et al.* (2019) suggested that school leaders must be vigilant and evaluate all elements that influence the staff's productivity, effectiveness, and work satisfaction. As curriculum managers, school leaders should explain upcoming changes to their employees and urge them to discard outmoded teaching techniques while encouraging more study and attendance at professional development seminars and workshops (Cooper, 2017; Donaldson, 2014; Lahdemaki, 2019; Tong, 2010). According to Hall and Whitaker (1998, cited in Donaldson, 2020), school improvement and adaptability cannot be accomplished without the professional development of both school leaders and teaching personnel. Mafora and Phorabatho (2013) concurred, noting that continual training for school leaders is essential in order to improve the internal conditions of schools since leaders play a significant role in assisting teachers and other staff members.

4.6. *Curriculum implementation evaluation*

Evaluation is a fundamental process of systematically assessing the value and quality of something. As Caldwell & Spinks (1992) noted, the primary aim of evaluation is to assist schools in reflecting on their objectives, measuring their achievements, and identifying areas for improvement. However, for evaluation to be effective, it needs to be an ongoing process integrated throughout the implementation process, rather than only at the end (Alkahtani, 2017; Keesing-Styles *et al.*, 2014; Mafora & Phorabatho, 2013).

The implementation of the National Curriculum Framework (NCF) in schools requires a continuous assessment system, as outlined by the Ministry of Education of Maldives in 2015. Principals are responsible for developing this system to measure the extent to which teaching and learning objectives are met. By doing so, they can identify potential obstacles that might impede curricular changes and offer appropriate solutions. In addition, leaders can recognize and sustain excellent teaching practices that have shown positive results (Alkahtani, 2017).

Failing to assess the curriculum systematically may lead to curriculum failure, as emphasized by several studies (Cheung & Man Wong, 2011; Donaldson, 2020; Gleeson *et al.*, 2020; Harding *et al.*, 1976;

Memon, 1997). Therefore, it is crucial to have a continuous evaluation process in place to ensure the success of the curriculum implementation. The continuous evaluation of the curriculum is necessary for reflecting on objectives, identifying areas for improvement, and recognizing best practices. It is an ongoing process that needs to be integrated into the implementation of the curriculum to ensure its effectiveness. By doing so, schools can avoid potential obstacles and guarantee the success of the curriculum implementation.

5. Theoretical Perspective in Relation to Curriculum Management

In the field of curriculum management, Decker Walker's naturalistic approach emphasizes the importance of understanding the diversity of activities and responsibilities involved. As Marsh (2003) pointed out, this model reflects the actual obligations of curriculum directors, rather than simply offering suggestions on how they should carry out their tasks. The naturalistic approach demonstrates the process of curriculum administration in action, taking into account the various views, beliefs, and ideas that curriculum leaders may bring to their work (Marsh, 2003).

The first phase of this approach involves debating and discussing possible difficulties in curriculum management with the aim of reaching an agreement on the subsequent steps. The team platform, according to Walker, is where the group as a whole undertakes the administration of a course's fundamental elements. During this phase, the functions of curriculum management are described and any negative attitudes are identified. The second step of this approach is discussion, which involves problem-solving through learning and action, with debates leading to a deeper understanding of the actions to be performed. Marsh (2003) noted that principals recognize that educational activities and conditions have diverse value for team members. The last step of this methodology is action decision-making, which includes instructional design, selecting appropriate materials, defining suitable tasks for students, organizing and grading their work, and assessing their progress. The potential for success is dependent on students' ability to effectively execute, attain, and demonstrate the desired goals in their academic work.

Walker's naturalistic approach to curriculum management acknowledges the diversity of activities and responsibilities involved and provides a practical model for curriculum directors. By recognizing the importance of open discussion and problem-solving, this approach enables curriculum leaders to work together effectively, taking into account the various perspectives and beliefs they bring to their work. Through instructional design and effective assessment, this approach ultimately aims to ensure that students can achieve their academic goals.

In the field of curriculum management, Ralph Tyler's approach emphasizes the importance of student behavior and learning experiences (Marsh, 2003). This approach involves four steps that curriculum leaders must consider while developing curricula: determining the school's objectives, identifying educational experiences related to those objectives, organizing these experiences, and evaluating the outcomes. These steps are reflected not only in the goals and objectives but also in the school's vision and mission (Slattery, 2006). The collaborative approach of Tyler's theory involves including instructors in discussions and debates, as well as understanding the roles and expectations of other team members. This approach is intended to establish academic norms that contribute to student success.

Curriculum designers must determine how students can demonstrate mastery of required skills and knowledge, as well as how to evaluate the effectiveness of their preparation for future work. They must establish guidelines that benefit instruction and student growth, such as those regarding homework assignments and classroom behavior, and ensure that all educators are using effective time management techniques. In addition, they should encourage parental involvement and regularly assess the curriculum to identify strengths and weaknesses and implement necessary improvements. Critics of Tyler's paradigm have questioned its rationality. However, the theory is not inflexible; it poses questions that may be adapted to meet the needs of a school and guides curriculum leaders in facilitating conversations about curricular concerns. The theory emphasizes visionary leadership, strategic management of curriculum, cooperation, teamwork, and the decentralization of curricular decision-making to curriculum implementers. It also highlights the importance of understanding roles and responsibilities in curriculum management for successful implementation.

As suggested by these theories, it is the responsibility of school management to establish and maintain a strategic management process in educational institutions (Cheong Cheng, 1994). Leadership is responsible for managing instructional programs, promoting a positive learning climate, and coordinating curriculum across individual, program, and school

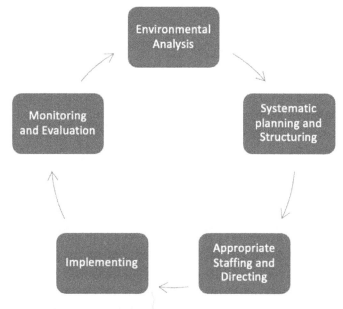

Figure 1. Strategic curriculum management process.

levels to ensure congruence (Hulpia & Devos, 2009). To successfully implement a new curriculum, educators must be willing to adjust their own attitudes, practices, and perspectives on leadership, instruction, and student achievement. Slattery (2006) argued that the global community is undergoing a paradigm shift in curriculum development and leadership, which is necessary for a new understanding of best practices. Figure 1 depicts the strategic management process (Cheong Cheng, 1994) that will lead to the curriculum change.

Strategic management is a cyclical process that can help schools improve their performance, achieve objectives, and fulfill their mission within the context of their environment (Cheong Cheng, 1994). This process involves several steps, including environmental analysis, systematic planning and construction, personnel selection and direction, implementation, monitoring, and evaluation. To begin, it is necessary to monitor the internal and external environment and collect data for planning purposes. Based on the results of the environmental analysis, a plan of action is developed and resources are allocated to support individual, program, and school objectives. Competent personnel are selected and trained to achieve the goals outlined in the plan. Performance is monitored and assessed at the individual, program, and school levels to ensure that goals are being met. The results of monitoring and evaluation contribute to the next cycle of the strategic management process.

The strategic management process is an educational activity that contributes to the growth and development of students at the individual, programmatic, and institutional levels. Effective administration requires the participation of school personnel and administrative leadership throughout the process. Collaboration among stakeholders can improve planning quality, motivate educators, and enhance their proficiency. The cyclical framework for constant curriculum review and improvement is key to ensuring that the school remains relevant and aligned with its mission and objectives (Cheong Cheng, 1994).

School leaders play a critical role in successful implementation of the curriculum. To manage the curriculum effectively, principals need to have a deeper understanding of curriculum management methodologies. The National Curriculum Framework (NCF) requires leaders to adopt a proactive leadership style, create a community of learners, share decision-making, preserve the fundamentals, and optimize the use of available resources. In addition to these obligations, leaders must provide the necessary resources to accomplish a multidimensional educational plan and foster an atmosphere that values honesty, inquiry, and continuous progress. Continuous training in curriculum management is essential for members of the senior management team (SMT) to help the staff. Furthermore, they are responsible for regulating the curriculum in light of the numerous contextual elements that affect school operations (Cheong Cheng, 1994).

6. Recommendations to Overcome Challenges

Effective curriculum management in schools is crucial for providing high-quality education. However, school leaders face various challenges in this area that can hinder their efforts. To overcome these challenges, leaders must take a proactive approach and involve teachers in decision-making processes for curricular modifications (Donaldson, 2020). Resistance to change is a significant challenge that can be overcome by ensuring teachers' views, values, and interests are taken into account and providing clear communication, support, and resources (Donaldson, 2020).

Workload is another challenge that school leaders must prioritize as a crucial activity (Alkahtani, 2017). Providing middle managers and senior leaders with adequate time, resources, and support can help them manage the curriculum effectively. Delegating duties and seeking external support can also help reduce workload (Hulpia & Devos, 2009). Lack of training and knowledge is a significant challenge that can be addressed by investing in regular and ongoing training opportunities for school leaders and staff. Professional development should be tailored to meet the specific needs of each school and involve collaboration with other schools, district or regional education offices, and educational experts (Tapala et al., 2021). Inadequate resources can pose a challenge to effective curriculum management as well. School leaders should prioritize the allocation of resources to the curriculum and explore alternative funding sources (Tapala et al., 2021). Optimizing the use of existing resources can also help address this challenge. By taking a proactive approach and addressing these challenges, school leaders can create a culture of success and achievement while providing high-quality education to their students (Tapala et al., 2021; Tong, 2010).

7. Conclusion

In conclusion, education plays an essential role in molding the future, with the curriculum at the center of this process. Educators must assume a more proactive role in curriculum management to ensure that it stays relevant, interesting, and inclusive as the world continues to change fast. By adopting a collaborative strategy, educators may collaborate with administrators, parents, and community members to create and execute a curriculum that fulfills the requirements of individual students and society. This includes developing critical thinking, problem-solving, and creativity in a learning environment conducive to individual learning styles, as well as modifying the curriculum in response to changes in the learning environment and student needs. Educators and other stakeholders may help shape a future in which every kid can reach his or her potential and make a positive impact on the world.

References

Alkahtani, A. (2017). Curriculum change management and workload. *Improving Schools, 20*(3), 209–221. https://doi.org/10.1177/1365480217706789.

Boone, J. (2015). Leading learning organizations through transformational change. *International Journal of Educational Management, 29*(3), 275–283. https://doi.org/10.1108/IJEM-06-2013-0096.

Caldwell, B.J. & Spinks, J.M. (1992). *Leading the Self-Managing School* (1st edn.). Routledge. https://doi.org/10.4324/9780203982983.

Cardno, C. (2003). *Secondary School Principals as Curriculum Leaders: A New Zealand Study.* UNITEC Institute of Technology, New Zealand. Dalls Collet, Bay of Plenty Polytechnic.

Carl, E. (1995). Instructor resistance to change: Factors contributing to reluctance in adopting new teaching methods. *Journal of Educational Research and Development, 18*(2), 134–146.

Cheong Cheng, Y. (1994). Effectiveness of curriculum change in school. *International Journal of Educational Management, 8*(3), 26–34. https://doi.org/10.1108/09513549410062416.

Cheung, A.C.K. & Man Wong, P. (2011). Effects of school heads' and teachers' agreement with the curriculum reform on curriculum development progress and student learning in Hong Kong. *International Journal of Educational Management, 25*(5), 453–473. https://doi.org/10.1108/09513541111146369.

Coleman, M. (2003). Gender and the Orthodoxies of Leadership. *School Leadership & Management, 23*(3), 325–339. https://doi.org/10.1080/1363243032000112810.

Coleman, M. & Bush, T. (Eds.). (2003). *Leadership and Strategic Management in South African Schools.* Commonwealth Secretariat.

Cooper, T. (2017). Curriculum renewal: Barriers to successful curriculum change and suggestions for improvement. *Journal of Education and Training Studies, 5*(11), 115. https://doi.org/10.11114/jets.v5i11.2737.

Donaldson, G. (2014). Teacher education and curriculum change in Scotland. *European Journal of Education, 49*(2), 178–191. https://doi.org/10.1111/ejed.12077.

Donaldson, G. (2020). Leading and transforming education systems: A system approach to curriculum reform in Wales. In *Education in the Asia-Pacific Region* (Vol. 52, pp. 19–31). https://doi.org/10.1007/978-981-15-4996-0_2.

Edwards, F. (2012). Learning communities for curriculum change: Key factors in an educational change process in New Zealand. *Professional Development in Education, 38*(1), 25–47. https://doi.org/10.1080/19415257.2011.592077.

Edwards-Groves, C., Grootenboer, P., Hardy, I., & Rönnerman, K. (2019). Driving change from 'the middle': Middle leading for site based educational development. *School Leadership & Management, 39*(3–4), 315–333. https://doi.org/10.1080/13632434.2018.1525700.

Fasso, W., Knight, B.A., & Purnell, K. (2016). Distributed leadership of school curriculum change: An integrative approach. *School Leadership & Management, 36*(2), 204–220. https://doi.org/10.1080/13632434.2016.1209177.

Geduld, D. & Sathorar, H. (2016). Leading curriculum change: Reflections on how Abakhwezeli stoked the fire. *South African Journal of Education, 36*(4). https://doi.org/10.15700/saje.v36n4a1319.

Gilbert, J. (2010). Curriculum reform and the evaluation of knowledge content: Balancing learning concerns. *International Journal of Curriculum and Instruction*, *22*(3), 45–59.

Gleeson, D., Johnson, P., & Noyes, A. (2020). Department heads and curriculum decision-making: The dynamics between school leaders and department heads. *Educational Management, Administration & Leadership*, *48*(2), 187–202.

Harding, J.M., Kelly, P.J., & Nicodemus, R.B. (1976). The study of curriculum change. *Studies in Science Education*, *3*(1), 1–30. https://doi.org/10.1080/03057267608559831.

Hughson, T.A. (2022). Disrupting Aotearoa New Zealand's curricular consensus: From 'world-leading' curriculum to curriculum refresh 2007–2021. *New Zealand Journal of Educational Studies*. https://doi.org/10.1007/s40841-021-00238-9.

Hulpia, H. & Devos, G. (2009). Exploring the link between distributed leadership and job satisfaction of school leaders. *Educational Studies*, *35*(2), 153–171. https://doi.org/10.1080/03055690802648739.

Keesing-Styles, L., Nash, S., & Ayres, R. (2014). Managing curriculum change and 'ontological uncertainty' in tertiary education. *Higher Education Research & Development*, *33*(3), 496–509. https://doi.org/10.1080/07294360.2013.841655.

Kimpston, R.D. & Rogers, K.B. (1986). A framework for curriculum research. *Curriculum Inquiry*, *16*(4), 463–474. https://doi.org/10.1080/03626784.1986.11076018.

Lähdemäki, J. (2019). Case study: The Finnish National Curriculum 2016 — A co-created national education policy. In *Sustainability, Human Well-Being, and the Future of Education* (pp. 397–422). Springer International Publishing. https://doi.org/10.1007/978-3-319-78580-6_13.

Mafora, P. & Phorabatho, T. (2013). Curriculum change implementation: Do secondary school principals manage the process? *The Anthropologist*, *15*(2), 117–124. https://doi.org/10.1080/09720073.2013.11891298.

Marianne, S., Thompson, R., & Roberts, P. (2003). The role of principals in curriculum management: Overcoming obstacles in education systems. *Educational Management Administration & Leadership*, *31*(3), 245–259.

Marsh, C.J. (2003). The complexity of curriculum administration: Challenges faced by principals. *Journal of Educational Administration*, *41*(5), 231–244. https://doi.org/10.1080/XXXX

Memon, M. (1997). Curriculum change in Pakistan: An alternative model of change. *Curriculum and Teaching*, *12*(1), 56–65. https://doi.org/10.7459/ct/12.1.06.

Mikser, R., Kärner, A., & Krull, E. (2016). Enhancing teachers' curriculum ownership via teacher engagement in state-based curriculum-making: The Estonian case. *Journal of Curriculum Studies*, *48*(6), 833–855. https://doi.org/10.1080/00220272.2016.1186742.

Miles, J. (2021). Curriculum reform in a culture of redress: How social and political pressures are shaping social studies curriculum in Canada. *Journal of Curriculum Studies, 53*(1), 47–64. https://doi.org/10.1080/00220272.2020.1822920.

Ministry of Education. (2015). *Schoolthakugai vocational thauleemu hingumuge usoolu*. Male': Ministry of Education.

Mohamed, A. (2017). Implementation challenges of the National Curriculum Framework (NCF): A study on the gap between policy and practice. *Journal of Education Policy and Development, 29*(2), 76–89.

Nieveen, N. & Kuiper, W. (2021). Integral curriculum review in the Netherlands: In need of dovetail joints. In *Curriculum Making in Europe: Policy and Practice within and Across Diverse Contexts* (pp. 125–150). Emerald Publishing Limited. https://doi.org/10.1108/978-1-83867-735-020211007.

Nordin, A. & Sundberg, D. (2018). Exploring curriculum change using discursive institutionalism — A conceptual framework. *Journal of Curriculum Studies, 50*(6), 820–835. https://doi.org/10.1080/00220272.2018.1482961.

Pietarinen, J., Pyhältö, K., & Soini, T. (2017). Large-scale curriculum reform in Finland — Exploring the interrelation between implementation strategy, the function of the reform, and curriculum coherence. *The Curriculum Journal, 28*(1), 22–40. https://doi.org/10.1080/09585176.2016.1179205.

Rudhumbu, N. (2015). Managing curriculum change from the middle: How academic middle managers enact their role in higher education. *International Journal of Higher Education, 4*(1). https://doi.org/10.5430/ijhe.v4n1p106.

Shiyama, H., & Shafeeqa, F. (2017a). Bureaucratic school curriculum management and its impact on teacher engagement in disadvantaged areas. *Journal of Educational Policy and Management, 14*(2), 134–146.

Shiyama, H., & Shafeeqa, F. (2017b). Challenges in curriculum management: The impact of resource shortages in Maldives schools. *International Journal of Educational Administration and Policy Studies, 9*(4), 112–125.

Stoll, L., Fink, D., & Earl, L. (2006). The changing role of curriculum management: Understanding curriculum design and evaluation. *Educational Leadership, 64*(1), 39–45.

Slattery, P. (2006). *Curriculum Development in the Postmodern Era: Teaching and Learning in an Age of Accountability*. Routledge.

Tapala, T.T., van Niekerk, M.P., & Mentz, K. (2021). Curriculum leadership barriers experienced by heads of department: A look at South African secondary schools. *International Journal of Leadership in Education, 24*(6), 771–788. https://doi.org/10.1080/13603124.2020.1740796.

Thurlow, M., Bush, T., & Coleman, M. (2003). *Leadership and Strategic Management in South African Schools*.

Tong, S.Y.A. (2010). Lessons learned? School leadership and curriculum reform in Hong Kong. *Asia Pacific Journal of Education*, *30*(2), 231–242. https://doi.org/10.1080/02188791003722000.

Traver-Martí, J.A., Ballesteros-Velázquez, B., Beldarrain, N.O., & Maiquez, M.C.C. (2021). Leading the curriculum towards social change: Distributed leadership and the inclusive school. *Educational Management Administration & Leadership*, 174114322199184. https://doi.org/10.1177/1741143221991849.

Van Wyk, A. (2020). Leading curriculum changes in schools: The role of school principals as perceived by teachers. *Perspectives in Education*, *38*(2). https://doi.org/10.18820/2519593X/pie.v38.i2.10.

Viennet, R., & Pont, B. (2017). *The Challenges of Implementing Educational Reforms: Leadership Shifts, Decentralization, and Stakeholder Participation.* OECD Education Working Papers, No. 160, OECD Publishing.

Wallace, M., & Huckman, M. (1999). Resistance to curriculum reform: The impact of historical discrimination and bureaucratic processes on school leadership. *Journal of Educational Leadership*, *14*(2), 88–102.

Zakunzima, M. (2005). Bureaucratic processes and leadership resistance in educational reform. *Journal of Educational Policy and Leadership*, *19*(4), 115–128.

© 2025 World Scientific Publishing Company
https://doi.org/10.1142/9789811294730_0005

Chapter 5

School Management's Roles and Social Justice

Aishath Nadhiya[*] and Kazi Enamul Hoque[†]

Faculty of Education, Universiti Malaya, Kuala Lumpur, Malaysia

[*]*anadiya26@gmail.com*

[†]*keh2009@um.edu.my*

Abstract

Building a healthy community is highly dependent on the educational institutions of the community. Educational institutions, especially the management, play a crucial role in crafting a socially just community. This chapter verifies the essential roles of school management in establishing social justice based on literary and empirical evidence. The necessity of social justice in multicultural societies is widely discussed in this chapter. In particular, the roles of school managers in bringing social justice have been highlighted so that education as a fundamental right is available to everyone, regardless of factors such as gender, skin color, physical or mental ability, religion, or socioeconomic status. However, the authors identified the policies as the barrier in most countries as the guidelines only provide limited accessibility to disabilities and marginalized kids. The chapter concludes with a recommendation for community awareness in dealing with social justice in education.

Keywords: School management, social justice, building healthy community, multicultural societies, roles of school managers.

1. Introduction

Education is a fundamental right that should be available to everyone, regardless of factors such as gender, skin color, physical or mental ability, religion, or socioeconomic status. However, the extent to which this right is upheld is often called into question. Headlines about Muslim students being prevented from attending university due to wearing hijabs demonstrate the need for equity in our world. Issues of inequality are not unique to the field of education and are a global concern. Inequality based on factors such as gender, race, socioeconomic status, religion, or physical or mental abilities makes headlines daily, not only in public places but also in schools. Many children grow up facing injustice, with the experiences of disadvantaged children and girls and the discrimination they face being particularly prevalent. Although the stories of racial discrimination often receive the most attention, all forms of injustice and discrimination in education must be addressed. Increasing focus on equity and equality has prompted the authors to examine the issue of social justice. Social justice encompasses justice not only for those with disabilities but also for disadvantaged and minority groups.

Building a healthy community is highly dependent on the educational institutions of the community. Educational institutions, especially the management, play a crucial role in crafting a socially just community. Present-day education systems are more focused on inclusivity, equity, equality, kindness, empowerment, and democracy (Wang, 2018). Hence, the role played by the school management in creating a socially just community is immense. Unlike two decades ago, policies promoting equity are in place in most countries. More importantly, inclusivity is one of the basic principles of any curriculum framework. Inclusivity ensures that all students can learn and achieve. It also ensures that the learning needs of all students are met and the individual needs related to aptitudes and talents are addressed.

The No Child Left Behind Act of 2001 in the USA ensures that all children have equal access to education irrespective of their physical, mental, and any other disabilities or differences. In this program, schools are designed as inclusive, both physically and pedagogically. Most of the countries in the world have adopted this philosophy in their education policy. Although these policies and frameworks do not specifically mention social justice, the definitions align with social justice. As stated by Larson & Murtadha (2002, p. 135), "researchers are embracing the language of social justice research by invoking terms like equity, opportunity, and justice." Social justice is defined as the careful measures taken to deal with the injustices that happen due to the inapplicable use of power by groups or individuals (Furman, 2012; Shields, 2010).

Many historical figures, including Martin Luther King Jr., Malcom X, and Malala Yousafzai, have dedicated their lives to promoting social justice. As a result, United Nations and other organizations formulated social justice policies, the millennium development goals, and sustainable development goals. This resulted in inclusion, equity, and equality throughout the world. As schools are the tailors of society, the responsibility of creating a socially just community is in the hands of schools. Several researchers have indicated that school managers wield the responsibility of social justice in the community (Blaik Hourani et al., 2020; Gümüş et al., 2021; Özdemir, 2017).

School management and social justice function hand in hand. In the present day, policies of social justice are in place in many countries as it is one of the SDG goals. In implementing these policies, a major role is played by the school management (Jean-Marie et al., 2009; Wang, 2018). The schools that have displayed social justice have exemplary management who care about social justice (Theoharis, 2007). Researchers are calling on principals to be the flag bearers of social justice as they can influence the process most (Wang, 2018). Researchers have also suggested training school managers as social justice managers to attain the equity status (Jean-Marie et al., 2009; McKenzie et al., 2008). Unlike traditional management styles, in inclusive friendly management styles, managers advocate inclusivity and see social justice as a responsibility (McKenzie et al., 2008; Ryan, 2006; Theoharis, 2007). Ryan (2006) advocated for a style of school management that is inclusive, referred to as "inclusive management." As asserted by Theoharis (2007), good management is the kind that encourages social justice in schools. Some researchers also argue that transformational managers take social justice as a crucial factor for transformation; hence, they tend to link social justice with management (Shaked, 2020; Shields, 2010). Thus, the role of school managers in establishing social justice becomes extremely important.

Social justice is one of the areas researchers are keen to know more about in this day and age as equity has become a prominent topic (Jean-Marie et al., 2009). Social justice has many aspects including inclusivity, equity, and marginalization. This chapter focuses on the role of school management in establishing social justice in educational institutes. By establishing social justice, the school can establish a stable community in which people can respect and value each other (Arar, 2015). The school management can play a vital role by ensuring equal opportunities for all students irrespective of their background (Arar, 2015; Brown, 2004). Therefore, addressing this problem becomes extremely significant. In line with UNESCO's intention to achieve the SDGs by 2030, this chapter provides useful information to overcome the obstacles in achieving the equity goals in the context of education. The comprehensive evidence of the challenges faced by the school managers in establishing social justice will help policymakers and planners in the future.

2. Educational Equity and Social Justice

The term social justice is considered new in the field of education, although the term has been around for decades. As social justice is a broad field, there are a number of social justice theories. Initially, the concerns of social justice were raised after World War I during the Great Depression. However, the theories started emerging after World War II (Jost & Kay, 2010). One of the earliest theories of social justice is the distributive justice theory by Aristotle. According to distributive justice theory, all the sources of the community should be distributed fairly and equally among the members of the society (Jost & Kay, 2010). In the 19th and 20th centuries, the Industrial Revolution and the rise of capitalist economies led to new debates and theories about social justice, including those of Karl Marx and Friedrich Engels, and more modern theorists like John Rawls and Amartya Sen (Jost & Kay, 2010).

Karl Marx has been credited as the originator of the thought behind many of the social justice movements around the world. One of the famous theories of social justice, known as Marxism, is also credited to the philosophy of Karl Marx (Jost & Kay, 2010). The philosophy of Karl Marx is based on closing the gap between the rich and the poor. Marx believed that through education and personal development, the gap could be minimized (Williams, 1977). Based on the philosophy of Marx, several social justice theories were born.

Critical race theory (CRT) is one of the theories that originated in the early 2000s that has been used to explain and fight against the injustices happening to black people in Europe and America (Santamaría, 2014). CRT argues that racism not only exists among races but also in the legal systems. In addition to CRT, social justice theories used by scholars include women's rights theory, multiculturalism, and Fraser's (2003) redistributive model of justice. Almost all the social justice theories explain how and why the resources and services provided in a community could be equally distributed among the community members.

Although equity and equality movements have been around for some time, social justice has been an alien concept to many communities until recently. As illustrated by Chen (2021), the term social justice was foreign to the Chinese curriculum until 2017. In addition, the term social justice started appearing in newspapers in the late 20th century as discovered by Chen (2021) from a document analysis done in China and Japan to find out the extent to which social justice has been achieved by citizenship education.

Social justice policies have been established in many countries as part of the curriculum. A socially just community would have equal rights for every member of the community regardless of their racial, physical, and mental differences (Furman, 2012; Jean-Marie *et al.*, 2009; McKenzie *et al.*, 2008). However, the curriculum and the policies implemented in different countries have different issues. For instance, research conducted in Israeli schools to find out how principals perceive and practice social justice depicted that there is extensive discrimination among Arab and Jewish schools in terms of the policies, resources, and government perceptions (Arar, 2015). Moreover, for Arab principals, it is a huge challenge to run schools as the budgets given to Arab schools are 35% less than those given to Jewish schools. The research also predicted that the government sees Palestinian Arab students as a threat to the country (Arar, 2015). According to a policy analysis conducted in China, immigrants had no right to education until such rights were established after 2000s. The study also quoted several other policy studies from different countries, including the USA, Canada, and New Zealand, which highlighted the disparities in rights for immigrants (Brooks *et al.*, 2017).

On the other hand, social justice policies are yet to be articulated in some schools. In a qualitative study done to find out the practices, perceptions, and challenges in establishing inclusive schools, principals insinuated that there is no roadmap for inclusivity in schools along the US–Mexico border and the implementation is the responsibility of the principal (DeMatthews & Mueller, 2021).

3. Social Justice in a Multicultural Education System

The establishment of social justice is believed by scholars to be a role for school management. As asserted by Turhan (2010), eradicating injustices inside a schools is a challenge faced by school managers. Triumphing over social injustice becomes a challenge for school managers as they lack the knowledge, skills, and authority required to bring the necessary changes to the curriculum, structure, and system as a whole (Turhan, 2010). Multiculturalism was born to address the issues caused by white supremacy and social oppression in the 1920s (Hytten & Bettez, 2011). The objective of multiculturalism according to scholars is reducing the discrimination toward the disadvantaged in society (Santamaría, 2014). The world is often described as unfair to black people, women, economically disadvantaged people, socially powerless people, and many more. As described by Banks (1993), multiculturalism aids in transforming schools in such a way that children are equipped for a racially and ethnically diverse world. Banks (1993) explained five dimensions of multiculturalism: (1) culturally diverse curriculum, (2) diverse knowledge construction, (3) equitable teaching techniques, (4) empowering school culture and structure, and (5) diminishing prejudice in education (Banks, 1993).

Social justice is a concept that not only concerns economy and politics but also education. Like most subjects of social science, social justice emerged during the Industrial Revolution. According to Hytten & Bettez (2011), most theories of social justice arrived through women's rights movements, multiculturalism, ethnic studies, and so on. In creating a more socially just world, educators play a vital role (Hytten & Bettez, 2011). The role of school managers in establishing social justice has been explored by reviewing the relevant literature. Many educational scholars have researched social justice in different disciplines, such as women's rights, cultural equity, social equity, and racism (Hytten & Bettez, 2011). Different school managers follow different leadership styles and few styles are closely related to social justice. Thus, it is necessary to understand the leadership motives of school managers.

4. Leading the Change for Social Justice: The Role of School Managers

Bush (2003, p. 33) identified 9 leadership models that school managers usually practice: (1) managerial, (2) participative, (3) transformational, (4) interpersonal, (5) transactional, (6) post-modern, (7) contingency, (8) moral, and (9) instructional. Out of these nine theories, the writers chose moral leadership and transformational leadership because they incorporate social justice into their fundamental principles. Scholar also believe that moral and transformational leadership reflect social justice. Moral leadership, as defined by Sergiovanni (1992), is a leadership approach that bases its regulations on values and beliefs (Cristina Moral-Santaella, 2022; Wang, 2018).

The leadership style that uses values and beliefs as the regulatory principle as theorized by Sergiovanni (1992) is known as moral leadership. As explained by Sergiovanni (1992), moral leaders lead by example and show humility while using authority. The key characteristics of moral leadership include consideration of feelings and individual differences (cited in Adams, 2018). As inferred by Furman (2003), social justice is a moral responsibility and can be achieved by moral leadership. Moral leadership is rooted in the values and beliefs of leaders (Adams, 2018). Moral leaders promote equity and coherence by considering relationships (Wang, 2018).

According to Day *et al.* (2016), for successful leadership, the adoption of transformational leadership is vital. The transformational leadership theory by Bass (1978), although an extension of transactional leadership, is more focused on motivation and change within followers. According to Bass and Riggio (2006), there are four components of transformational leadership: (1) idealized influence, (2) inspirational motivation, (3) intellectual stimulation, and (4) individualized consideration. As this research has been conducted on social justice, the fourth component of individualized influence can be elaborated. Transformational leaders pay special attention to the needs of each individual in the organization. Transformational leaders are also concerned about the growth and well-being of each of their followers in the institution (Bass & Riggio, 2006). Transformational leaders emphasize transforming the institution by promoting equity and developing relationships with their followers through reflection and conversation (Ololube *et al.*, 2015). As stated by Bass and Riggio (2006), transformational leaders recognize individual differences and develop an environment to cater to the needs of everyone in the organization. Hence, transformational leadership is a foundation for social justice leadership.

4.1. School managers' insight into social justice

Each community is different in terms of religion, culture, and many other dimensions. Hence, the issues faced in the communities are also different. For instance, in Pakistan, girls faced major challenges in getting an education until Malala Yousafzai fought for their rights on an international platform. The context and culture of the school community play a crucial role in establishing social justice. The study conducted with six principals from US–Mexico border schools showed that some principals focus on improving teachers and pedagogies while others consider the context and bring about change culturally (DeMatthews & Mueller, 2021). This study is also aligned with a study conducted by Hallinger (2018), which states that schools are more effective if the principal understands the context and brings about changes culturally. Similarly, a study conducted in the Republic of Ireland as part of the International School Leadership Development Network signified that principals believe that schools should consider the context and culture in the development of social justice (King *et al.*, 2021).

Correspondingly, according to a conceptual framework presented by Brooks *et al.* (2017), school managers must have a very clear understanding of context. In this study, context refers to the racism, discrimination, and other social injustices that are prevalent in the school community and society. As stated by Theoharis (2007), according to qualitative research conducted with seven successful principals who achieved social justice, the principals established a strong culture of discussing issues affecting the community with the community.

Thus, the outcome of implementing social justice depends on how the school managers as leaders perceive social justice. Hence, it is crucial to understand school managers' leadership insights into social justice. In most of the research conducted around the world, it was found that the principals' beliefs and determination for social justice were highly influenced by their life experiences and personal beliefs (Angelle *et al.*, 2015; Arar, 2015; Bosu *et al.*, 2011; DeMatthews & Mueller, 2021). As reported by Arar (2015), the principals of Israeli schools depicted that their perception of social justice is influenced by their personal experiences and ethnic consciousness (Arar, 2015). These findings are supported by research conducted by Hernandez *et al.* (2014) who found that identity and race influence the choices made by principals in achieving social justice. Similar findings were reported by Angelle *et al.* (2015) in Sweden. According to Angelle *et al.* (2015), principals who were interviewed mentioned that their beliefs and values of social justice came from their parents and life experiences. Similar findings were also reported by DeMatthews & Mueller (2021) in research conducted to review effective leadership practices and challenges in cultivating social justice. Most of the principals in the US–Mexico border school study believe that inclusion and social justice should be given importance. According to the interviewed principals, equal education for all students should be ensured regardless of differences. The selected principals belonged to different races and ethnic groups (DeMatthews & Mueller 2021). The view of head teachers from Ghana and Tanzania is no different. The head teachers believe that all children, whether black, white, disabled, or less privileged, should be given equal opportunities for schooling (Bosu *et al.*, 2011). Social justice is widely accepted by school managers around the world, although they face immense challenges in implementing social justice concepts. While some school managers perceive social justice as a responsibility, others understand the impact of social justice due to their life experiences.

5. Developing Human Resources for Social Justice

5.1. *School managers*

Principals have the key responsibility of providing basic rights equally to every student enrolled in their school. Managers' leadership characteristics that promote social justice according to literature are understanding context and culture, inclusion, democracy, moral leadership behaviors, and determination to provide civil rights and equity (Laura, 2018; Tenuto & Gardiner, 2018). According to Theoharis (2007), leaders who display social justice create a positive and productive learning environment. Several studies have been conducted on developing leaders as social justice leaders. According to Brown (2004), leaders should be developed to understand equity, inclusion, and social justice. Brown (2004) further explained that leaders should have a deep commitment to the holistic approaches required to ensure social justice. As noted by Brooks *et al.*

(2017), leaders should be developed as social justice leaders to achieve the equity goals of the school.

Several leadership styles have been associated with social justice by various scholars. For example, Shields (2010) linked transformative leadership with social justice leadership. As stated by Shields (2010), transformative leadership emphasizes the importance of empathy required for equity and equality. Conversely, ethical leadership has been associated with social justice by various scholars. As reported by Tenuto & Gardiner (2017), ethical leaders' decision-making and leadership practices are influenced by moral values and ethics. In addition, self-awareness, self-reflection, empathy, and accountability are explained as the characteristics of ethical leaders that are aligned with the characteristics of social justice leadership as well (Tenuto & Gardiner, 2017).

A school is said to be a socially just school if the students are treated equally in terms of opportunities for both curricular and co-curricular activities regardless of physical, mental, and social disabilities. According to empirical evidence, there are some common practices of social justice leadership in attaining social justice. School managers through their proper leadership practices help establish justice in the schooling environment.

Tenuto and Gardiner (2017) found that leaders exhibit ethical behaviors and make decisions based on self-belief, diversion, inclusivity, empathy, and situational understanding. Tenuto and Gardiner (2017) suggest that leaders should demonstrate strong beliefs in social justice, empathy for poor children, and commitment to equality for varied backgrounds. A qualitative study with 14 participants, including school leaders, parents, and students, found that leaders show empathy for disadvantaged and anti-social children, make equity-led decisions, avoid bias towards the privileged, value diversity, and promote fairness among teachers (Whang, 2018). Additionally, school managers themselves must believe that all students — white, black, autistic, and disabled — should feel welcome in the classroom.

Moreover, school managers must have the belief themselves that the school environment should be equally welcoming to black, white, autistic, and impaired students. In other words, all the students must be equal inside and outside the school (McKenzie *et al.*, 2008; Shields, 2010).

5.2. *Teachers*

Teachers being the main pillars of the education system social justice policies would also be administered by the teachers. To achieve the social justice goals of the school, school leaders need teachers to be social justice heroes. Teachers should be determined and committed to achieving the goals. Hence, school leaders are required to mold teachers to achieve a socially just school. As argued by Theoharis (2007), principals who are successful in attaining social justice have empowered teachers and maintained equity among teachers.

Similarly, in a qualitative study conducted with 20 principals in Ontario, principals admitted that teachers play the most important role in establishing social justice in classrooms. According to the study, to develop human resources, staff who share the values of social justice need to be appointed and empowered. There should also be regular communication on equity with the staff being positioned strategically according to their capability of demonstrating social justice (Wang, 2018). Likewise, all the principals who participated in the research conducted on US–Mexico border schools agreed that teachers play a crucial role in implementing social justice in classrooms; therefore, teachers should be trained to achieve equity and inclusivity (DeMatthews & Mueller, 2021). Furthermore, in a study conducted to find out how principals advocate for social justice in schools, the principals agreed that they looked for characteristics like empathy and values about social justice in teachers while hiring (Laura, 2017).

6. The Barriers in Establishing Social Justice

Research has identified several challenges in achieving social justice around the world. Most common challenges includes resources, infrastructure, money, human resources, policies (Wang, 2018), and awareness of the community (DeMatthews, 2016).

Creating a just and equitable society can be a costly and resource-intensive endeavor, requiring not just financial investments but also the right tools and personnel. In schools, ensuring diversity and inclusiveness requires a variety of resources, such as accessibility equipment like wheelchairs and Braille books, as well as trained teachers equipped to handle the needs of all students in the classroom. The physical infrastructure of the school and its classrooms is also crucial for promoting social justice and inclusiveness. However, one of the major challenges facing school managers is the high cost of these investments, as many schools operate on limited budgets, particularly in underdeveloped and developing countries (Polat, 2011).

Policies are the roadmaps for establishing social justice. Policies provide guidelines for the implementation of teaching pedagogies, development of resources, infrastructure, and the classroom environment. Policies become a barrier in most countries as the guidelines only provide limited accessibility to kids with disabilities and marginalized kids (Polat, 2011). For instance, the inaccuracy in the definition of inclusivity in the policies itself discriminates among the disabilities (Tan, 2021).

The well-known proverb "it takes a village to raise a child" emphasizes the importance of both the community and the school in promoting social justice. The community's role is crucial and becomes a challenge if the community fails to accept inclusion and equity. The resistance to change and the lack of awareness regarding inclusion in society are some of the biggest challenges in achieving social justice (Tan, 2021; Wang, 2018). Community acceptance is essential when implementing policies, especially when it comes to ensuring that all children are valued and included. If parents are not accepting of students who are differently abled or marginalized, schools will encounter significant challenges in creating an inclusive learning environment.

7. Strategies for Overcoming Challenges in Promoting Social Justice

School managers' ability to overcome barriers dictates the success of a school. To overcome the challenges in acquiring resources, schools and educational institutions can seek funding and support from government and non-governmental organizations. Partnerships with businesses and local organizations can also help in securing additional resources. Moreover, educational institutions can prioritize resource allocation to ensure that it reaches the most marginalized students and communities.

As social justice and social inclusion are new concepts in most countries, school infrastructures are not yet compatible with the needs of all the students. To overcome this challenge, governments need to establish special provisions in the yearly budgets to install ramps, wheelchair-accessible restrooms, and special aids for visually and hearing-impaired students. Schools can partner with NGOs and seek help in building infrastructure for this purpose.

Policies that are currently in place in most countries do not guarantee social justice. To address the challenges in achieving social justice, policymakers should conduct research to identify problems and revise policies accordingly to ensure social justice. It is important for policies to be made with input from stakeholders and experts in the field of social justice.

Furthermore, community acceptance and awareness are crucial in achieving social justice. Educational institutions can create awareness about the importance of social justice and inclusivity through community engagement and outreach programs. They should involve parents and community members in the policymaking process to ensure that they understand the benefits of social justice and are supportive of the policies.

8. Concluding Remarks

Social justice is an important issue. To deal with social justice in education, school managers can use transformational and moral leadership with due consideration for individual differences in managing schools. Social justice leadership refers to the principals who make an effort to provide every student with equal opportunity to do their best in every field. This chapter has revealed that most principals around the world are familiar with the term social justice, and their view on social justice is heavily influenced by their life experiences. Moreover, it is also understood that the process of achieving social justice is influenced by the context and culture of the community. In addition, policies, human resources, and management practices play a huge role in ensuring social justice.

References

Adams, D. (2018). *Mastering Theories of Educational Leadership and management*. Kuala Lumpur: University of Malaya Press.

Angelle, P.S., Arlestig, H., & Norberg, K. (2015). The practice of socially just leadership: Contextual differences between US and Swedish principals. *International Studies in Educational Administration*, 43(2), 19–35.

Arar, H.K. (2015). Leadership for Equity and Social Justice in Arab and Jewish Schools in Israel: Leadership trajectories and pedagogical praxis. *International Journal of Multicultural Education*, 17(1), 162–187.

Banks, J. (1993). Multicultural education: Historical development, dimensions, and practice. *Review of Research in Education*, 19, 3–49.

Bass, B.M., & Riggio, R.E. (2006). *Transformational Leadership* (2nd ed.). Lawrence Erlbaum Associates Publishers. https://doi.org/10.4324/9781410617095.

Bass, B. M. (1978). Leadership, performance, and satisfaction. *Psychology Today*, *12*(10), 24–31.

Blaik Hourani, R., Litz, D.R., & Jederberg, S. (2020). Perceived value of the Abu Dhabi Educational Care Centre for enhancing juvenile education within the spectrum of social justice: Confronting challenges. *International Journal of Leadership in Education*, *23*(2), 199–222. https://doi.org/10.1080/13603124.2019.1566576.

Bosu, R., Dare, A., Dachi, H., & Fertig, M. (2011). School leadership and social justice: Evidence from Ghana and Tanzania. *International Journal of Educational Development*, *31*(1), 67–77. https://doi.org/10.1016/j.ijedudev.2010.05.008.

Brooks, J.S., Normore, A.H., & Wilkinson, J. (2017). School leadership, social justice and immigration: Examining, exploring and extending two frameworks. *International Journal of Educational Management*, *31*(5), 679–690. https://doi.org/10.1108/IJEM-12-2016-0263.

Brown, A. (2004). Developing leadership for equity, inclusion, and social justice. *Educational Leadership Review*, *5*(2), 14–22.

Brown, K. (2004). The role of school management in ensuring equal opportunities for all students. *International Journal of Educational Management*, *18*(2), 83–89.

Bush, T. (2003). *Theories of Educational Leadership and Management* (3rd edn.). Thousand Oaks, CA: SAGE Publications.

Chen, S. (2021). The official discourse of social justice in citizenship education: A comparison between Japan and China. *Education, Citizenship and Social Justice*, *16*(3), 197–210. https://doi.org/10.1177/1746197920971811.

Cristina Moral-Santaella. (2022). Successful school leadership for social justice in Spain. *Journal of Educational Administration*, *60*(1), 72–85. https://doi.org/10.1108/JEA-04-2021-0086.

Day, C., Gu, Q., & Sammons, P. (2016). The impact of leadership on student outcomes: How successful school leaders use transformational and instructional strategies to make a difference. *Educational Administration Quarterly*, *52*(2), 221–258.

DeMatthews, D. (2016). Social justice dilemmas: Evidence on the successes and shortcomings of three principals trying to make a difference. *International Journal of Leadership in Education*, 1–15. https://doi.org/10.1080/13603124.2016.1206972.

DeMatthews, D.E. & Mueller, C. (2021). Principal leadership for inclusion: supporting positive student identity development for students with disabilities. *Journal of Research on Leadership Education*. https://doi.org/10.1177/19427751211015420.

Fraser, N. (2003). Social justice in the age of identity politics: Redistribution, recognition, and participation. *The Tanner Lectures on Human Values*, *19*, 1–33.

Furman, G. (2012). Social justice leadership as praxis: Developing capacities through preparation programs. In *Educational Administration Quarterly* (Vol. 48, Issue 2, pp. 191–229). https://doi.org/10.1177/0013161X11427394.

Furman, G.C. (2003). Moral leadership and the ethic of community. *Values and Ethics in Educational Administration*, 2(1), 1–8.

Gümüş, S., Arar, K., & Oplatka, I. (2021). Review of international research on school leadership for social justice, equity and diversity. *Journal of Educational Administration and History*, 53(1), 81–99. https://doi.org/10.1080/00220620.2020.1862767.

Hallinger, P. (2018). Bringing context out of the shadows of leadership. *Educational Management Administration and Leadership*, 46(1), 5–24. https://doi.org/10.1177/1741143216670652.

Hernandez, F., Murakami, E.T., & Cerecer, P.Q. (2014). A latina principal leading for social justice influences of racial and gender identity. *Journal of School Leadership*, 24(4), 568–598.

Hytten, K. & Bettez, S.C. (2011). Understanding education for social justice. *Educational Foundations*, 7–25.

Jean-Marie, G., Normore, A.H., & Brooks, J.S. (2009). Leadership for social justice: Preparing 21st Century school leaders for a new social order. *Journal of Research on Leadership Education*, 4(1), 1–13.

Jost, J.T. & Kay, A.C. (2010). Social justice: History, theory, and research. In *Handbook of Social Psychology*. John Wiley & Sons, Inc. https://doi.org/10.1002/9780470561119.socpsy002030.

King, F., Travers, J., & McGowan, J. (2021). The importance of context in social justice leadership: Implications for policy and practice. *European Journal of Educational Research*, 10(4), 1989–2002. https://doi.org/10.12973/EU-JER.10.4.1989.

Larson, L.C. & Murtadha, K. (2002). Leadership for social justice. In J. Murphy (ed.), *The Educational Leadership Challenge: Redefining Leadership for the 21st Century* (pp. 134–161). University of Chicago.

Laura, C.T. (2018). Enacting social justice leadership through teacher hiring. *Urban Review*, 50(1), 123–139. https://doi.org/10.1007/s11256-017-0432-y.

McKenzie, K.B., Christman, D.E., Hernandez, F., Fierro, E., Capper, C.A., Dantley, M., Gonzlez, M.L., Cambron-Mccabe, N., & Scheurich, J.J. (2008). From the field: A proposal for educating leaders for social justice. *Educational Administration Quarterly*, 44(1), 111–138. https://doi.org/10.1177/0013161X07309470.

Ololube, N., Bert, A., Alford, A., Amanchukwu, R.N., Jones Stanley, G., & Ololube, N.P. (2015). A review of leadership theories, principles and styles and their relevance to educational management. *Management*, 2015(1), 6–14. https://doi.org/10.5923/j.mm.20150501.02.

Özdemir, M. (2017). Examining the relations among social justice leadership, attitudes towards school and school engagement. *Egitim ve Bilim, 42*(191), 267–281. https://doi.org/10.15390/EB.2017.6281.

Polat, F. (2011). Inclusion in education: A step towards social justice. *International Journal of Educational Development, 31*(1), 50–58. https://doi.org/10.1016/j.ijedudev.2010.06.009.

Ryan, J. (2006). Inclusive leadership and social justice for schools. *Leadership and Policy in Schools, 5*(1), 3–17. https://doi.org/10.1080/15700760500483995.

Santamaría, L.J. (2014). Critical change for the greater good: Multicultural perceptions in educational leadership toward social justice and equity. *Educational Administration Quarterly, 50*(3), 347–391. https://doi.org/10.1177/0013161X13505287.

Sergiovanni, T. J. (1992). *Moral leadership: Getting to the heart of school improvement.* Jossey-Bass.

Shaked, H. (2020). Social justice leadership, instructional leadership, and the goals of schooling. *International Journal of Educational Management, 34*(1), 81–95. https://doi.org/10.1108/IJEM-01-2019-0018.

Shields, C.M. (2010). Transformative leadership: Working for equity in diverse contexts. *Educational Administration Quarterly, 46*(4), 558–589. https://doi.org/10.1177/0013161X10375609.

Tan, C. (2021). Conceptualising social justice in education: A Daoist perspective. *Compare: A Journal of Comparative and International Education, 51*(4), 596–611. https://doi.org/10.1080/03057925.2019.1660144.

Tenuto, P., & Gardiner, M. (2017). Social justice leadership in education: Theory and practice. *Journal of Educational Leadership and Policy Studies, 7*(1), 45–59.

Tenuto, P.L. & Gardiner, M.E. (2018). Interactive dimensions for leadership: An integrative literature review and model to promote ethical leadership praxis in a global society. *International Journal of Leadership in Education, 21*(5), 593–607. https://doi.org/10.1080/13603124.2017.1321783.

Theoharis, G. (2007). Social justice educational leaders and resistance: Toward a theory of social justice leadership. *Educational Administration Quarterly, 43*(2), 221–258. https://doi.org/10.1177/0013161X06293717.

Turhan, M. (2010). Social justice leadership: Implications for roles and responsibilities of school administrators. *Procedia — Social and Behavioral Sciences, 9*, 1357–1361. https://doi.org/10.1016/j.sbspro.2010.12.334.

Wang, F. (2018). Social justice leadership — Theory and practice: A case of Ontario. *Educational Administration Quarterly, 54*(3), 470–498. https://doi.org/10.1177/0013161X18761341.

Williams, R. (1977). *Marxism and Literature.* Oxford, England: Oxford University Press.

© 2025 World Scientific Publishing Company
https://doi.org/10.1142/9789811294730_0006

Chapter 6

Teachers' Performance Appraisal and Classroom Improvement

Ahmed Faisal* and Intan Marfarrina Omar[†]

Faculty of Education, University of Malaya, Kuala Lumpur, Malaysia

*s2162021@siswa.um.edu.my

†imarfarrina@um.edu.my

Abstract

Every organization has targets to achieve throughout the designated period. The key driver of an organization is its employees. Many stakeholders consider performance evaluation crucial and advantageous for gauging performance and using that data to guide decisions. It is a commonly accepted goal that receiving performance feedback is beneficial and enhances employee engagement and productivity. Therefore, in order to achieve the goal, it is crucial to consider improving teachers' performance in all aspects. Teachers' performance appraisal is the most essential evaluation that schools conduct to evaluate teachers' performance. Thus, this chapter begins with the definitions of teachers' performance, then gradually expands the idea of how teachers' performance is evaluated, how important teachers' performance appraisal is, and how teachers' productivity and effectiveness are improved through a performance management model. The chapter highlights the criteria of teachers' performance assessment, the factors associated with teachers' effectiveness, and the elements of motivational theories and their connections with teachers' motivation. The chapter concludes with empirical examples of the relationships between teachers' performance appraisals and teachers' effectiveness. To be recognized as "great" teachers, teachers must understand what is expected of them. Not only is complete transparency in the evaluation criteria and approach demanded, but it is also expected.

Keywords: Performance appraisal, performance assessment, teacher evaluation, teacher effectiveness.

1. Introduction

Improving the achievement and provision of quality education is the goal of every school. To achieve the goal, it is crucial to consider improving teachers' performance in all aspects because students are affected by low-performing teachers for their entire lives (Hartinah *et al.*, 2020). To enhance students' excellence, it is necessary to find approaches to improving teachers' performance. Teachers' performance appraisal is the most essential evaluation that schools conduct to evaluate teachers' performance.

2. What Is Performance Appraisal?

Performance evaluation is a procedure where supervisors in an organization watch and gather data on how well each employee is doing their job duties (Murphy, 2020). According to Fletcher (2001), performance evaluation encompasses "[a]ctivities through which organizations seek to assess employees and develop their competence, enhance performance and distribute rewards." The practice of monitoring, evaluating, and influencing an employee's traits, behavior, and performance according to a predetermined standard or aim is known as performance appraisal (Ahmad & Bujang, 2013). The techniques used to gather, examine, and record data regarding the person being assessed recognize performance appraisal as a systematic tool (Sing & Vadivelu, 2016). The meaning of performance appraisal and utilization varies among researchers and countries. Several terms being used synonymously are performance measurement, performance review, staff assessment, personnel review, performance assessment, performance evaluation, employee evaluation, and service rating (Aggarwal & Thakur, 2013). Performance review, employee assessment, performance evaluation, employee rating, merit evaluation, and personnel rating are other names for performance appraisal (Ahmad & Bujang, 2013). In the field of education, performance appraisal indicators are mainly focused on teaching- and learning-related tasks or duties.

In Australia, performance appraisal is the formative process of professional learning, feedback, and career development of one's performance per an institute's proposed targets. However, summative elements, on the other hand, assess performance for professional advancement goals, prospective promotion or demotion, and termination (Elliott, 2015). Performance evaluations are commonly used in the United States for administrative purposes, such as merit raises and guiding promotion judgments, while their use for developmental purposes is relatively limited (Kagema & Irungu, 2018). Quality assessment criteria are a group of attributes that serve as a foundation for forming quality assessments (Anatolyevna-Stepanova et al., 2018).

The fairness of the performance review process and employee faith in the supervisor are used to gauge performance. Clarity, communication, trust, and impartiality are critical components of an effective performance appraisal system (Su & Baird, 2017). A structured teacher-appraisal approach designed to ensure that specific organizational targets are met is known as performance management. This incorporates any sort of evaluation linked to a teacher's career management and development. As a result, performance management is part of a more extensive process and system for assessing, monitoring, and improving teachers' performance. It covers teacher registration, regular appraisals, and promotion appraisals (OECD, 2013). Therefore, the purpose of performance appraisals is to evaluate individual teachers' performance or provide support to improve their practice in the classroom. Furthermore, countries utilize a variety of appraisal approaches: appraisal as a probationary term, appraisal for registration, appraisal for promotion and incentive programs.

2.1. *Performance management model*

According to Gruman & Saks (2011), performance management process models usually comprise structured activities or stages, such as goal setting, performance monitoring, appraisal and feedback, and improving performance. Figure 1 provides a performance management process

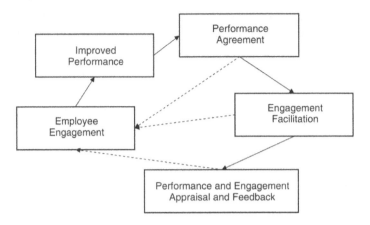

Figure 1. Performance management process.

model that considers employee involvement. Cultivating engagement as a prerequisite to outstanding performance is the model's primary goal. Performance management necessitates a comprehensive approach that considers all aspects of the company and the performance's constituent parts.

The performance model suggested by Gruman & Saks (2011) starts with a performance agreement that outlines employees' expectations. What sets it apart is that the job parameters, goals, and performance indicators are negotiable to boost engagement.

During this process, the psychological contract is also reviewed to enhance engagement. The next part of the model deals with engagement facilitation, which includes job design, leadership, coaching, supervisory support, and training, to help employees develop engagement. An innovative aspect of this component is creating psychological capital, which can enhance employee engagement.

Performance and engagement appraisal and feedback then concentrate on the impact of justice and trust on engagement instead of the conventional focus on rating accuracy. As the model suggests, each component contributes to employee engagement, leading to improved performance.

2.2. Importance of performance appraisal

Every organization has targets to achieve throughout the designated period. The key driver of an organization is its employees. Many stakeholders consider performance evaluation crucial and advantageous for gauging performance and using that data to guide decisions. It is commonly accepted that receiving performance feedback is beneficial and enhances employee engagement and productivity. The type of evaluation approach that the majority of firms employ does not appear to have an obvious alternative (Murphy, 2020). The performance evaluation process and the clarity and fairness of the evaluation standards are associated with higher levels of satisfaction with the evaluation process, more favorable views about performance bonuses, and higher levels of job satisfaction and motivation. Using controllable assessment criteria is linked to increased job satisfaction and motivation, as well as greater satisfaction with the system, reduced stress from the system, and reduced use of subjective criteria (Ong Kelly et al., 2008).

As more parents strive for excellent education for their children, teacher evaluations provide a method for schools to be held accountable for the quality of teaching in their classes and to focus on underperformance among teachers (Schleicher, 2015). Therefore, they must be assessed to determine their working quality. According to Hallinger et al. (2014), "teacher appraisal is an important vehicle for promoting educational quality." The major goal of teacher evaluation is to identify areas where individual teachers need to improve, which leads to the creation of individual improvement plans and a school-wide improvement plan (OECD, 2013). The appraisal system provides a pathway for self-evaluation and organizational evaluation. The addition of the strategic role of the school has purposefully broadened the scope of performance appraisal as a human resources function. Performance appraisal practices and research, which were earlier considered secondary, have recently gained prominence in developmental function (Iqbal et al., 2015). Performance appraisal strategies have evolved over time to aid in determining an employee's performance. In recent years, performance evaluations have expanded beyond analyzing an employee's performance to include characteristics such as motivation (Idowu, 2017). Teachers' performance has a particular responsibility in the education field because, in academia, teachers' performance is an important area (Mwangi & Njuguna, 2019).

Since no endeavor at educational improvement can be effective without classrooms staffed by capable, excellent instructors, teacher evaluation is crucial. Teaching and learning are the two main components of education, and they may be accomplished by having good teachers

(Samuel & Berhanu, 2019). Hence, it is only possible to identify effective teachers when there exist reliable evaluation systems. Therefore, to effectively accomplish the goals and objectives of education and enhance the quality of teaching, teachers must be consistently motivated and up to date.

A low performance by teachers causes a significant decline in the academic career of students, which has a long-term impact on the education sector. As a result, teachers' performance plays an important role in the education sector, which scholars and practitioners must address (Hartinah *et al.*, 2020). Thus, performance appraisal needs to be implemented as an ongoing process to improve teachers in their classroom teaching and related activities. Therefore, it would be beneficial for teachers as well as students.

3. Factors Which Improve Teachers' Effectiveness

Teacher effectiveness and teacher qualification have a direct relationship with interpersonal skills and work ethics. A competent teacher must possess professional qualifications and academic competencies, as well as effective communication skills with students, the ability to inspire creativity and productivity, a strong work ethic, and a strong commitment to the job (Sidi, as cited in Hartinah *et al.*, 2020). Moreover, ongoing performance appraisal was more effective in assessing teacher quality and effectiveness in the classroom over a longer period of time (Lee, 2018). Furthermore, implementing effective performance appraisal practices offers a significant opportunity to identify high-caliber individuals who can be added to the talent pool of future prospective leaders, allowing them to participate in targeted professional development opportunities (Williams, 2019).

The relationship between teacher professional development and school improvement is a key component of teacher assessment systems (Samuel & Berhanu, 2019). Teacher effectiveness improves by providing mentoring programs for teachers, but it depends on the proper guidance of the head teacher and the time provided to complete assigned tasks (OECD, 2013). Performance evaluation merely covers collaboration, cooperation, communication, and commitment. All of these elements influence the quality of teachers (Stronge, 2005). In other words, it's crucial to consider how both appraisers and appraisees view the appraisal process and their relationship if a quality system is to be built.

Bandura (1997) stated that goal setting and self-efficacy are essential sources of motivation, with efficacy affecting the types of objectives people choose to stick with tasks. Performance of International Students Assessment (PISA) results show a significant influence on students' self-efficacy, their faith, and their capability for academic performance and behavior (OECD, 2013). There is evidence that teachers' self-efficacy, or confidence in their talent to teach, involve students, and manage a classroom, influences students' achievements and motivation, as well as teachers' own practices, enthusiasm, dedication, work satisfaction, and classroom behavior (Schleicher, 2015). Moreover, intrinsic and extrinsic motivation are also factors which affect teacher effectiveness. While intrinsic motivation promotes motivation through personal satisfaction or enjoyment, extrinsic motivation describes the importance of external rewards, including salary increases and promotions (Idowu, 2017). Therefore, if performance appraisals are linked with salary increments and promotions, teachers' focus would be on correcting their mistakes in the classroom to get higher scores in appraisals.

Optimistic belief promotes acceptance of the task. Likewise, teacher trust in performance appraisals encourages the involvement of teachers. According to Finster & Milanowski (2018), several researchers have looked into the relations among teacher assessment perceptions and found that the reasons are linked. Teacher perceptions of these elements' quality are equally crucial in making PA work. In addition, it supports a shared leadership style that gives teachers the power to improve their own instruction and develop trust between teachers and principals in the school culture (Mette, 2015). Failure to consider and accommodate teachers' perspectives throughout the design and application stages can lead to views of misalignment or disagreement with teachers' concerns, beliefs, and values, thereby leading to social invalidity (Reddy *et al.*, 2018). It is critical to include teachers' perspectives in the appraisal process to engage them in the process and empower their performance. To be recognized as "good" teachers, teachers must understand what is expected of them. This demands not only complete simplicity in the evaluation standards and process but also complete confidentiality (OECD, 2013). While the performance appraisal is directly related to the teachers, it is important to include teachers' voices in the performance appraisal framework in the design stage.

Teachers who provided students with a step-by-step explanation of how to complete their work, provided time for practice, gave students time to reflect on the material, informed students about the lesson objectives, reviewed the material, asked questions to determine whether students understood the material, appropriately answered student questions, repeated things when students did not understand, and presented the lesson logically are believed to be effective teacher (Nussbaum, 1992). Clearly stating the lesson's objective, incorporating students' prior knowledge, using more than one delivery method or modality, using numerous examples, providing feedback on the learning process, and asking how and why questions are all good ways to improve instruction (Strong *et al.*, 2011). Today's effective teachers work hard to accommodate students' particular needs while maintaining high standards for students' performance (Blair *et al.*, 2007).

3.1. *Teachers' effectiveness model*

The teacher effectiveness model suggested by McBer (2000) confirms already-known effective teaching attributes and some new dimensions that demonstrate the extent to which effective teachers improve their pupils' performance. The three main factors that teachers can considerably manage and have an impact on students' success are teaching skills, professional characteristics, and classroom climate (Figure 2).

Each offers unique and complementary means for teachers to comprehend their contribution. To provide teaching with added value, none can be relied upon alone.

The three factors each have a distinct nature. Professional characteristics and teaching skills are two fundamental factors which are considered while offering a teaching job. The consistent behavioral patterns that generally motivate performance are the professional characteristics. These include the "micro-behaviors" that teaching skills address. Though teaching skills can be learned, maintaining these behaviors throughout a career will require more in-built professional characteristics. On the other hand, the classroom climate may be measured. It enables teachers to comprehend how the students in their class feel about the aspects of the learning environment the teacher has produced and which affect the students' motivation to learn.

The effective teacher regularly performs "micro-behaviors," including teaching skills in class. Such behaviors include involving the whole class in the lesson and using differentiated learning approaches to involve

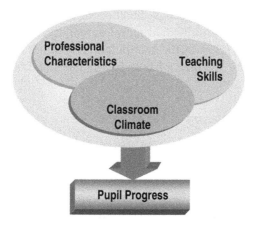

Figure 2. The measures of teacher effectiveness.

all pupils in the class equally. Using different types of learning methods and activities, employing instructional strategies aligned with the goals of the national curriculum, and utilizing a variety of questioning tactics to test students' understanding and knowledge contribute to creating a dynamic and engaging learning environment.

3.2. *Motivation theory*

Motivation theory is a broad field of study that aims to understand why individuals behave as they do. There are many different theories of motivation, each with its own unique perspective on the forces that drive behavior.

Motivation is a psychological process resulting from the interaction between the individual and the environment. Work motivation is a collection of energy factors that arise within and without a person's being. Its purpose is to initiate behavior linked to work and to control its form, direction, intensity, and duration (Latham & Pinder, 2005). People tend to seek out or avoid particular types of stimuli, whether they are innate or learned. These tendencies, sometimes known as motives or needs, significantly impact behavior and performance. Work motivation is described as a broad concept that refers to the circumstances and mechanisms that explain the arousal, focus, intensity, and maintenance of effort in a person's line of work (Katzell & Thompson, 1990). Motivational efforts can exert control over individual moral autonomy. Among other things, motivation usually involves the manipulation of values that motivate individuals to work for organizational ends (Michaelson, 2005).

3.3. *Goal-setting theory*

Goal-setting theory is a motivation theory developed by Edwin A. Locke and Gary P. Latham. It states that specific, challenging goals lead to higher performance than easy or general goals. The theory also posits that the process of setting goals leads to increased motivation and engagement.

As stated in goal-setting theory, a goal is the purpose or aim of an action. It might be a standard of performance to be met in the workplace (Locke & Latham, 2013). A goal is what a person is working toward; it is the purpose or aim of an action. Goal acceptance and commitment are two distinct but related ideas. Goal commitment suggests a resolve to make an effort toward a goal, but the source of the goal is not stated. It can be a goal that was given, one that you created on your own, or one that was collaboratively set (Saari *et al.*, 1981). The goal-setting theory of motivation explains why some people perform better than others on tasks linked to their jobs. While goal-setting theory contends that the goal itself is the main source of a person's motivation, control theorists consider discrepancy reduction as the driving force for action (Locke & Latham, 2013). The core idea behind goal-setting theory is that setting challenging, precise, and alluring goals will improve performance. To keep performing at a high level, people want feedback. Money, another tangible reward, or involvement in establishing work goals can boost commitment to a goal (Katzell & Thompson, 1990). The most important finding is that when provided goals are approved, challenging goals lead to more excellent task performance. But most goals in research are set by a supervisor and specified by performance standards, quotas, work norms, or deadlines (Erez & Kanfer, 1983).

3.4. *Conceptual framework*

This conceptual framework consists of two variables: performance appraisal is an independent variable (IV), and teacher effectiveness is a dependent variable (DV). These are performance appraisal targets assessed during the year as formative assessments (Figure 3).

Figure 3. Conceptual framework.

4. Relationship between Teachers' Performance Appraisal and Teachers' Effectiveness

Every organization desires to be a pioneer in its specialized field of service, but to reach that goal, certain things need to be improved. One of the most essential things required to improve is their staff performance. Otherwise, designated goals for the staff may not be achieved, and it will affect the organization's goals. Evaluating employees' work aims to enhance their work to achieve organizational goals. A survey done in OCED countries shows that it is essential to combine teachers' performance appraisals with primary teacher training and skill development programs. Some countries were concerned that the teachers' preparations were poorly aligned with the standard and "good teaching" criteria of appraisal. But later, teachers explored the standard well and reached the goal (OECD, 2013). A study conducted to examine the Turkish evaluation system for teachers found that teacher effectiveness improves when the administrator's viewpoint is positive because teachers expressed a need for performance comments, particularly administrators' acknowledgment and support of positive performance. On the other hand, administrators had a "no problem, no feedback" attitude, and their refusal to provide recorded feedback did not affect teaching, learning, teacher development, or overall school progress (Reddy et al., 2018).

Performance evaluation is an important management approach for evaluating employee work performance, clarifying personnel decisions such as promotion, demotion, or retention, and aiding people in increasing their capabilities through feedback or training. Furthermore, successful performance appraisals motivate staff to strive for improvement by linking appraisals to performance-based incentives. Despite widespread agreement that performance appraisals can benefit businesses, their theorized benefits appear to be underrealized in some circumstances (Lee, 2018). Effective teacher evaluation can also assist schools in becoming more aware of individual potential, performance, and motivation and permitting teachers to advance in their professions and take on new tasks and obligations based on performance evaluations (OECD, 2013). The success of teachers and staff in assisting their pupils to achieve academically, socially, emotionally, and behaviorally is increased when working conditions in a school are improved. The performance of each educator appears to be enhanced by a good working environment (Havik & Westergård, 2020).

Contrary to popular belief, a teacher's effectiveness cannot be consistently determined by their place of education, level of certification, or length of service. Examining a teacher's on-the-job performance, such as what they do in the classroom and how much improvement their pupils make on achievement tests, is a better approach to judging their effectiveness. This has led to rules that mandate evaluating teachers' effectiveness while on the job, based partly on data regarding their pupils' academic progress (Opper, 2019).

Based on the research, there is a direct link between teachers' performance appraisals and teachers' effectiveness because performance appraisals lead to correcting mistakes in their teaching with supervisors' feedback.

5. Conclusion

The literature review indicates that performance appraisal can be a formative or summative process. In most cases, the summative approach is being used because performance assessments are generally utilized for administrative objectives. Summative elements assess performance for professional advancement goals, prospective promotion or demotion, and termination. Although, among teachers, the formative approach is more respectable. It leads to more corrective measures than evaluation alone. Teachers' appraisals provide a framework for schools to be held accountable for the educational quality of their students. Self-assessment and organizational evaluation are both possible with the appraisal system. Along with interpersonal skills and work ethics, teacher effectiveness and credentials are directly related. Professional qualities and academic competence are demanded of a professional teacher. There is a chance to find individuals of high caliber who can be added to the talent pool of possible leadership prospects. Employee work is evaluated to improve and fulfill organizational goals. Teachers' efficacy and performance ratings have a direct relationship. To be recognized as "great" teachers, teachers must understand what is expected of them. Not only is complete transparency in the evaluation criteria and approach demanded, but it is also expected.

References

Aggarwal, A. & Thakur, G.S.M. (2013). Techniques of performance appraisal — A review. *International Journal of Engineering and Advanced Technology*, *2*(3), 617–621.

Ahmad, R. & Bujang, S. (2013). Issues and challenges in the practice of performance appraisal activities in the 21st century. *International Journal of Education and Research*, *1*(4), 1–8.

Anatolyevna-Stepanova, N., Nailevna-Sannikova, L., Ivanovna-Levshina, N., Nikolayevna-Yurevich, S., & Vyacheslavovna-Ilyina, G. (2018). Methodological performance evaluation by teachers in preschool educational institutions. *International Journal of Cognitive Research in Science Engineering and Education*, *6*(2), 67–79. https://doi.org/10.5937/ijcrsee1802067A.

Bandura, A. (1997). *Self-Efficacy: The Exercise of Control*. New York: Freeman.

Blair, T.R., Rupley, W.H., & Nichols, W.D. (2007). The effective teacher of reading: Considering the "what" and "how" of instruction. *The Reading Teacher*, *60*(5), 432–438. https://doi.org/10.1598/RT.60.5.3.

Elliott, K. (2015). Teacher performance appraisal: More about performance or development? *Australian Journal of Teacher Education*, *40*(40). https://doi.org/10.14221/ajte.2015v40n9.6.

Erez, M. & Kanfer, F.H. (1983). The role of goal acceptance in goal setting and task performance. *Academy of Management Review*, *8*(3), 454–463.

Finster, M. & Milanowski, A. (2018). Teacher perceptions of a new performance evaluation system and their influence on practice: A within- and between-school level analysis. *Education Policy Analysis Archives*, *26*, 41. https://doi.org/10.14507/epaa.26.3500.

Fletcher, C. (2001). Performance appraisal and management: The developing research agenda. *Journal of Occupational and Organizational Psychology*, *74*(4), 473–487.
Gruman, J.A. & Saks, A.M. (2011). Performance management and employee engagement. *Human Resource Management Review*, *21*(2), 123–136. https://doi.org/10.1016/j.hrmr.2010.09.004.
Hallinger, P., Heck, R.H., & Murphy, J. (2014). Teacher evaluation and school improvement: An analysis of the evidence. *Educational Assessment, Evaluation and Accountability*, *26*(1), 5–28. https://doi.org/10.1007/s11092-013-9179-5.
Hartinah, S., Suharso, P., Umam, R., Syazali, M., Lestari, B.D., Roslina, R., & Jermsittiparsert, K. (2020). Teacher's performance management: The role of principal's leadership, work environment and motivation in Tegal City, Indonesia. *Management Science Letters*, 235–246. https://doi.org/10.5267/j.msl.2019.7.038.
Havik, T. & Westergård, E. (2020). Do teachers matter? Students' perceptions of classroom interactions and student engagement. *Scandinavian Journal of Educational Research*, *64*(4), 488–507. https://doi.org/10.1080/00313831.2019.1577754.
Idowu, A. (2017). Effectiveness of performance appraisal system and its effect on employee motivation. *Nile Journal of Business and Economics*, *3*(5), 15. https://doi.org/10.20321/nilejbe.v3i5.88.
Iqbal, M.Z., Akbar, S., & Budhwar, P. (2015). Effectiveness of performance appraisal: An integrated framework: Effectiveness of performance appraisal. *International Journal of Management Reviews*, *17*(4), 510–533. https://doi.org/10.1111/ijmr.12050.
Kagema, J. & Irungu, C. (2018). An analysis of teacher performance appraisals and their influence on teacher performance in secondary schools in Kenya. *International Journal of Education*, *11*(1), 93. https://doi.org/10.17509/ije.v11i1.11148.
Katzell, R.A. & Thompson, D.E. (1990). Work motivation: Theory and practice. *American Psychologist*, *45*(2), 144–153. https://doi.org/10.1037/0003-066X.45.2.144.
Latham, G.P. & Pinder, C.C. (2005). Work motivation theory and research at the dawn of the twenty-first century. *Annual Review of Psychology*, *56*(1), 485–516. https://doi.org/10.1146/annurev.psych.55.090902.142105.
Lee, S.W. (2018). Pulling back the curtain: Revealing the cumulative importance of high-performing, highly qualified teachers on students' educational outcome. *Educational Evaluation and Policy Analysis*, *40*(3), 359–381. https://doi.org/10.3102/0162373718769379.

Locke, E.A. & Latham, G.P. (2013). *New Developments in Goal Setting and Task Performance* (1st edn.). London: Routledge. https://doi.org/10.4324/9780203082744.

McBer, H. (2000). Research into Teacher Effectiveness: A Model of Teacher Effectiveness. Crown Copyright. https://dera.ioe.ac.uk/4566/1/RR216.pdf.

Mette, I.M. (2015). Teachers' perceptions of teacher supervision and evaluation: a reflection of school improvement practices in the age of reform.

Michaelson, C. (2005). Meaningful motivation for work motivation theory. *Academy of Management Review*, *30*(2), 235–238. https://doi.org/10.5465/amr.2005.16387881.

Murphy, K.R. (2020). Performance evaluation will not die, but it should. *Human Resource Management Journal*, *30*(1), 13–31. https://doi.org/10.1111/1748-8583.12259.

Mwangi, B.W. & Njuguna, R. (2019). Performance appraisal strategies on performance of teachers in public secondary schools in Kiambu County, Kenya. *International Journal of Current Aspects*, *3*(II), 218–230. https://doi.org/10.35942/ijcab.v3iII.19.

Nussbaum, J.F. (1992). Effective teacher behaviors. *Communication Education*, *41*(2), 167–180. https://doi.org/10.1080/03634529209378878.

OECD. (2013). *Teachers for the 21st Century: Using Evaluation to Improve Teaching*. Paris: OECD. https://doi.org/10.1787/9789264193864-en.

Ong Kelly, K., Yun Angela Ang, S., Ling Chong, W., & Sheng Hu, W. (2008). Teacher appraisal and its outcomes in Singapore primary schools. *Journal of Educational Administration*, *46*(1), 39–54. https://doi.org/10.1108/09578230810849808.

Opper, I.M. (2019). Teachers Matter: Understanding Teachers' Impact on Student Achievement (RR-4312, 2019). RAND Corporation. https://www.rand.org/pubs/research_reports/RR4312.html.

Reddy, L.A., Dudek, C.M., Peters, S., Alperin, A., Kettler, R.J., & Kurz, A. (2018). Teachers' and school administrators' attitudes and beliefs of teacher evaluation: A preliminary investigation of high poverty school districts. *Educational Assessment, Evaluation and Accountability*, *30*(1), 47–70. https://doi.org/10.1007/s11092-017-9263-3.

Saari, M., Latham, G.P., Locke, E.A., & Shaw, K.N. (1981). Goal setting and task performance: 1969–1980. *Psychological Bulletin*, *90*(1), 125–152.

Samuel, C. & Berhanu, E. (2019). Practices and challenges of appraising teacher's performance appraisal in government preparatory schools of Wolaita Zone, South Ethiopia. *Research on Humanities and Social Sciences*, *9*(7), 47–62. https://doi.org/10.7176/RHSS/9-7-07.

Schleicher, A. (2015). *Schools for 21st-Century Learners: Strong Leaders, Confident Teachers, Innovative Approaches*. Paris: OECD. https://doi.org/10.1787/9789264231191-en.

Sing, R.R. & Vadivelu, S. (2016). Performance appraisal in India — A review. *International Journal of Applied Engineering Research, 11*(5), 3229–3234.

Strong, M., Gargani, J., & Hacifazlioğlu, Ö. (2011). Do we know a successful teacher when we see one? Experiments in the identification of effective teachers. *Journal of Teacher Education, 62*(4), 367–382. https://doi.org/10.1177/0022487110390221.

Stronge, J.H. (2005). *Evaluating Teaching: A Guide to Current Thinking and Best Practice*. Thousand Oaks, California: Corwin Press.

Su, S. & Baird, K. (2017). The association between performance appraisal systems, work-related attitudes and academic performance. *Financial Accountability & Management, 33*(4), 356–372. https://doi.org/10.1111/faam.12128.

Williams, P. (2019). Current and ideal performance appraisal: Employee perceptions in an Australian faith-based education system. *TEACH Journal of Christian Education, 13*(1), 21–28.

© 2025 World Scientific Publishing Company
https://doi.org/10.1142/9789811294730_0007

Chapter 7

Teachers' Motivation and Job Performance

Rafiu Jameel* and Intan Marfarrina Omar†

Faculty of Education, University of Malaya, Kuala Lumpur, Malaysia
*s2160527@siswa.um.edu.mu
†marfarrina@um.edu.my

Abstract

Motivation is a key factor that determines not only the well-being of the staff but also their performance in the organization. Intrinsic motivation, which has its roots in the early 20th century, explains some of the reasons for lower performance and how to tackle them. When compared to a peer who is not intrinsically motivated, an intrinsically motivated teacher can bring innovative teaching pedagogies and high performance. School leaders can consider a positive work environment where authority and autonomy are given, learning is encouraged, and professional development is provided in order to successfully bring out the potential of staff and achieve the overall objectives of the organization. It is worthwhile to note the importance of intrinsic motivation and at the same time give due attention to other factors that can contribute to or lead to teacher performance.

Keywords: Motivation, intrinsic motivation, teacher performance, teachers' effectiveness, successful teacher.

1. Introduction

Motivation remains a vital factor in effective and efficient job performance in every area of employment. In an ever-changing world, individuals need to be well motivated to perform their responsibilities best, to reach their potential and the expectations of their stakeholders, and to keep themselves efficient and equipped to survive in the job market. It is a key factor in human psychology and behavior that influences how an individual in a normal work environment will spend their time, decide the amount of effort that they will put into a task, and most importantly how they will think and feel about their work, which often determines how long they will pursue it (Filgona *et al.*, 2020). Motivation is of two major types: intrinsic motivation, which is the practice of engaging in a task for one's own internal satisfaction rather than for a physical or financial benefit, and extrinsic motivation, which applies when a task is performed in order to achieve a specific result that one wishes to obtain, often in physical or monetary form (Ryan & Deci, 2000). Job performance is a result of employee motivation, competence, and how they adapt to the constraints of their situation and unfriendly environment (Al-Omari & Okasheh, 2017). Motivation is essential for staff, including teachers, to perform well in various settings. The ability to successfully convey knowledge, uphold moral ideals, and perform superbly academically distinguishes job performance in teaching (Omar *et al.*, 2020).

Intrinsic motivation has its roots in Maslow's esteem and self-actualization needs (Maslow, 1943) and it facilitates the drive of perseverance and eagerness toward the tasks (Vansteenkiste *et al.*, 2020). In the early 20th century, researchers began to understand that, more than extrinsic motivation that is obtained with rewards or punishments, humans tend to get involved even in the absence of the previously mentioned factors if an activity gives them joy, satisfaction, or is associated with positive feelings (Krijgsman *et al.*, 2017). Some prominent research, such as Abraham Maslow's theory of motivation, McGregor Gregor's theory of X and Y, Fredrick Herzberg's two-factor theory, and Campbell's hierarchical model of job performance, help us comprehend both motivation and job performance in various human interactions.

The job performance of employees can be defined as the total of an employee's actions in a given situation that are pertinent to the goals of the organization (Yilmaz, 2015). It is the degree to which an individual performs their responsibilities and duties effectively and efficiently to achieve the goals of the employer (Inayat & Khan, 2021) (Millacci *et al.*, 2019). It includes a number of elements, such as task competence, work quality, job commitment, and organizational civic behavior. Job performance is a key dimension in both management and psychology as well as other organizational studies. In this chapter, the focus is on the intrinsic motivation factor and how it impacts the performance of a teacher. It is the right of every student to get a teacher who is knowledgeable, well prepared, and motivated to ensure that the content is well delivered to students. A teacher who is well prepared has the skills, resources, and self-assurance necessary to effectively engage students, foster learning, and manage the classroom (Franklin & Harrington, 2019). Teachers devote a lot of time and energy to their careers because they have a huge impact on how their students will thrive in the future (Lee & Yuen, 2019). Someone who is intrinsically motivated sees the job or the tasks at hand as a challenge that she/he needs to successfully achieve, which enhances the desire to complete the activity and makes it more rewarding upon successful achievement (Fishbach & Woolley, 2022).

Every student, once they enter a class, will have high expectations from the teachers, i.e. the teachers will perform well and deliver content to them in a good environment with the right techniques so that students are able to grasp the most amount of information. The impact intrinsic motivation has on the teacher's performance is an area of interest for every organization and employer.

2. Elements of Intrinsic Motivation

Teachers need intrinsic motivation for a successful career as it is a vital part of their work life and is a significant determinant of performance in a variety of ways. They can boost their intrinsic motivation and enhance their overall performance and success by recognizing and using some of the elements involved in intrinsic motivation as follows:

(1) **Autonomy:** Autonomy is the perception of control and independence over one's actions and decisions, and it has been recognized as an important element of motivation that gives meaning to work (Martela & Riekk, 2018). This is visible as an esteem need in Maslow's hierarchy of needs and is visible in the self-concordance model as it proposes that autonomous motivation is best supported

by goals that are self-concordant. The need for autonomy to bring out the best performance can also be determined based on the self-determination theory, which concludes that giving someone the authority to control their behavior and destiny will encourage them to perform better.

Teachers will need autonomy in conducting lessons. They will be more motivated when they are able to decide how the delivery of lessons will be done, the teaching techniques they will use, or the materials they will use. This can also include decisions such as taking students on field trips and the authority to tackle the challenges faced during the class.

(2) **Challenge:** A challenge motivates people to engage in an activity with a sense of meaning and purpose as opposed to just doing it for the sake of getting something for free. It is the feeling of challenge that often brings out the motivation within us to dare and do. Challenge–Skills Balance refers to the idea that for individuals to feel motivated and engaged, the level of challenge must be appropriate for their current level of skill (Larche & Dixon, 2020). Such a challenge can fulfill the need for competence by providing an opportunity for individuals to test their abilities and develop their skills according to the self-determination theory.

A teacher with high expectations will be motivated to work toward meeting them, which will enhance their performance. The challenge must be reasonable and achievable, and it is ideal to decide on it with the teacher's approval. This will help students feel like they belong to the challenge and will motivate them to complete it.

(3) **Competition:** Competition is a strong motivator for many people and has been researched from various angles in motivational psychology. When it comes to their most coveted qualities, people think more of themselves than their average peer, which leads to rivalry (Fishbach & Woolley, 2022). Competition can influence the intrinsic motivation of a person by providing various opportunities for the individual to experience a sense of autonomy, competence, and belonging to a group. Competition can provide opportunities for individuals to meet their esteem needs by demonstrating their competence and skills. It also allows people to aim for self-actualization by striving to be their best as in Maslow's hierarchy of needs, to view their work as a challenge, and to strive for personal growth and

development as suggested by McGregor's X and Y theories. Competition can also provide external motivation in the form of rewards and recognition, which can further enhance intrinsic motivation as predicted by Frederick Herzberg's two-factor theory.

A teacher in a competitive environment where they are expected to continuously improve, and that improvement is noticed and appreciated by the superiors, has a higher chance of being intrinsically motivated. That way, competition as a dimension of intrinsic motivation will lead to higher performance.

(4) **Enjoyment:** Intrinsic motivation is driven by the internal enjoyment one gets from an activity and a sense of fulfillment or personal growth. Such enjoyment within the self is less likely to be achieved if the task is to obtain rewards or avoid a punishment or consequence. People tend to continue longer on a task that gives them joy or satisfaction at the end of the day. While Herzberg's theory sees enjoyment as a motivator that offers fulfillment and satisfaction beyond basic job satisfaction, Maslow's theory asserts that enjoyment serves higher-order needs in addition to basic physiological needs.

A teacher who enjoys teaching and working with students will tend to work harder in order to bring out the best in the students. This encourages the teachers to perform well, be prepared, and be up to date for every lesson. It provides a sense of fulfillment and satisfaction that goes beyond the basic job satisfaction of finishing an assigned task, thus being more related to intrinsic motivation.

(5) **Interest:** Interest could be described as the drive to engage in an activity for its own sake, without external rewards or pressure (Bontempi, 2019). According to curiosity theory, the drive to seek information and knowledge leads to the exploration of new and challenging activities and can lead to increased attention and exploration of the object or event, and the subsequent satisfaction of the need for knowledge and understanding (Kashdan *et al.*, 2020). Interest is a motivator for learning and exploration, and more learning and exploration in general will make one more effective and efficient, leading to higher job performance.

A teacher's interest in being the best teacher, bringing the best results, or even using the best available teaching pedagogies will make the teacher more successful. It will lead to intrinsic motivation and job satisfaction, both contributing to the better performance of the teacher. In this way, interest as a dimension of intrinsic motivation will lead to better performance on the part of teachers.

(6) **Mastery:** Development and progress are what everyone looks forward to in their career. Mastery is driven by a desire to have a sense of personal advancement and growth through the achievement of excellence and the completion of challenging tasks (Hammond et al., 2020). Once an individual is intrinsically motivated toward a task, they engage more in learning the means, skills, and knowledge to improve and enhance the task performance. In Maslow's hierarchy of needs, mastery is considered as a source of strength and freedom that come with the esteem need. People who are driven by mastery experience a sense of joy throughout the learning and improvement processes, and they are often more likely to keep trying in spite of the failures and setbacks they may come across in the process.

Teachers will require the right skills, knowledge, information, and teaching methodologies in order to be successful in teaching and to bring out a good academic performance from students. Regardless of the motivation one holds, delivering the content and ensuring that students are able to grasp the knowledge demand the teacher to be knowledgeable. It is equally important to consider that with the availability of free access to information for students, it is essential for teachers to get the latest information to minimize, if not avoid, challenges in the classroom.

(7) **Personal growth:** Personal growth can be defined as the ambition of a person to achieve their maximum potential and improve themselves in their career. It is a long and continuous process if one needs to ensure that personal growth does not halt. Since personal growth is driven by the desire to develop one's own skills, interests, and goals and also to grow, learn, and improve, it demands intrinsic motivation (Fishbach & Woolley, 2022). Additionally, one is more likely to approach learning and self-development independently and in a self-directed manner, similar to the "Y" type individuals in McGregor's X and Y theory and the self-esteem stage of Maslow's hierarchy of needs. Personal growth occurs with one's own creativity, readiness to take risk, and the will to move out of the comfort zone and face challenges.

Teachers, upon completion of their studies, have to undergo continuous improvements and professional development. For instance, a teacher who does not undergo personal growth after studies and simply continues to teach for 10 years is not attaining a decade of experience, rather repeating one year of expertise 10 times. Expertise is not merely about time but also about how much personal growth and improvement were made in that duration.

(8) **Purpose:** Motivation can exist only when one has a real aim or purpose for doing something. It is driven by a sense of purpose and direction in life, in addition to a goal to have a significant impact on the world. According to self-determination theory, purposeful activities are those that promote one's personal development, foster a sense of fulfillment, and add meaning to one's life. It is also critical that the purpose for which one aims and works aligns with the visions of the school or organization, so that the purposeful act can be reflected as good performance within the organization. It gives meaning to a person's life and thus enhances self-actualization, as in Maslow's hierarchy of needs. The importance of purpose in motivation is also acknowledged in Douglas McGregor's theory of X and Y.

A teacher who is intrinsically motivated will have a purpose and an aim to achieve. It is this purpose that acts as a driving force for teachers to face challenges, tackle issues, aim higher, and perform well. Regular assessment of students, setting targets for individual students, making plans to improve, and bringing required changes to teaching methods and strategies or class environment are some of the factors a motivated teacher will need to consider in the race toward reaching a purpose. Teachers also will have their own personal purposes such as moving up the career ladder, which demand good performance and intrinsic motivation.

(9) **Recognition:** In Maslow's hierarchy of needs, recognition is a lower-level need related to the need for self-actualization and self-esteem. Recognition can be referred to as the acknowledgment or appreciation of an individual's efforts, abilities, or accomplishments. People must feel a sense of purpose and expertise or skill in their work in order to be effectively recognized for their performance (Wiles, 2022). According to the expectancy theory, people are more motivated to work hard if they feel that their efforts will be well recognized by their superiors. Similarly, McGregor's theory of X and Y also identifies the role of recognition in motivation. Giving the right recognition can be a powerful tool in an organization to keep the staff motivated and bring out the best in performance.

(10) **Responsibility:** Responsibility is about every task that one is expected to do on the job and how it is done (Lin & Tsai, 2020). It is about how one looks at and works toward the duties and obligations they have to fulfill as a member of an organization. According to the self-determination theory, responsibility and a sense of obligation are crucial parts of intrinsic motivation since they enhance a person's tendency to be driven by inner forces like growth and meaning in their performance. The role of responsibility in motivation is also addressed by Douglas McGregor's theory of X and Y, where theory Y sees people as autonomous and motivated by internal factors like commitment and goals that they set for themselves to achieve in their careers.

3. Intrinsic Motivation and Job Performance

A motivated teacher will work to achieve success and bring out the best in performance, not just for the teacher but also for the student and school or academic institution. A study examining the relationship between teacher motivation and student academic performance in public secondary schools in Gem sub-county, Kenya, showed that teacher motivation had a moderate, positive, and significant relationship (Oluoch & Gogo, 2022). Similar results were found in studies on Nigeria's TVET colleges, intermediate and secondary education in Lahore, Pakistan, schools located in the city center of Kars Province in Turkey, and secondary schools in Tabora municipality, Tanzania. A research of 357 Pakistani secondary school teachers revealed a link between intrinsic motivation and teacher effectiveness (Manzoor *et al.*, 2021). Several investigations (Manzoor *et al.*, 2021; Bukhari *et al.*, 2021; Hafızoglu & Yerdelen, 2019) found similar results in their contexts.

4. Drawbacks

Intrinsic motivation is not the only factor that could determine the motivation of teachers and their performance. In their study, Miao *et al.* (2020) observed that both intrinsic and extrinsic motivation have an impact on job performance and involvement, but they also mentioned that the latter's level of influence is anticipated to decrease in the future.

Work–life balance is very important for every employee in order to perform well for a sustained period of time. Regardless of the motivation a staff member has toward the job, performance could be negatively affected when work–life balance is not maintained (Roopavathi & Kishore, 2020).

Working conditions and the environment have a significant impact on job performance. A positive and friendly environment is essential for performance where there is mutual respect and support between subordinates and superiors. The absence of fair and timely encouragement, appreciation, and support can lower the performance of, if not demotivate, an already intrinsically motivated member of the organization.

Therefore, it is essential to note that regardless of the important role of intrinsic motivation in the job performance of teachers, there is no magic wand to bring out the best performance. Intrinsic motivation is a vital factor, but the need for other factors has to be equally considered.

5. Solutions

As previously stated, intrinsic motivation and job performance are related, although performance is determined by more than one factor.

Building a positive work environment can improve the performance as well as the mental well-being of the staff. Factors such as indoor and outdoor nature exposure in the work environment not only lead to increased motivation and reduced stress but also have an overall impact on employee well-being and performance (Sadick & Kamardeen, 2020).

Staff members will be highly motivated to develop goals if they are given responsibility and autonomy (Blom *et al.*, 2022). It will help teachers shape the lesson according to the performance of students so allowing them to attain a greater level of knowledge. Teachers with authority and autonomy can also practice new techniques and strategies that will enhance and improve their overall performance.

Encouraging learning and creating a continuous learning environment are considered a vital function of the human resource department of an organization (Parding & Jansson, 2018). Giving staff the resources and incentives to study and improve themselves in their profession will not only improve their performance on the job but also lead to staff loyalty and improve the school's reputation. Moreover, it is important that teachers are equipped with every skill or knowledge they require to perform well; thus, professional development programs can help to fill the gap and improve performance. With the aid of a continuous learning environment within the organization, it is possible to bring out the best performance or potential of the staff.

6. Conclusion

In conclusion, intrinsic motivation plays an important role in determining how well teachers perform their jobs. Teachers who are intrinsically motivated generally put more effort and commitment into their work, which improves performance and has a greater beneficial effect on students. However, it is important to remember that other aspects of a career, such as work–life balance, working conditions, and the environment in which a teacher works, can also have a big impact on how well teachers perform. Organizations and employers must realize the importance of intrinsic motivation, consider other factors, and establish an environment that encourages and supports it to get the best possible performance from teachers.

References

Al-Omari, K. & Okasheh, H. (2017). The influence of work environment on job performance: A case study of engineering company in Jordan. *International Journal of Applied Engineering Research*, *12*(24), 15544–15550. Retrieved from http://www.ripublication.com.

Blom, M., Smith, L., & Johnson, P. (2022). The role of responsibility and autonomy in staff motivation and goal development. *Journal of Organizational Psychology*, *30*(1), 45–58.

Bontempi, E. (2019, May 21). Intrinsic and extrinsic motivation: Implications in school, work, and psychological well-being. Retrieved from https://www.excelsior.edu/: https://www.excelsior.edu/article/types-of-motivation/.

Bukhari, S.G., Jamali, S.G., Larik, A.R., & Chang, M.S. (2021). Fostering intrinsic motivation among teachers: Importance of work environment and individual differences. *International Journal of School & Educational Psychology*, *11*(1), 1–19. https://doi.org/10.1080/21683603.2021.1925182.

Filgona, J., Sakiyo, J., Gwany, D., & Okoronka, A. (2020). Motivation in learning. *Asian Journal of Education and Social Studies*, *10*(4), 16–37. https://doi.org/10.9734/AJESS/2020/v10i430273.

Fishbach, A. & Woolley, K. (2022). The structure of intrinsic motivation. *Annual Review of Organizational Psychology and Organizational Behavior*, *9*(1), 1–38. https://doi.org/10.1146/annurev-orgpsych-012420-091122.

Franklin, H. & Harrington, I. (2019). A review into effective classroom management and strategies for student engagement: Teacher and student roles in today's classrooms. *Journal of Education and Training Studies*, *7*(12), 1. https://doi.org/10.11114/jets.v7i12.4491.

Hafızoglu, A. & Yerdelen, S. (2019). The role of students' motivation in the relationship between perceived learning environment and achievement in science: A mediation analysis. *Science Education International*, *30*(4), 51–260. Retrieved from https://files.eric.ed.gov/fulltext/EJ1236386.pdf.

Hammond, D.L., Flook, L., Harvey, C.C., Barron, B., & Osher, D. (2020). Implications for educational practice of the science of learning and development. *Applied Developmental Science*, *24*(2), 97–140. https://doi.org/10.1080/10888691.2018.1537791.

Inayat, W. & Khan, M.J. (2021). A Study of job satisfaction and its effect on the performance of employees working in private sector organizations, Peshawar. *Education Research International*, *2021*(1), 1–9.

Kashdan, T., Goodman, F., Disabato, D., McKnight, P., Kelso, K., & Naughton, C. (2020). Curiosity has comprehensive benefits in the workplace: Developing and validating a multidimensional workplace curiosity scale in United States and German employees. *Personality and Individual Differences*, *155*(2), 109717. https://doi.org/10.1016/j.paid.2019.109717.

Krijgsman, C., Vansteenkiste, M., Tartwijk, J.V., Maes, J., Borghouts, L., Cardon, G., ... Haerens, L. (2017). Performance grading and motivational functioning and fear in physical education: A self-determination theory perspective. *Learning and Individual Difference*, *55*, 202–211. https://doi.org/10.1016/j.lindif.2017.03.017.

Larche, C. & Dixon, M. (2020). The relationship between the skill-challenge balance, game expertise, flow and the urge to keep playing complex mobile games. *Journal of Behavioral Addictions*, *9*(3), 606–616. https://doi.org/10.1556/2006.2020.00070.

Lee, Q. & Yuen, M. (2019). The role of teacher care in determining academic success of community college students: A case study from Hong Kong. *International Journal of Personal, Social and Emotional Development*, *37*(2), 94–107.

Lin, Y., & Tsai, P. (2020). Responsibility and task execution in professional environments: Understanding performance expectations. *Journal of Vocational Education and Training*, *72*(1), 78–92.

Manzoor, F., Wei, L., & Asif, M. (2021). Intrinsic rewards and employee's performance with the mediating mechanism of employee's motivation. *Frontier in Education-Organizational Psychology*, *12*, 1–12. https://doi.org/10.3389/fpsyg.2021.563070.

Martela, F. & Riekk, T. (2018). Autonomy, competence, relatedness, and beneficence: A multicultural comparison of the four pathways to meaningful work. *Frontiers in Psychology*, *9*, 1–14. https://doi.org/10.3389/fpsyg.2018.01157.

Maslow, A. (1943). A theory of human motivation. *Psychological Review*, *50*(4), 370–396. https://doi.org/10.1037/h0054346.

Miao, S., Rhee, J., & Jun, I. (2020). How much does extrinsic motivation or intrinsic motivation affect job engagement or turnover intention? A comparison study in China. *Sustainability*, *12*(9), 3630. https://doi.org/10.3390/su12093630.

Millacci, T.S. (2019, April 9). What is goal setting and how to do it well. Retrieved from https://positivepsychology.com/; https://positivepsychology.com/goal-setting/.

Oluoch, O.D. & Gogo, J.O. (2022). Relationship between intrinsic teacher motivation and teacher amotivation and student academic performance in public secondary schools in Gem Sub-County, Kenya. *African Educational Research Journal*, *10*(2), 134–142. https://doi.org/10.30918/AERJ.102.22.020.

Omar, I.M., Zulazmi, N.L., & Zainal, M.F. (2020). Extrinsic motivational factors and teachers' job performance in Kepala Batas's secondary schools, Pulau Pinang. *Malaysian Online Journal of Psychology & Counseling*, *7*(1), 27–47. Retrieved from https://mojc.um.edu.my/index.php/MOJC/article/view/24180/11655.

Parding, K., & Jansson, A. (2018). Encouraging learning and creating a continuous learning environment: The role of human resource departments. *Human Resource Development International*, *21*(4), 310–324.

Quinoso, D. (2019). The impact of bonuses on teacher retention: A study of monotonic and non-monotonic effects. *Journal of Educational Policy and Practice*, *33*(2), 112–125.

Roopavathi, S. & Kishore, D. (2020). The impact of work life balance on employee performance. *Journal of Interdisciplinary Cycle Research*, *12*(10), 31–38.

Ryan, R.M. & Deci, E.L. (2000). Intrinsic and extrinsic motivations: Classic definitions and new directions. *Contemporary Educational Psychology*, *25*, 54–67. https://doi.org/10.1006/ceps.1999.1020.

Sadick, R., & Kamardeen, I. (2020). The impact of nature exposure on employee well-being and performance: A review of work environment factors. *Journal of Workplace Well-being*, *14*(3), 155–170.

Vansteenkiste, M., Ryan, R.M., & Soenens, B. (2020). Basic psychological need theory: Advancements, critical themes, and future directions. *Motivation and Emotion*, *44*, 1–31. https://doi.org/10.1007/s11031-019-09818-1.

Wiles, R. (2022). The role of purpose and expertise in recognizing performance. *Journal of Organizational Behavior*, *35*(4), 210–220.

Yilmaz, O.D. (2015). Revisiting the impact of perceived empowerment on job performance: Results from front-line employees. *Turizam*, *19*(1), 34–46.

Chapter 8

Human Resource Leaders in a Post-COVID-19 Era

Ahmad Zabidi bin Abdul Razak

Department of Educational Management, Planning and Policy Faculty of Education, University of Malaya, Kuala Lumpur, Malaysia

zabidi@um.edu.my

Abstract

As one of the most unpredictable worldwide public health crises, the COVID-19 pandemic, caused enormous damage to various sectors, including all levels of organizations. This crisis compelled organization systems around the world to find alternative methods to remain competitive. Organizations were forced to adapt and relocate many activities to online settings as a result of lockdown measures implemented in many countries around the world in order to control the spread of the coronavirus. As a result, organizational leaders at all levels including Human Resource Leaders (HRLs) had to think clearly, make the best and fast decisions, and act appropriately in order to meet not only the needs of staff but also the needs of society. This paper examines the characteristics of effective organizational leadership, particularly HRLs, in the post-COVID-19 era through a review of the literature on organizational leadership studies. Previous literature on organizational leadership in the post-COVID-19 era is still limited. According to the literature, the most effective leaders are those who are emotionally stable, have emotional intelligence, are responsible, concentrate on learning experiences, are flexible, adaptable, and open to changes, provide meaningful roles, give teams power, account for emotions, have emotional agility, pay attention to other opinions, recognize fear, and are engaged in what they do. In summary, the critical discussion provided in this paper will contribute to the body of knowledge on HRL studies, as well as serve as a reference for research in other countries. The findings of this study shed some light on how to improve the skills of HRLs, especially in today's challenging world.

Keywords: Human resource leaders, leadership skills, post-COVID-19, pandemic, literature review.

1. Introduction

The COVID-19 pandemic posed numerous unpredictable global challenges, forcing people to develop and implement flexible solutions to adapt to the new reality. The crisis has had a strong and profound impact on all levels of organizations. Given the complexity of organizations, managing change during the pandemic proved to be a significant challenge for leaders. Organizational leaders are increasingly called upon to make critical decisions on a daily basis to shape their organizations' future. With more complex and critical situations that need immediate solutions, organizations leaders should make innovative decisions and respond to the needs of the hour (Al-Dabbagh, 2020). However, during a pandemic, leaders are under intense psychological pressure. Furthermore, ambiguity, time constraints, a lack of information, and a high level of stress all contribute to the difficulty of decision-making. In this situation, effective organizational leadership can assist organizations in dealing with the challenges. Therefore, this review investigates the most effective HRL characteristics in times of crisis.

2. Characteristics of Effective Human Resource Leaders

2.1. *Emotional stability and emotional intelligence*

The most effective organizational leaders, according to Fernandez & Shaw (2020), are those who have emotional stability and emotional intelligence. Emotionally stable people are more reliable and calmer than neurotics, who are more vulnerable and anxious (Olsen et al., 2020). Several studies have found that emotional stability is a predictor of leader effectiveness (van Heesch & Søreide, 2018) as well as the ideal type of politician (Aichholzer & Willmann, 2020). This positive relationship between emotional stability and leader effectiveness can be attributed to followers' perception of the leader mastering difficult situations and making sound and good judgments even under pressure, which in turn can boost confidence and optimism in followers (Olsen, 2018). Emotional intelligence is defined by Gignac (2010) as the ability to purposefully adapt, shape, and select environments via the use of processes related to emotions. Emotional intelligence, according to Boyatzis (2009), is the ability to recognize, comprehend, and apply emotional information about oneself to achieve or cause superior performance. Numerous academicians have investigated the association between emotional intelligence and leadership effectiveness in a variety of organizational settings. For instance, emotional intelligence has been studied in connection with transformational leadership (Barling et al., 2000; Gardner & Stough, 2002), organizational leadership (Zaccaro, 2002), and leadership emergence in small groups (Côté et al., 2010). Rosete & Ciarrochi (2005) conducted a survey of 41 executives from a large Australian government organization to investigate the relationship between emotional intelligence and leadership effectiveness. They discovered statistically significant correlations between emotional intelligence and leadership effectiveness. This finding supports the claim that emotional intelligence is related to a leader's ability to achieve organizational goals. In addition, another study found that emotional intelligence accurately predicts effectiveness in management and leadership roles across various sectors (Boyatzis, 2009). Therefore, emotional stability and emotional intelligence are essential characteristics for effective HRLs, especially in critical and unexpected situations.

2.2. *Responsibility and adaptability*

The need for responsible leadership is even more pressing during times of crisis (Mascia et al., 2013). Responsibility is seen as a catalyst for effective organizational leadership (Dumulescu & Mu, 2021; Yukl et al., 2002). Responsible leadership, according to Pless & Maak (2011) is concerned with the well-being of others. Szczepańska-Woszczyna et al. (2015) defined responsible leadership as a way of interacting with stakeholders to integrate a common goal based on ethical values and principles, both within and outside the company. This characteristic contributes significantly to long-term business or organizational success. Adaptability is also perceived as an important and crucial personal factor in addressing various educational, communication, and administrative situations (Dumulescu & Mu, 2021). Adaptability, according to Birkinshaw & Gibson (2018), is the ability to easily shift toward new opportunities and adjust to volatile markets. This is one of the main characteristics of effective leadership, as HRLs must analyze a given situation and respond appropriately.

2.3. *Flexibility and accounting for emotions*

Schwantes (2020) stated that providing flexibility for employees and accounting for their emotions are the key competencies of an effective leader to overcome COVID-19-related challenges. In this context, flexibility is defined as the ability for employees to make choices on when, where, and for how long to work, including flexibility in their work schedules, working hours, and the management of unexpected personal and family responsibilities (Hill *et al.*, 2008). According to Halpern (2005), employees who have time-flexible work policies are less stressed and more committed to their employer. Torres (2009) revealed that followers want leaders who care about them, which means leaders viewing their followers as partners. Therefore an effective HRL can provide personalized attention to her or his followers.

2.4. *Concentrating on learning experience*

Previous leadership experience has been viewed as an effective factor in crisis management, particularly during the COVID-19 pandemic (Dumulescu & Mu, 2021). Concentrating on learning from their lived experience is the most powerful source of leadership development (Ashford & Derue, 2012), where leadership development is a continuous process through which people take the initiative and capitalize on the developmental value of a broad range of life experiences in their actions. Experience-based knowledge enables an individual to define novel problems they face in an environment that works in the same way as the knowledge acquired (Amit *et al.*, 2009).

2.5. *Team's power*

Great leaders believe in the strength and the power of teams (Dumulescu & Mu, 2021; Gleeson, 2016). They stress the importance of confidence in the competence and cooperation of others (Dumulescu & Mu, 2021). Greer *et al.* (2011) defined team power as the team's collective capacity to modify the states of others by withholding or providing actual resources or punishments to others. The higher the level of the teams' power, the easier it is for members to express their opinions, and the more they are motivated, which improves team performance.

2.6. *Emotional agility*

Emotional agility is one of the team leader's engaging behaviors. Emotional agility is a competency developed by effective leaders to face their negative feelings productively to perform better and be innovative (David & Congleton, 2013). The ability to be healthy with our emotions, thoughts, and stories is at the heart of emotional agility (David, 2016). Emotional agility will help HRLs share their positive ideas and motivate teams to achieve team objectives rather than use negative emotions like fear and threats. An emotionally agile team leader can thus assist the team in high-pressure situations (Sharma & Bhatnagar, 2017).

3. Conclusion

This paper conducted a literature review on the characteristics of effective organizational leadership in times of crisis. This review contributed significantly to organizational leadership research by giving a clearer picture of key characteristics of effective HRLs, especially during the COVID-19 pandemic crisis. Intending to explore the most effective leader characteristics concerning HRL processes during the crisis, our research contributed to a better understanding of leadership, specifically in the most difficult times in the last few decades. Future research should empirically investigate these characteristics, as human resource leadership characteristics may vary across institutions due to differences in mission, organizational culture, and more.

References

Aichholzer, J. & Willmann, J. (2020). Desired personality traits in politicians: Similar to me but more of a leader. *Journal of Research in Personality, 88*, 103990. https://doi.org/10.1016/j.jrp.2020.103990.

Al-Dabbagh, Z.S. (2020). The role of decision-maker in crisis management: A qualitative study using grounded theory (COVID-19 pandemic crisis as a model). *Journal of Public Affairs, 20*(4). https://doi.org/10.1002/pa.2186.

Amit, K., Hefer, E., Gal, R., Mamane-levy, T., & Lisak, A. (2009). Leadership-shaping experiences: A comparative study of leaders and non-leaders. *Leadership & Organization Development Journal, 30*(4), 302–318. https://doi.org/10.1108/01437730910961658.

Ashford, S.J. & Derue, D.S. (2012). Developing as a leader: The power of mindful engagement. *Organizational Dynamics, 41*(2), 146–154. https://doi.org/10.1016/j.orgdyn.2012.01.008.

Barling, J., Slater, F., & Kevin Kelloway, E. (2000). Transformational leadership and emotional intelligence: An exploratory study. *Leadership & Organization Development Journal, 21*(3), 157–161. https://doi.org/10.1108/01437730010325040.

Birkinshaw, J. & Gibson, C. (2018). Building an ambidextrous organisation. In *AIM Research Working Paper Series*. https://doi.org/10.4324/9781315716084-8.

Boyatzis, R.E. (2009). Competencies as a behavioral approach to emotional intelligence. *Journal of Management Development, 28*(9), 749–770. https://doi.org/10.1108/02621710910987647.

Côté, S., Lopes, P.N., Salovey, P., & Miners, C.T.H. (2010). Emotional intelligence and leadership emergence in small groups. *The Leadership Quarterly, 21*(3), 496–508. https://doi.org/10.1016/j.leaqua.2010.03.012.

David, S. (2016). *Emotional Agility: Get Unstuck, Embrace Change, and Thrive in Work and Life*. Avery.

David, S. & Congleton, C. (2013). Emotional agility. *Harvard Business Review*. https://hbr.org/2013/11/emotional-agility.

Dumulescu, D. & Mu, A.I. (2021). Academic leadership in the time of COVID-19 — experiences and perspectives. *Frontiers in Psychology, 12*. https://doi.org/10.3389/fpsyg.2021.648344.

Fernandez, A.A. & Shaw, G.P. (2020). Academic leadership in a time of crisis: The coronavirus and COVID-19. *Journal of Leadership Studies, 14*(1), 39–45. https://doi.org/10.1002/jls.21684.

Gardner, L. & Stough, C. (2002). Examining the relationship between leadership and emotional intelligence in senior level managers. *Leadership & Organization Development Journal, 23*(2), 68–78. https://doi.org/10.1108/01437730210419198.

Gignac, G.E. (2010). On a Nomenclature for emotional intelligence research. *Industrial and Organizational Psychology*, *3*(2), 131–135. https://doi.org/10.1111/j.1754-9434.2010.01212.x.

Gleeson, B. (2016). 10 Unique perspectives on what makes a great leader. *Forbes*. https://www.forbes.com/sites/brentgleeson/2016/11/09/10-unique-perspectives-on-what-makes-a-great-leader/?sh=49263f2c5dd1.

Greer, L.L., Caruso, H.M., & Jehn, K.A. (2011). The bigger they are, the harder they fall: Linking team power, team conflict, and performance. *Organizational Behavior and Human Decision Processes*, *116*(1), 116–128. https://doi.org/10.1016/j.obhdp.2011.03.005.

Halpern, D.F. (2005). How time-flexible work policies can reduce stress, improve health, and save money. *Stress and Health*, *21*(3), 157–168. https://doi.org/10.1002/smi.1049.

Hill, E.J., Grzywacz, J.G., Allen, S., Blanchard, V.L., Matz-Costa, C., Shulkin, S., & Pitt-Catsouphes, M. (2008). Defining and conceptualizing workplace flexibility. *Community, Work & Family*, *11*(2), 149–163. https://doi.org/10.1080/13668800802024678.

Mascia, A., Sartori, M., & Dal Pubel, L. (2013). A vision of effective leadership: An Italian perspective. In *Collective Efficacy: Interdisciplinary Perspectives on International Leadership* (Vol. 20, pp. 215–228). Emerald Group Publishing Limited. https://doi.org/10.1108/S1479-3660(2013)0000020012.

Olsen, O.K. (2018). Effective cooperation between strangers in unexpected and dangerous situations — A matter of "swift trust." In G.-E. Torgersen (ed.), *Interaction: "Samhandling" Under Risk. A Step Ahead of the Unforseen* (pp. 399–412). Olso: Cappelen Damm Akademik. https://doi.org/10.23865/noasp.36.ch21.

Olsen, O.K., Heesch, P., Søreide, C., & Hystad, S.W. (2020). Trust after just 45 seconds? An experimental vignette study of how leader behavior and emotional states influence immediate trust in strangers. *Frontiers in Psychology*, *10*. https://doi.org/10.3389/fpsyg.2019.02921.

Pless, N.M. & Maak, T. (2011). Responsible leadership: Pathways to the future. *Journal of Business Ethics*, *98*, 3–13. https://doi.org/10.1007/s10551-011-1114-4.

Rosete, D. & Ciarrochi, J. (2005). Emotional intelligence and its relationship to workplace performance outcomes of leadership effectiveness. *Leadership & Organization Development Journal*, *26*(5), 388–399. https://doi.org/10.1108/01437730510607871.

Schwantes, M. (2020). 4 sign to instantly identify a great leader during crisis. Inc. https://www.inc.com/marcel-schwantes/great-leader-time-of-crisis.html.

Sharma, A. & Bhatnagar, J. (2017). Emergence of team engagement under time pressure: Role of team leader and team climate. *Team Performance*

Management, *23*(3–4), 171–185. https://doi.org/10.1108/TPM-06-2016-0031.

Szczepańska-Woszczyna, K., Dacko-Pikiewicz, Z., & Lis, M. (2015). Responsible leadership: A real need or transient curiosity. *Procedia — Social and Behavioral Sciences*, *213*, 546–551. https://doi.org/10.1016/j.sbspro.2015.11.448.

Torres, R.Z. (2009). What followers want from their leaders an analytical perspectivas lo que los seguidores esperan de sus líderes Una perspectiva analítica. *Cuadernos de Administracion*, *42*, 11–23.

van Heesch, P. & Søreide, C. (2018). *Cooperation in the Heat of the Moment: The Effect of Leadership Behavior on Swift Trust*. University of Bergen.

Yukl, G., Gordon, A., & Taber, T. (2002). A hierarchical taxonomy of leadership behavior: Integrating a half century of behavior research. *Journal of Leadership & Organizational Studies*, *9*(1), 15–32. https://doi.org/10.1177/107179190200900102.

Zaccaro, S.J. (2002). Organizational leadership and social intelligence. In *Multiple Intelligences and Leadership* (pp. 29–54). Lawrence Erlbaum Associates Publishers.

Chapter 9

Extrinsic Benefits and Teacher Retention

Kazi Enamul Hoque

Faculty of Education, University of Malaya, Kuala Lumpur, Malaysia

keh2009@um.edu.my

Abstract

Teacher attrition has a negative impact on student achievement, teaching quality, and school culture, and increases the school's human resource costs for recruitment and training. Therefore, teacher retention is important to enhance education quality and student achievement. This chapter attempts to provide a framework for whether extrinsic benefits help teacher retention. To achieve this aim, the author portrays empirical evidence sourced from Web of Science, Scopus, and Google Scholar. The PRISMA method was used to screen articles on extrinsic benefits and teacher retention published from 2010 to 2021 to ensure the authenticity of the review results. A total of 21 articles were selected as the sample articles for thematic analysis. This chapter summarizes a total of six external benefits that highly influence teacher retention, i.e. salary, bonus, performance pay, stipend, accommodation/housing, and other monetary incentives. This chapter concludes that salary is not the main reason for retention; trust and recognition of the school and career assistance for teachers' career aspirations were more likely to increase retention rates. It is worth emphasizing that in rural areas, teachers are more likely to make the decision to stay when the school offers good accommodation than if they are paid a better salary.

Keywords: Teacher attrition, teacher retention, teachers' extrinsic benefits, teachers' allowance.

1. Introduction

Teacher stability is an important factor affecting the educational quality in schools. Building a stable and high-quality teaching force is an inevitable requirement for the sustainable and healthy development of education in the new era. Teacher turnover can negatively impact student achievement and teaching quality, as well as increase human resource costs such as recruitment and training for schools (Starnes, 2018). Teacher turnover has a considerable effect on the quality of school education, especially in schools that have poor performance, have difficulty recruiting teachers, and are in poor areas (Marston, 2014). Frequent teacher turnover can also negatively impact school culture, increase student discipline problems and principal departures, inhibit the learning environment in schools, and decrease student desire and ability to learn (Campbell, 2013). Examining the elements that affect teacher retention is crucial for boosting retention intentions, enhancing stability, and, most importantly, keeping talented educators.

Teacher attrition or teacher turnover in remote, poor, rural schools and low-performing schools is a common problem in many countries around the world (Darling-Hammond, 2010). Compensation incentives are an important part of modern human resource management. It is a standard method of compensation that is designed according to the characteristics and results of employees' work and can fully motivate them to work (Khan *et al.*, 2011). In today's environment of market economy, whether teachers are willing to stick to their teaching positions and devote themselves to teaching depends on whether the monetary benefits they can receive are competitive and motivating (Duflo *et al.*, 2012; Starnes, 2018). According to the human nature assumption in the economic man theory, the purpose of teachers' work is to obtain the maximum financial income (Cohen, 1967). According to Maslow's hierarchy of needs theory, human beings always have various needs that happen to be supported by physical conditions (Maslow, 1943). Therefore, this literature review explores the extrinsic factors that affect teacher retention from the perspective of monetary incentives and summarizes the research on external predictors of teacher retention from 2010 to 2021 to fill the research gap in this area.

2. Methodology

TGynpochis study followed PRISMA guidelines to conduct a systematic review. This methodology was chosen because it ensures the quality of the review and allows replication of the review methodology (Shamseer et al., 2015).

2.1. Data collection

To ensure the high quality of the searched articles to enhance the credibility of this literature review, large comprehensive electronic databases and core journals were prioritized. Web of Science and Scopus were identified for use in this study. Since Google Scholar contains more comprehensive articles and covers a very wide range of research areas (Saadatdoost et al., 2015), Google Scholar was also used as an important addition to the literature sources.

In the search process, the language of the publication was set to English and the year of publication was restricted from 2010 to 2021 to ensure reviewing the latest works of literature. Two basic concepts were considered for the search keywords: ("extrinsic incentives"/"monetary incentives"/"financial incentives") and ("teacher retention"/"retain teachers"). Synonyms, alternative spellings, and related terms were considered in identifying keywords for each concept. The different keywords were combined in the two different databases, namely, Web of Science and Scopus, and Google Scholar when conducting the search.

The inclusion criteria for the articles used in this study were as follows: (1) the language was English; (2) the year of publication was from 2010 to 2021; (3) the type of research was empirical rather than essentially non-empirical such as viewpoints, editorials, opinions, or books; (4) the core journal articles were on the topic of education; and (5) the articles were considered to be more relevant to the topic if they mentioned more extrinsic factors that influenced teacher retention. Since PRISMA has the advantages of allowing replication of review methods and facilitating transparency of the research process (Shamseer et al., 2015), the process of selecting articles for this study was based on the PRISMA statement for reporting systematic reviews and meta-analysis. The specific screening process is shown in Figure 1.

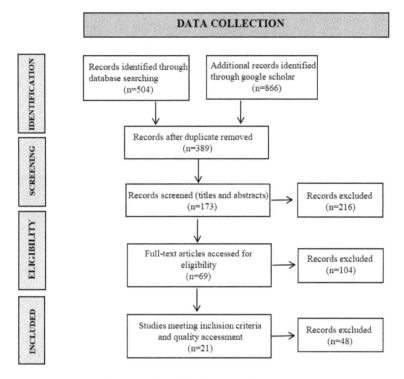

Figure 1. PRISMA data collection process.

2.2. *Data analysis*

Since the purpose of this study is to systematically review the extrinsic incentives that influence teacher retention, this study utilized a widely used software for qualitative data analysis: ATLAS.ti. This software was chosen for data analysis because it has the following advantages: It is easy to learn and has an intuitive interface; it has powerful data analysis capabilities and excellent presentation of results, which is very helpful in improving the scientific and normative nature of qualitative research (Anna Guidry, 2002); and the software helps to build networks and relationships, allowing users to combine and decompose data according to themes, categories, and visualize pertinent questions (Ngalande & Mkwinda, 2014).

The details of the data analysis are as follows: First, install software ATLAS.ti.22.0.0 and create a project named "Extrinsic Benefits as the

Predictor of Teachers' Retention." Second, place the selected high-quality papers in a folder and add this folder to ATLAS.ti. Third, code or write memos and comments separately for each article in the folder. When coding, distill the main idea of the selected content or paragraph in concise language as much as possible and group these codes into different categories. These categories are the extrinsic incentives that affect teacher retention, such as salaries, wages, fees, rewards, free accommodation, free medical assistance, free meals, paid leave, and extra teaching allowances. Fourth, explore the links between the different categories and generalize the links into different themes. Finally, write a report based on the themes established and the results of the analysis.

2.3. *Results*

In selecting the articles to be reviewed, firstly, a total of 1370 articles were identified by keywords. Second, 981 duplicate articles were eliminated, leaving 389 articles. Third, 216 articles that were not related to the topic were eliminated by reading the article titles and abstracts, leaving 173 articles. Fourth, 104 articles were not eligible as access to the full text was unavailable, leaving 69 articles. Finally, the articles related to the topic were further finely screened, resulting in a total of 21 high-quality sample papers for this study.

In the 21 journal articles, the extrinsic incentives influencing teacher retention were salaries, bonuses, merit pay, allowances, accommodation/housing, and other monetary incentives. Of these, nine articles addressed the effect of salaries on retaining teachers, five articles mentioned the effect of bonuses on retaining teachers, three articles mentioned the effect of allowances and accommodation/housing on retaining teachers, one article mentioned the effect of merit pay on retaining teachers, and five articles mentioned the effect of other monetary incentives on retaining teachers.

A vast majority of studies on factors influencing teacher retention have been conducted in the context of rural or poor areas (e.g. Acheampong & Gyasi, 2019; Miller *et al.*, 2020; Opoku *et al.*, 2020; Vincent, 2018). Whether in urban or rural areas, monetary incentives are important extrinsic factors that improve teachers' retention (Duflo *et al.*, 2012; Starnes, 2018). Table 1 summarizes the six monetary incentives that influence teacher retention and the specific findings.

Table 1. Six monetary incentives affecting teacher retention and specific findings.

Factors	Findings	Sources
Salaries	Salaries are one of the main factors in a teacher's decision to continue teaching in a high-poverty school.	Burtsfield (2021)
	Salaries have been successful in attracting many new teachers to rural areas, but are unlikely to improve teacher retention in rural Tennessee.	Campbell (2013)
	Salaries are beneficial in improving faculty retention.	Hughes (2012)
	Teachers' salaries are the most important consideration when deciding whether or not to accept and stay at a given school.	Kolbe & Strunk (2012)
	Competitive salaries are one of the key factors influencing teachers' decisions to remain in their current roles at East Alabama rural schools.	Lucy (2018)
	In the Bekwai Municipality of Ghana, prompt payment of monthly salaries is the most effective incentive for teacher retention in public senior high schools.	Ofori (2021)
	Remuneration of teachers can motivate teachers to remain in their schools in Nigeria.	Oke *et al.* (2016)
	Salaries are one of the five major factors affecting teacher retention.	Podolsky *et al.* (2016)
	Salary or wage is one of the external incentives influencing teacher retention.	Tehseen & Hadi (2015)
Bonuses	Bonuses reduce math and science teachers' attrition by 18 to 28 percent in Georgia.	Bueno & Sass (2018)
	Bonuses have no monotony effect on teacher retention.	Quinoso (2019)
	Bonuses positively and directly affect teacher retention in Peruvian rural schools.	Castro & Esposito (2022)
	Retention bonuses can increase teachers' retention in Tennessee.	Springer *et al.* (2016)
	Bonuses help improve the retention of teachers.	Podolsky *et al.* (2016)
Merit Pay	Merit pay helps improve teacher retention.	Ryu & Jinnai (2021)

Table 1. (*Continued*)

Factors	Findings	Sources
Allowances	Teaching allowances help reduce teacher attrition in Chhukha District, Bhutan.	Hu (2021)
	The current amount of the rural allowance is insufficient to retain teachers in rural schools in Malawi's Salima District.	Mwenda & Mgomezulu (2018)
	Allowances for car maintenance have the least effect on teacher retention in public senior high schools in the Bekwai Municipality of Ghana.	Ofori (2021)
Accommodation/ Housing	In the Salima District of Malawi, housing has a greater influence on teacher retention in rural schools than other monetary incentives.	Mwenda & Mgomezulu (2018)
	Providing free housing or housing loans and grants for teachers is key to retaining teachers, especially in remote areas in the Rukwa region of Tanzania.	Swai (2013)
	Free accommodation is one of the factors increasing teacher retention.	Tehseen & Hadi (2015)
Other Monetary Incentives	Alternative compensation programs (ACPs) were in place for about five years before having an impact on teacher retention rates and the effects may vary by school type in Minnesota.	Choi (2015)
	The availability of incentives, such as money incentives, trips to recreational sites, and gifts, enhances teacher retention in Kathonzweni Subcounty, Makueni County, Kenya.	Mbuno (2019)
	Other compensation in addition to salary is a key element influencing teacher retention.	Podolsky *et al.* (2016)
	The Governor's Teaching Fellowship (GTF) makes it more likely for teachers in California to choose to stay in low-performing schools.	Steele *et al.* (2010)
	Paid leave and free medical assistance are extrinsic incentives for teacher retention.	Tehseen & Hadi (2015)

2.4. Factor 1 — *Salaries*

A vast majority of scholars agree that salary is the most important factor in promoting teacher retention (Burtsfield, 2021; Kolbe & Strunk, 2012; Lucy, 2018; Ofori, 2021; Podolsky *et al.*, 2016). Salary is often used as an important measure of the value and status of the employee in the organization (Burtsfield, 2021). At the same time, employees' job satisfaction and commitment to the organization are enhanced when they feel they are being paid at a level similar to that offered at the same or a similar organization, or when they are paid in line with their personal values (Robbins, 2001). Sekyere (2009) also pointed out that when employees are paid less for their work and payment is delayed, this may affect teachers' morale and acceptance of the organization, leading to a degree of strife, which may have a negative impact on students or, in more serious cases, cause teachers to leave their jobs (Ofori, 2021). However, Campbell (2013) drew contradictory inferences from a study of teachers in rural Tennessee, concluding that salaries can successfully attract new teachers to teach in rural areas but are unlikely to increase teacher retention.

2.5. Factor 2 — *Bonuses*

In a majority of studies, bonuses have been found to largely reduce teacher turnover (Bueno & Sass, 2018; Castro & Esposito, 2018; Feng & Sass, 2017) and positively and directly impact teacher retention (Springer *et al.*, 2016; Podolsky *et al.*, 2016). Williams *et al.* (2016) and Cowan & Goldhaber (2018) explained that for schools, relevant incentives will be used as a policy orientation to attract teachers to capture human resource needs. Springer *et al.* (2016) suggested that targeted bonus payments have a positive effect on teacher retention. However, a few scholars, such as Quinoso (2019), found that bonuses have no monotonic effect on teacher retention.

2.6. Factor 3 — *Merit pay*

Merit pay was mentioned rarely in the selected articles, with Ryu & Jinnai (2021) finding that merit pay could help teachers make retention decisions. Of course, they also stressed that increasing performance compensation could result in losing competent or good teachers. When a teacher performs well, they may consider leaving the organization for a larger income. Thus, teacher retention has been a significant concern. Bridges (2018) concluded in his study that in the teacher salary scale, the policies on salary increases or bonus payment conditions for teachers are often based on the assessment of students' academic performance, whether the teacher has achieved the teaching objectives set by the school, and the overall job evaluation of the teacher.

2.7. Factor 4 — *Allowances*

Allowances can help reduce teacher turnover (Hu, 2021), but the amount of the allowances in some districts is not sufficiently attractive and has less impact on their decision to remain in a particular school. Hu (2021) explained that there is a positive correlation between the salary status of teachers and their turnover rate. As for the teaching stipend, it is effective in helping professional teachers who meet the teaching quality requirements to be better engaged in their teaching activities. At the same time, stipends can be a morale booster, which can reduce the likelihood of teachers leaving the school. Mwenda & Mgomezulu (2018) pointed out that rural schools do not have enough allowances to retain teachers. It is also because of the lack of allowances that rural schools are not able to attract teachers from urban areas to teach in rural areas.

2.8. Factor 5 — *Accommodation/Housing*

Free accommodation or housing is considered to be one of the key factors that can retain teachers, especially in rural areas (Mwenda & Mgomezulu, 2018; Swai, 2013; Tehseen & Hadi, 2015). In Mwenda & Mgomezulu's (2018) study, in addition to the issue of stipends, when teachers teaching in rural areas were asked how they could stay in their schools, they noted that the provision of a decent house, as opposed to a stipend, could make them want to stay. When teachers are provided with good accommodation support and livelihood support in the form of bicycles, furniture, etc., they are more likely to remain (Swai, 2013). At the same time, Marry (2010) referred to the availability of dormitory or residential accommodation as an extrinsic motivation for teacher effectiveness and retention.

2.9. Factor 6 — *Other monetary incentives*

Other monetary incentives such as trips to recreational sites, gifts, paid leave, free medical assistance, and programs specifically for teachers were shown to attract teachers to remain in their schools (Choi, 2015; Mbuno, 2019; Podolsky et al., 2016; Steele et al., 2010). Choi (2015) conducted a study on the implementation of alternative compensation programs to certify that although the policy support can improve teacher retention, the implementation and enforcement of the policy take more time to be reflected in action. Mbuno (2019) provided an exhaustive study on how to improve teacher retention, showing that teachers are more likely to choose to stay in their positions when they are satisfied with salary incentives, when they are trusted, when they are satisfied with the duties and tasks given to them by the organization, when they are satisfied with the provision of school premises, and when the award is made public. Teachers are also more willing to continue working with the school in the future when they are satisfied with the continuing education opportunities offered by the school. Finally, Mbuno (2019) stated that teachers' retention rates are increased to a limited extent when they have flexible working hours and when their career aspirations are realized.

3. Discussion

Teachers' salaries are a reflection of the price of their labor and have a direct effect on attracting, retaining, and motivating good teachers to work hard (Xuehui, 2018). However, the magnitude of the effect of teacher salaries on teacher attrition, and whether it contributes to the retention of quality teachers, is controversial. The reason may be related to the level of economic development in the area investigated by the researchers. In countries and regions with better economic development, the effect of salary on teacher retention is relatively small. In less economically developed countries and regions, salaries have a greater impact on teacher retention. There is already evidence that in developed countries, teachers are willing to give up higher salaries for a more desirable work environment despite being more sensitive to salary. Non-monetary incentives such as student group characteristics, teacher professional development, school management and organizational climate, and campus environment are important in influencing teacher retention (Bernard, 2012; Mata et al.,

2021; Tehseen & Hadi, 2015; Tumaini, 2015). In contrast, in developing countries, monetary incentives such as salary play a significant role in teacher retention in most cases (DeJaeghere *et al.*, 2006).

Bonuses can reduce teacher turnover to a great extent, especially retention bonuses. Retention bonuses are one-time payments made by a company or organization to employees as an incentive to stay with the company for a period of time (Goswami & Jha, 2012) and have been shown to be an effective tool that can reduce teacher turnover and make employees remain (Goswami & Jha, 2012; Law, 2016; Osibanjo *et al.*, 2014). There have been studies demonstrating that retention bonuses can increase teacher retention intentions (Springer *et al.*, 2016; Swain *et al.*, 2019), especially in rural and poor areas.

Some scholars have found that bonuses and stipends have less effect on teacher retention or do not work alone because the amount of the bonus is not enough to attract teachers. Free accommodation or housing is one of the determinants that can attract teachers to stay in rural and remote regions because almost no housing is available for rent in remote areas (Swai, 2013).

In summary, monetary incentives, such as increased salaries, bonuses, allowances, or other monetary benefits, are necessary to retain teachers, but they alone are not sufficient (Greenlee & Brown, 2009). Teachers' intentions to remain are also influenced by other extrinsic factors as well as internal factors, for example, working conditions, work environment and climate, management and leadership, career prospects and promotion, training and development opportunities, student engagement and behavior, and professional identity (Alexander *et al.*, 2020; Bernard, 2012; Billingsley & Bettini, 2019). These factors come from a variety of sources, including teachers, students, families, and organizations.

4. Conclusions

This study provides a systematic review of six categories of monetary motivations that influence teacher retention: salaries, bonuses, merit pay, allowances, accommodation/housing, and other monetary incentives. Of these, a vast majority of scholars believe that salary is the most significant factor that can retain teachers.

The limitation of this paper is that only Web of Science, Scopus, and Google Scholar were selected for conducting the search due to the constraints of time and circumstances, and other electronic databases and paper journals on the topic of teacher retention were not systematically explored. This may have made this study less comprehensive and detailed. In addition, the search for keywords may have missed other synonymous terms, resulting in incomplete articles being extracted. In future studies, it is hoped that more journal articles and related keywords can be searched to increase the credibility of this literature review.

References

Acheampong, P. & Gyasi, J. (2019). Teacher retention: A review of policies for motivating rural basic school teachers in Ghana. *Asian Journal of Education and Training*, *5*(1), 86–92. https://doi.org/10.20448/journal.522.2019.51.86.92.

Alexander, C., Wyatt-Smith, C., & Du Plessis, A. (2020). The role of motivations and perceptions on the retention of inservice teachers. *Teaching And Teacher Education*, *96*, 103186. https://doi.org/10.1016/j.tate.2020.103186.

Anna Guidry, J. (2002). LibQUAL+™ spring 2001 comments: A qualitative analysis using Atlas.ti. *Performance Measurement and Metrics*, *3*(2), 100–107. https://doi.org/10.1108/14678040210429008.

Bernard, B. (2012). Factors that determine academic staff retention and commitment in private tertiary institutions in Botswana: Empirical review. *Global Advanced Research Journal of Management and Business Studies*, *1*(9), 278–299.

Billingsley, B. & Bettini, E. (2019). Special education teacher attrition and retention: A review of the literature. *Review of Educational Research*, *89*(5), 697–744. https://doi.org/10.3102/0034654319862495.

Bridges, C. (2018). Novice teacher retention in relation to merit pay: A phenomenological study. Doctoral dissertation, University of Phoenix.

Bueno, C. & Sass, T. (2018). The effects of differential pay on teacher recruitment and retention. *SSRN Electronic Journal*. https://doi.org/10.2139/ssrn.3296427.

Burtsfield, A.H. (2021). Teachers with longevity in high-poverty schools: Factors that influence their retention. Doctoral dissertation, Purdue University Graduate School.

Campbell, J. (2013). Improving low teacher retention in rural Tennessee: Cultural education. Milligan, TN: Milligan College.

Castro, J. & Esposito, B. (2018). The effect of bonuses on teacher behavior: A story with spillovers. Working Paper 104, Peruvian Economic Association.

Castro, J. & Esposito, B. (2022). The effect of bonuses on teacher retention and student learning in rural schools: A story of spillovers. *Education Finance and Policy, 17*(4), 693–718. https://doi.org/10.1162/edfp_a_00348.

Choi, W.S. (2015). The effect of alternative compensation programs on teacher retention and student achievement: The case of Q Comp in Minnesota. Retrieved from https://hdl.handle.net/11299/171082.

Cohen, P.S. (1967). Economic analysis and economic man. *Themes in Economic Anthropology, 5*, 91–118.

Cowan, J. & Goldhaber, D. (2018). Do bonuses affect teacher staffing and student achievement in high poverty schools? Evidence from an incentive for national board certified teachers in Washington State. *Economics of Education Review, 65*, 138–152. https://doi.org/10.1016/j.econedurev.2018.06.010.

Darling-Hammond, L. (2010). Recruiting and retaining teachers: Turning around the race to the bottom in high-need schools. *Journal of Curriculum and Instruction, 4*(1), 16–32. https://doi.org/10.3776/joci.2010.v4n1p16-32.

DeJaeghere, J., Chapman, D., & Mulkeen, A. (2006). Increasing the supply of secondary teachers in sub-Saharan Africa: A stakeholder assessment of policy options in six countries. *Journal of Education Policy, 21*(5), 515–533. https://doi.org/10.1080/02680930600866116.

Duflo, E., Hanna, R., & Ryan, S. (2012). Incentives work: Getting teachers to come to school. *American Economic Review, 102*(4), 1241–1278. https://doi.org/10.1257/aer.102.4.1241.

Feng, L. & Sass, T. (2017). The impact of incentives to recruit and retain teachers in "hard-to-staff" subjects. *Journal of Policy Analysis and Management, 37*(1), 112–135. https://doi.org/10.1002/pam.22037.

Goswami, B.K. & Jha, S. (2012). Attrition issues and retention challenges of employees. *International Journal of Scientific & Engineering Research, 3*(4), 1–6. Retrieved from http://www.ijser.org.

Greenlee, B. & Brown Jr, J.J. (2009). Retaining teachers in challenging schools. *Education, 130*(1), 96–109.

Hu, R. (2021). Impact of teaching allowance on teacher retention in and attraction to teaching profession: A case under Chhukha District, Bhutan. Doctoral Dissertation, University of Canberra.

Hughes, G. (2012). Teacher retention: Teacher characteristics, school characteristics, organizational characteristics, and teacher efficacy. *The Journal of Educational Research, 105*(4), 245–255. https://doi.org/10.1080/00220671.2011.584922.

Khan, R., Aslam, H., & Lodhi, I. (2011). Compensation management: A strategic conduit towards achieving employee retention and job satisfaction in banking sector of Pakistan. *International Journal of Human Resource Studies, 1*(1), 89. https://doi.org/10.5296/ijhrs.v1i1.809.

Kolbe, T. & Strunk, K. (2012). Economic incentives as a strategy for responding to teacher staffing problems: A typology of policies and practices. *Educational Administration Quarterly*, *48*(5), 779–813. https://doi.org/10.1177/0013161x12441011.

Law, C. (2016). Using bonus and awards for motivating project employees. *Human Resource Management International Digest*, *24*(7), 4–7. https://doi.org/10.1108/hrmid-05-2016-0073.

Lucy, T. (2018). An investigation of factors that affect teacher retention in East Alabama rural schools. PhD Dissertation, Auburn University. Retrieved from http://hdl.handle.net/10415/6383.

Marry, A. (2010). Motivation and the performance of primary school teachers in Uganda:A case of Kimaanya-Kyabankuza division, Madaka District. Unpublished (Master of arts) dissertation Makerere University, Kampala, Uganda.

Marston, T.M. (2014). Factors that contribute to teacher retention in high poverty middle schools. Doctoral dissertation, East Tennessee State University. Retrieved from https://www.proquest.com/pagepdf/1547732310?accountid=28930.

Maslow, A.H. (1943). A theory of human motivation. *Psychological Review*, *50*(4), 370.

Mata, M.N., Anees, S.S.T., Martins, J.M., Haider, S.A., Jabeen, S., Correia, A.B., & Rita, J.X. (2021). Impact of non-monetary factors on retention of higher education institutes teachers through mediating role of motivation. *Academy of Strategic Management Journal*, *20*, 1–17.

Mbuno, S.W. (2019). Governance practices influencing teacher retention in public secondary schools in Kathonzweni sub county, Makueni County, Kenya. Doctoral dissertation, University of Nairobi. Retrieved from http://erepository.uonbi.ac.ke/handle/11295/107170.

Miller, J., Youngs, P., Perrone, F., & Grogan, E. (2020). Using measures of fit to predict beginning teacher retention. *The Elementary School Journal*, *120*(3), 399–421. https://doi.org/10.1086/707094.

Mwenda, D. & Mgomezulu, V. (2018). Impact of monetary incentives on teacher retention in and attraction to rural primary schools: Case of the rural allowance in Salima District of Malawi. *African Educational Research Journal*, *6*(3), 120–129. https://doi.org/10.30918/aerj.63.18.028.

Ngalande, R.C. & Mkwinda, E. (2014). Benefits and challenges of using ATLAS.ti. Berlin: Technische Universitat.

Ofori, K.N. (2021). The effect of motivation on teacher retention in public senior high schools: The case of Bekwai municipality of Ghana. *Asian Journal of Education and Social Studies*, *23*(1), 28–39. https://doi.org/10.9734/AJESS/2021/v23i130544.

Oke, A.O., Ajagbe, M.A., Ogbari, M.E., & Adeyeye, J.O. (2016). Teacher retention and attrition: A review of the literature. *Mediterranean Journal of Social Sciences*, 7(2 S1), 371. https://doi.org/10.5901/mjss.2016.v7n2s1p371.

Opoku, M., Asare-Nuamah, P., Nketsia, W., Asibey, B., & Arinaitwe, G. (2020). Exploring the factors that enhance teacher retention in rural schools in Ghana. *Cambridge Journal of Education*, 50(2), 201–217. https://doi.org/10.1080/0305764x.2019.1661973.

Osibanjo, A.O., Adeniji, A.A., Falola, H.O., & Heirsmac, P.T. (2014). Compensation packages: A strategic tool for employees' performance and retention. *Leonardo Journal of Sciences*, 25, 65–84. Retrieved from http://ljs.academicdirect.org/.

Podolsky, A., Kini, T., Bishop, J., & Darling-Hammond, L. (2016). Solving the teacher shortage: How to attract and retain excellent educators. *Learning Policy Institute*. Retrieved from https://learningpolicyinstitute.org.

Quinoso, D. (2019). The impact of bonuses on teacher retention: A study of monotonic and non-monotonic effects. *Journal of Educational Policy and Practice*, 33(2), 112–125.

Quinoso, M.A.P.L. (2019). Estimating teacher retention in remote locations under boundary discontinuity design. Doctoral dissertation, Yale University. Retrieved from https://www.proquest.com/docview/2392443221?pqorigsite=gscholar&fromopenview=true.

Robbins, S.P. (2001). *Organisational Behaviour: Global and Southern African Perspectives*. South Africa: Pearson.

Ryu, S. & Jinnai, Y. (2021). Effects of monetary incentives on teacher turnover: A longitudinal analysis. *Public Personnel Management*, 50(2), 205–231. https://doi.org/10.1177/0091026020921414.

Saadatdoost, R., Sim, A., Jafarkarimi, H., & Mei Hee, J. (2015). Exploring MOOC from education and Information Systems perspectives: A short literature review. *Educational Review*, 67(4), 505–518. https://doi.org/10.1080/00131911.2015.1058748.

Sekyere, E.A. (2009). *Teacher Guide on Tropical Issues for Promotion and Selection Interviews*. Kumasi: Cita Printing Press.

Shamseer, L., Moher, D., Clarke, M., Ghersi, D., Liberati, A., & Petticrew, M., et al. (2015). Preferred reporting items for systematic review and meta-analysis protocols (PRISMA-P) 2015: Elaboration and explanation. *BMJ*, 349. https://doi.org/10.1136/bmj.g7647.

Springer, M., Swain, W., & Rodriguez, L. (2016). Effective teacher retention bonuses. *Educational Evaluation and Policy Analysis*, 38(2), 199–221. https://doi.org/10.3102/0162373715609687.

Starnes, L. (2018). Factors impacting teacher retention in urban elementary schools. Doctoral dissertation, Carson-Newman University.

Steele, J., Murnane, R., & Willett, J. (2010). Do financial incentives help low-performing schools attract and keep academically talented teachers? Evidence from California. *Journal of Policy Analysis and Management*, *29*(3), 451–478. https://doi.org/10.1002/pam.20505.

Swai, A.E. (2013). The effects of incentive initiatives on teacher retention in Tanzania: A case of the Rukwa region. Retrieved from https://scholarworks.umass.edu/cie_capstones/35.

Swain, W., Rodriguez, L., & Springer, M. (2019). Selective retention bonuses for highly effective teachers in high poverty schools: Evidence from Tennessee. *Economics of Education Review*, *68*, 148–160. https://doi.org/10.1016/j.econedurev.2018.12.008.

Tehseen, S. & Ul Hadi, N. (2015). Factors influencing teachers' performance and retention. *Mediterranean Journal of Social Sciences*. https://doi.org/10.5901/mjss.2015.v6n1p233.

Tumaini, M. (2015). The contribution of non-monetary incentives to teachers' retention in public secondary schools in Korogwe Urban. Doctoral dissertation, The Open University of Tanzania.

Vincent, N. (2018). Factors and circumstances related to teacher retention in rural, high poverty districts in South Carolina. Doctoral dissertation, East Tennessee State University.

Williams, W., Adrien, R., Murthy, C., & Pietryka, D. (2016). *Equitable Access to Excellent Educators: An Analysis of States' Educator Equity Plans*. Washington, DC: Office of Elementary and Secondary Education, U.S. Department of Education.

Xuehui, A. (2018). Teacher salaries and the shortage of high-quality teachers in China's rural primary and secondary schools. *Chinese Education & Society*, *51*(2), 103–116. https://doi.org/10.1080/10611932.2018.1433411.

© 2025 World Scientific Publishing Company
https://doi.org/10.1142/9789811294730_0010

Chapter 10

Classroom Management and Teachers' Practices

Yang Yang Zhao[*], Kazi Enamul Hoque[†], and Intan Marfarrina Omar[§]

Faculty of Education, University of Malaya, Kuala Lumpur, Malaysia

[*]adainmalaysia@gmail.com
[†]keh2009@um.edu.my
[§]imarfarrina@um.edu.my

Abstract

Effective classroom management is the basis of successful teaching and learning. This chapter presents the definition of classroom management and groups the definition into four different categories. Then, the authors describe the five elements of classroom management: classroom arrangement, behavior management, teacher–student relationship, teaching–learning organization, and teachers–parent collaboration. The practice of classroom management is strongly related to student outcomes, such as decreasing misbehavior, more engagement, motivation and improvement, and increasing academic achievement. Most of the previous studies reported the positive effect of classroom management though the results varied based on different practice strategies; it is still necessary to know the potential factors that may hinder or promote teachers' classroom management which the authors list in three groups: personal, organizational, and social factors.

Keywords: Classroom management, teacher–student relationship, teacher–parent corporation.

1. Introduction

Effective classroom management is a prerequisite for effective teaching and learning and ensures that students learn effectively (Hằng et al., 2022; Lettink, 2020). It is also considered to be one of the most important indicators of a teacher's professionalism (Cho et al., 2020). Kyriacou (2018) stated that effective teaching/learning cannot simply happen when teachers fail to manage classrooms effectively. Kontor Owusu et al. (2021) mentioned in their study that students' learning depends to a great degree on the teacher's capability to appropriately manage the classroom. A teacher rightly thinks that effective classroom management is the basis of successful teaching and learning (Akhter & Akhter, 2021). Sieberer-Nagler (2015) stated that teachers are experts in their subject matter, but subject knowledge alone is not enough to ensure effective classrooms and successful student learning, so to ensure classroom effectiveness, teachers must understand students' interests and learning styles. Numerous prior research has demonstrated a strong correlation between effective classroom management and student performance (Herman et al., 2022; Manangan, 2022). Kontor Owusu et al. (2021) and Oppong-Sekyere et al. (2013) conducted research showing that in a supportive classroom and an atmosphere where they feel comfortable, secure, and involved, pupils perform better. Dwyer (2013) provided additional evidence in support of the idea that how a teacher handles issues in the classroom affects pupils' learning.

Kontor Owusu et al. (2021) and Hằng et al. (2022) claimed that teachers have the responsibility and obligation to build a good learning environment and create a positive learning atmosphere for students. According to Manangan (2022) and Zakaria et al. (2013), in order to succeed and ensure the success of their students, teachers must become proficient in classroom management. They need to organize and develop classroom life by encouraging student cooperation in ongoing activities and supervising their students for self-regulated learning processes that are centered on academic and social growth. Meanwhile, Dwyer (2013) reported that the teacher must create a classroom that encourages, enables, and supports teacher–parent, teacher–student, and peer relationships that will facilitate a supportive and successful academic environment. Also, the development of teacher–student relationships is a crucial component of contemporary classroom management in China, where society has progressively come to agree on the need to foster these relationships since the country's 2001 curriculum reform (Lei et al., 2022). Korpershoek et al. (2016) also emphasized that effective classroom management is typically built on the idea of creating a supportive learning environment that includes strong teacher–student interactions, and it was proven that building positive teacher–student relationships was effective in regulating students' behavior. Additionally, based on previous studies, Kontor Owusu et al. (2021) emphasized productive classroom management, which involves well-organized and effective planning, is beneficial helpful for high quality teaching and learning. Meanwhile, Evertson and Weinstein (2013) stated that in order to achieve a high level of classroom management, teachers must (a) cultivate nice, communicative relationships with and among students; (b) plan and carry out lessons in a way that maximizes students' access to learning; (c) encourage students' engagement in academic tasks by using group management techniques; (d) encourage the growth of students' social abilities and self-control; and (e) use appropriate interventions to aid pupils with behavior issues. Furthermore, Cheng & Chen (2018) measured classroom management in the following broad areas: (1) teaching management: managing teaching content; (2) discipline management: preparing for behavioral adjustments based on the ideals of creating learning individuals and school; and (3) cohesion management: enhancing students' well-being, teamwork skills, and engagement in school to support them in reaching their potential.

2. Definition of Classroom Management

Over the last few decades, experts and scholars have been trying to define classroom management. The definitions are varied and can be divided overall into the following types: The first is the process type. This type defines classroom management as the processes and steps that teachers practice in the classroom. The second is the technical strategic type. This type highlights the techniques and classroom strategies that teachers are expected to master in classroom management. The third is the role-oriented and goal-oriented type. This type highlights the role of the teacher and the relatively specific goals of classroom management. The fourth is the comprehensive definition. This type of definition tends to emphasize the comprehensive and holistic nature of classroom management and takes into account all aspects of student development, such as the physical, psychological, and social environments of classroom management.

3. Process-oriented View

In order to promote prosocial behavior and to avoid and prevent inappropriate behavior, classroom management is defined as "a collection of non-instructional classroom practices done by teachers in classroom settings with all pupils" (Oliver *et al.*, 2011). However, according to Alter & Haydon (2017) and Cooper *et al.* (2018), classroom management and instructional management are related because both involve the steps teachers take to create secure and effective learning environments that make the most of instructional time. Ahmed *et al.* (2018) stated that classroom management is a process that combines teachers and school administrations to develop as well as enforce suitable, appropriate, and assertive behaviors of the students in certain classroom settings. Collier-Meek *et al.* (2020) recognized classroom management as a core practice for instructors to effectively foster long-term student academic competency and whole-class academic engagement. Briefly stated, classroom management in education is generally believed to involve the structures and practices that create and preserve an emotionally balanced, academically productive atmosphere for learning (Evertson & Weinstein, 2006; Martin, 2021).

4. Technical Strategy View

Hirsch *et al.* (2021) viewed classroom management techniques as a group of instructional strategies linked to better academic and behavioral outcomes for students. Ahmad (2010) also listed the following crucial techniques for managing the classroom: (1) organization, which includes seating arrangements, material organization, equipment maintenance, and rules, routines, and procedures for the classroom, among other things; (2) communication, as effective classroom management depends greatly on strong communication; (3) watching, whether every student is involved and active; (4) instructional techniques and delivery; whether students are receptive to instruction and eager to learn more; and (5) inquiring which includes getting feedback from students. Gaias *et al.* (2019) reported that six classroom management strategies are used by teachers in high-level classrooms: control, anticipation and response, monitoring, active behavior management, meaningful involvement, and cultural responsiveness. Mitchell *et al.* (2017) summarized eight classroom management techniques based on empirical research: physical setup, expectations, routines, praise for specific behaviors, active observation, opportunities for response, behavioral reminders, and consistent reactions. Expectations and standing routines cover the development and instruction of rules and procedures for the classroom, whereas physical setup concentrates on the teacher's spatial organization and positioning of things. Specific praise for behavior means giving positive descriptive feedback when students show the expected behavior. Active monitoring is when the teacher moves and is aware of classroom behavior. Opportunities for response refers to providing varied opportunities for students to engage in learning. Behavioral reminder refers to alerting students to anticipate their behavior in advance and to pre-correct it. Finally, ongoing feedback refers to correcting students' misbehavior and re-teaching them the expected behavior. Meanwhile, developing routines and processes, setting up and enforcing a set of norms, and building classroom environments for learning are all examples of good classroom management techniques, according to Kowalski & Froiland (2020). Mitchell *et al.* (2017) further categorized these strategies as proactive or preventative, with the exception of consistent responding, which is reactive. Hepburn *et al.* (2020) found that unsupported reactive practices, such as detention and time-out, focus on responding to student behaviors after they occur and have been shown to be ineffective in reducing behavioral disruptions. In contrast, preventative classroom management practices focus on teaching and reinforcing expected behaviors, making the occurrence of unproductive behaviors less likely (Wills *et al.*, 2019). Martin (2021) further explained how proactive and reactive features are used in classroom management tactics. Proactive methods focus on taking preventative measures in the classroom that are intended to shape students' attitudes and conduct in a way that supports achieving different objectives. Reactive actions concentrate on the outcomes that result from expectations not being satisfied.

5. Role-Oriented and Goal-Oriented View

To achieve their goals, teachers must be able to establish appropriate student behavior in the classroom in order to maximize their and their students' learning time (Wiseman & Hunt, 2008). Nwankwo *et al.* (2019)

reported that managing a classroom involves more than just avoiding chaos; it also entails creating a schedule that makes it possible for learning activities to move through without interruption. Sieberer-Nagler (2015) argued that creating a supportive learning atmosphere in the classroom and setting clear academic and behavioral objectives are necessary for effective classroom management. The following are included in it: (a) Classroom behavior management: involves establishing expectations for behavior; (b) teachers serving as role models for pupils: Enthusiastic teachers encourage student participation in the classroom and have a powerful impact on student motivation; (c) setting expectations in the classroom: This is a strategy for encouraging kids to moderately push themselves academically; (d) clear classroom rules: include informing pupils of any behavioral infractions; (e) handling trouble: It is important to create a smooth and uninterrupted classroom environment; (f) handle mistakes well: Making mistakes is part of learning and teachers need to accept that students will make mistakes and build a trusting relationship with students; and (g) the teacher as a motivator: Teachers need to not only motivate students to learn but they should also inspire them on how to learn and practice in a way that is relevant, meaningful, and impressive. Wiseman and Hunt (2008) highlighted three key inquiries for effective teaching: Who are the individuals to teach? What do we expect students will learn? What should pupils do if they fail to learn?

6. Comprehensive Definition

School life is multifaceted and classroom management involves almost all the practical actions teachers take in (Díaz et al., 2018). The first definition depicts classroom management as a synonym for discipline; however, according to contemporary ideas, discipline is simply a facet of classroom management because classroom management is a broad term that covers numerous elements (Vairamidou & Stravakou, 2019). Classroom management now refers to creating a supportive learning environment for shaping and controlling instructors' actions rather than disciplinary measures and behavioral interventions (Ahmed et al., 2018). According to Sieberer-Nagler (2015), every action teachers take, such as setting up the atmosphere, decorating the space, setting up the chairs, conversing with the kids, and processing their responses, has an effect on classroom management. In order to give students additional opportunities to learn, routines and regulations must be established (and then followed through with implementation, modification, and reinstatement). In addition to this, some studies have shown that clear classroom expectations are the cornerstone of effective classroom management (Sailor *et al.*, 2009; Wills *et al.*, 2019).

In the modern age, classroom management is also linked to students' whole development, including their emotive, cognitive, and social emotions as well as the development of their inner discipline (Vairamidou & Stravakou, 2019). Also, according to Cho *et al.* (2020), there are several schools of thought about classroom management (e.g. ecological, behavioral, and social-emotional). In order to successfully provide a safe and effective learning environment for kids' quality education, Adedigba & Sulaiman (2020) classified management of the classroom as a key ability a teacher needs. Furthermore, according to Adedigba & Sulaiman (2020), the success of teaching and learning will depend on how the teacher organizes his daily schedule, organizes his classroom, schedules daily lessons, and establishes expectations for student behavior.

Cooper & Scott (2017) stated that the physical setup, procedures, and schedules in the classroom all contribute to the learning dynamics; however, the connections between the teacher and students are also very important. Ahmed *et al.* (2018) analyzed how physical setups, psychological conditions, and social and cultural interactions among students all affect how teachers perceive and rate their students. Effective management of the classroom entails the development of strong teacher–student relationships as well as knowledge of instructional techniques and environmental changes which go beyond just maintaining a sense of order or control (Hepburn *et al.*, 2020). Chaplain (2016) suggested three parts to effective classroom management for teachers: planning and setting up the environment, social skills that are useful for fostering relationships between students and teachers, and the application of instructional strategies and the development of professional skills. Three different types of classroom environments were also described by Vairamidou & Stravakou (2019): physical environments, psychological environments, and pedagogical environments. Physical environments include classroom supplies, activity equipment, and physical space. Psychological environments explain relationships between students and other students, students and teachers, teachers and other teachers, and teachers and parents. The pedagogical environment affects the teacher's selection of skills, strategies, and teaching and learning methodologies.

7. Elements of Classroom Management

Given the previous review of the research, it is clear that classroom management is fragmented and complex because teachers must deal with students who have a wide range of backgrounds, interests, behaviors, and skills (Adedigba & Sulaiman, 2020). As such, classroom management can be viewed as all the steps teachers take inside the classroom to promote learning, as well as all the decisions they make regarding students' education (Díaz et al., 2018; Marzano et al., 2003), which overall include classroom arrangements, behavior management, teacher–student relationship, teaching–learning organization, and teachers–parent collaboration.

A classroom arrangement that mainly focuses on the physical classroom environment is one of the key aspects of classroom management. In particular, it refers to the areas of seating, layout, wall color, and ambiance in the classroom (Storey, 2023). According to Maxwell (2010), the physical aspects of the classroom play a significant role in either fostering or limiting learning, with components like noise and crowding serving as the primary causes of chaotic learning environments. Teachers should take into account the tactics on noise levels, crowding, visual complexity, and class design for effective classroom management (Franklin & Harrington, 2019). In addition, as universities and schools move away from the traditional classroom setting, educators are left to negotiate not only how to incorporate technology into pedagogical content knowledge but also how to arrange the physical space to maximize education and manage student behavior (Donnelly & Berry, 2019). Understanding how the classroom environment affects inclusion and engagement is crucial for designing schools that fulfill the needs of all students since it has a substantial impact on pupils (Storey, 2023). Nyabando & Evanshen (2022) learned the perceptions of the physical classroom environment by observing 2nd grade students. Participants generally agreed that the ideal physical learning environments in the classroom were those that were interesting, promoted active learning and social interaction, and had simple access to tools and materials.

Discipline in the classroom is the first topic that comes to teachers' minds when discussing classroom management. It is one of the main concerns for student teachers and is also widely acknowledged as a critical area requiring in-service education for experienced teachers' (Kyriacou, 2018). However, classroom discipline and behavior management are comparable but distinct, as the former entails proactive measures to stop misbehavior and the teacher's response to it (Martin & Sass, 2010).

Therefore, this topic centers on preventive management tactics, which include disciplinary actions comparable to behavior management. Both teacher well-being and academic progress depend on efficient behavior control techniques (Franklin & Harrington, 2019). To enforce discipline and promote students self-control along with independence, teachers must employ a variety of behavior management strategies (Kyriacou, 2018). According to Kyriacou (2018), the majority of student misbehavior is relatively trivial including talking excessively or out of turn and not paying attention to the teacher. Nevertheless, to a large extent, these issues can be minimized by skillful teaching in general as well as by creating routines and conventions for behavior that are adhered to. Many studies have confirmed that effective classroom management can significantly reduce disruptive behavior in the classroom. For instance, a recent study of primary schools in Manchester, Jamaica, revealed that the use of tokens in reducing disruptive behavior was quite beneficial based on the behavior of the kids following the intervention (Shakespeare *et al.*, 2018).

Teaching–learning, which is also called lesson management by some other scholars, is another factor of classroom management. To maintain order in the classroom and ensure that students are learning, it requires a broad range of management and organizational skills (Kyriacou, 2018). It primarily refers to the abilities required for organizing and managing the learning activities in order to maximize students' productive participation in the class to the greatest extent possible (Haydn, 2012; Kyriacou, 2018). In terms of the strategies of teaching–learning organization and management, it is found that there are some abilities associated with lesson management, such as monitoring students' progress, providing feedback, and managing students' time (Kyriacou, 2018). In fact, in order to adapt to the student-centered class of the 21st century and to train a new generation of human resources with the knowledge and skills required for the development of a new era, teachers need to explore new and better ways to educate their students and also to teach them the skills they need to become innovators themselves (Yagyaeva & Zokirov, 2019).

7.1. *Teacher–student relationship*

The social environment that pupils experience at school, which has an impact on their academic development, includes relationships between teachers and students (Martin & Collie, 2019), which is acknowledged as the center of learning and teaching (Brinkworth *et al.*, 2018), especially in the modern class in the 21st century. Kyriacou (2018) reported that a well-managed lesson combined with a rapport- and respect-based connection will go a long way toward reducing student misbehavior. One of the closest levels of influence on a student's development at school is the relationship between the teacher and the student, which can be linked to a student's basic psychological needs (Froiland *et al.*, 2019). This relationship results from an ongoing interaction between the teachers themselves and the individual student (Sabol & Pianta, 2012). A quantitative study by Thornberg *et al.* (2022) in compulsory schools in Sweden found that, even after modifying for sex, age, and prior student engagement, the strength of the teacher–student interaction still predicted student engagement one year later. It was discovered that a strong link between effective teaching methods and student accomplishment was a crucial and fundamental component of the school's excellent performance on tests (Nisar *et al.*, 2022). Additionally, according to a prior study, student relationships with teachers are linked to improved cognitive abilities, a sense of belonging at school, and decreased behavioral issues (Allen *et al.*, 2016; Cook *et al.*, 2018; Lei *et al.*, 2016; Roorda *et al.*, 2019; Vandenbroucke *et al.*, 2017). Therefore, it is vital how teachers connect with, manage, and develop relationships with their students (Thornberg *et al.*, 2022). Teacher–student relationship building and development can be achieved through intervention (Cook *et al.*, 2018).

7.2. Teacher–parent collaboration

Nowadays, a holistic approach to education is heavily advocated in order to follow the prevalent global trend of the twenty-first century and adapt the objectives of educational systems to a constantly shifting and globalized world. As a result, the roles of both teachers and parents have been redefined since adopting a comprehensive approach to educational needs (de Oliveira Lima & Kuusisto, 2019). Teachers and parents frequently have complex relationships while cooperating to support children's learning and development (Gisewhite *et al.*, 2019). In order for teacher–parent partnerships to completely achieve their objectives, a holistic approach to pedagogy is necessary (de Oliveira Lima & Kuusisto, 2019).

Numerous studies have shown that interactions between teachers and parents are beneficial for students' academic progress (Englund *et al.*, 2004; Jeynes, 2005). According to studies, a positive parent–teacher relationship and parental involvement in a child's education have a significant impact on a range of outcomes for pupils, including academic success (Grace & Gerdes, 2019). In children's education, parents are crucial partners (Myende & Nhlumayo, 2022), though sometimes the research findings vary. Teachers are the primary participants in education and teaching, and because of their professionalism, extensive training, and educational background, teachers are formidable advocates for improvements in education (de Oliveira Lima & Kuusisto, 2019). Thus, building and maintaining good teacher–parent relationships in the management of teaching and learning is a need and a concern.

8. Practice of Classroom Management and Students' Performance

Numerous studies have confirmed the impact of classroom management practices on students' performance. Studies of classroom management over the previous 50 years found that classroom management has a considerable impact on students' learning and academic performance, even more so than student aptitude (George *et al.*, 2017). The association between classroom management and student performance has been demonstrated in a variety of recent studies, including those that looked at single classroom management practices, classroom management packages, and specific classroom management programs like CW-FIT (Class-Wide function-related Intervention Team) (Speight *et al.*, 2020), CHAMPS (CHAMPS is an acronym for the six dimensions: Conversation, Help, Activity, Movement, Participation, and Signal) (Herman *et al.*, 2022), and GBG (Good Behavior Game).

Classroom management is related to students' behavior. Several experimental investigations have shown that programs intended to increase instructors' utilization of efficient classroom management techniques have improved students' behavior and other outcomes (Gilmour *et al.*, 2018; Korpershoek *et al.*, 2016). Gaias *et al.* (2019) conducted a study about classroom management on 103 teachers at nine middle schools in one Maryland school district; as a result, students in classrooms with low levels of classroom management, in contrast to those in classrooms with medium and high levels of classroom management, displayed greater disruptive behavior. Also, compared to students in high-level classroom management classes, students in medium-level classroom management classrooms displayed more intrusive behaviors. Another research conducted by George *et al.* (2017) confirmed that four classroom management strategies

— verbal instruction from teachers, collective punishments, instructional supervision, and delegation of authority — significantly impacted students' performance. In addition, the study revealed that students' interest in learning increases when teachers engage in learning supervision, show concern for their academic performance, and encourage them. In Kalu-Mba's (2019) study, a similar positive impact on students was reported; specifically, teachers' classroom management ability including skills, teacher–student ratio, classroom communication, classroom discipline, instructional materials, and infrastructural/facilities can improve students' learning outcomes. Practices of classroom management not only reported that universal teacher classroom management intervention for aggressive kids is selectively beneficial but also revealed that it has good effects on math performance, prosocial conduct, and emotional control, with an observable decrease in aggressiveness (Chuang *et al.*, 2020). It was clearly verified by researchers in a survey of 1817 students and 105 teachers in the USA, conducted for a classroom management project named Incredible Years Teacher Classroom Management Program.

Student engagement is also influenced by classroom management. Collier-Meek *et al.* (2020) conducted classroom observations and surveys with 10 teachers and 177 students. The results suggested that teachers implemented specific classroom management strategies at varying levels and that two of these strategies — referring to schedules or routines and offering praise for specific behaviors — were associated with increases in academic engagement while the other — error corrections — was associated with decreases. Research by Gage *et al.* (2018) examined how primary school teachers in Nigeria used discrete classroom management techniques. The data showed that student engagement was much lower in classrooms with less interaction and few instructional management strategies. As can be observed, classroom management is also closely linked to student participation.

Student motivation varies based on the strategies of classroom management practices. This view is verified by Adedigba & Sulaiman (2020). A study was conducted in the Nigerian state of Kwara with the goal of determining how instructors' classroom management techniques affected students' motivation and academic performance. It involved 250 teachers and all of the students enrolled in their classrooms, numbering a total of 1248 participants. The findings revealed that classroom management style significantly influenced both students' academic achievement and motivation to learn. Meanwhile, Kowalski and Froiland (2020) used a mixed research strategy to validate and investigate the impact of instructors' autonomy support and classroom management strategies on children' motivation to learn from a parental perspective. However, the findings also revealed that students in classrooms with behavioral reward systems had lower autonomous motivation to learn, which included less enjoyment of learning. Parents were also less positive about the controlling nature of the behavioral form system, which they felt reduced or undermined students' internal motivation through external rewards. The results of this study corroborate Froiland, Worrell & Oh's (2019) assertion that restricted environments foster anxiety and external motivation, whereas autonomy-supportive situations strengthen students' internal drive for learning.

Teacher–student relationships as one of the classroom management strategies have an important impact on students. Research has indicated that good teacher–student relationships and pedagogical caring contribute to students' academic success and increased student learning, and that teachers' responsiveness to students' needs boosts student performance and improves students' social connections (Sengul *et al.*, 2019). Several recent studies in China have also suggested such a view. Xu & Qi (2019) conducted a study of year 8 students in 762 schools in mainland China showing that teacher–student relationship and self-efficacy can significantly predict mathematics academic achievement and both have a positive effect, but perceptions of teacher–student relationship differed significantly between urban and rural areas, with the findings showing higher perceived teacher–student relationship data in urban areas. A meta-analysis conducted by Lei *et al.* (2022) showed that teacher–student relationships have a substantial positive impact on student achievement in China and that the extent of this impact varies by subject, with the greatest impact in English classes, followed by mathematics, language, and science. The impact of teacher–student relationships on student learning is well documented by scientific research (Krane & Klevan, 2019), although findings vary (Lei *et al.*, 2022).

9. Factors Influence the Practice of Classroom Management

Teachers' strategies for managing classrooms are influenced by a wide range of circumstances since classroom management is a complex process that depends on many factors. Based on the previous studies, these influences can generally be grouped into three categories: personal factors, organizational factors, and social factors.

In terms of personal factors that constrain teachers' classroom management, it mainly refers to teachers' beliefs, experience, knowledge, skills, and even emotional intelligence. A study in Switzerland revealed that years of prior teaching experience, the motivation for choosing teaching, teacher education, the teaching context, and the influence of school norms all contributed to the practice of teachers' classroom management (Girardet & Jean-Louis, 2018). Valente *et al.* (2019) reported that emotional intelligence is one of the factors that influence behavior management in a classroom; meanwhile, gender, academic formation, and service time of teachers are all related to teachers' emotional intelligence, which ultimately impacts the management of the classroom. Moreover, the lack of classroom management skills also surfaced as a factor, which contributed to disorganization in the classroom (Brown, 2019). Besides, teachers' beliefs could be also a factor influencing classroom practices (Santos & Miguel, 2019).

Teachers' adoption of efficient classroom management techniques can also be influenced by organizational factors like school leadership and peer support. A study conducted by Sebastian *et al.* (2019) confirmed that teachers' sense of belonging to their school and the organizational effect have an impact on classroom management practices and student outcomes. Additionally, to manage a class, it is also necessary to receive formal instruction, support, and training in dealing with student behavior and creating productive learning environments. Brown (2019) argued that leadership and management at the school level are crucial in creating the conditions for successful classroom management to prevail.

Social problem is another aspect influencing teachers' performance and practice.

Teacher–parent relationship, relationships among teachers, and teacher–student relationship can promote or impede teachers' practice. Based on the self-efficacy theory, imagine that parents who are engaged and supportive can help reinforce classroom expectations and promote positive behavior, while parents who are disengaged or critical can undermine classroom management efforts. Then, similar as the teacher–parent relationship, if teachers are in a conducive environment with good colleagues and a cooperative culture, not only will classroom management be facilitated but so will other aspects. Furthermore, social problems in the community impact the learner population and in turn impact the classroom management of teachers (Brown, 2019).

10. Conclusion

In conclusion, the responsibilities of a teacher go far beyond simply conveying curriculum results to their pupils; they also have to provide them with the resources they need to succeed socially and academically both inside and outside the classroom (Franklin & Harrington, 2019). Thus, in classroom management practice, teachers must also consider the overall impact on students. More importantly, the old perspective, with its emphasis on establishing rules and applying them to control learner behavior, is no longer fully applicable to today's classrooms. The new view focuses more on the learner's need for nurturing relationships and opportunities for self-regulation in classroom management (Kontor Owusu *et al.*, 2021). Although behavioral management is the first thing that comes to mind when teachers think of a well-managed class (Martin, 2021), in an age of hope for the development of well-rounded students, classroom management needs to take into account both their cognitive and non-cognitive development. Successful classroom management is associated with student engagement, which includes (1) behavioral engagement, such as overall concentration and participation; (2) affective or emotional engagement, such as motivation, enjoyment, and interpersonal connections with others in the classroom; and (3) cognitive engagement, such as students' attention, interest, and engagement with the content (Fredricks *et al.*, 2004). Additionally, there is a need for educational stakeholders to be aware of the factors that potentially facilitate and hinder classroom management — personal, social, and organizational — in order to effectively inform the direction of classroom management from a practical perspective.

References

Adedigba, O. & Sulaiman, R.F. (2020). Influence of teachers' classroom management style on pupils' motivation for learning and academic achievement in Kwara State. *International Journal of Educational Methodology*, 6(2), 471–480. https://doi.org/10.12973/ijem.6.2.471.

Ahmad, M. (2010). Application of classroom management strategies in public and private sector at school level in Pakistan. *International Journal of Library and Information Science*, 2(9), 177–183.

Ahmed, M., Ambreen, M., & Hussain, I. (2018). Gender differentials among teachers' classroom management strategies in Pakistani context. *Journal of Education and Educational Development, 5*(2), 178.

Akhter, R., & Akhter, S. (2021). The role of effective classroom management in successful teaching and learning. *International Journal of Education and Pedagogy, 25*(2), 100–115.

Allen, K., Kern, M.L., Vella-Brodrick, D., Hattie, J., & Waters, L. (2016). What schools need to know about fostering school belonging: A meta-analysis. *Educational Psychology Review, 30*(1), 1–34. https://doi.org/10.1007/s10648-016-9389-8.

Alter, P. & Haydon, T. (2017). Characteristics of effective classroom rules: A review of the literature. *Teacher Education and Special Education, 40*(2), 114–127.

Brinkworth, M.E., McIntyre, J., Juraschek, A.D., & Gehlbach, H. (2018). Teacher-student relationships: The positives and negatives of assessing both perspectives. *Journal of Applied Developmental Psychology, 55*, 24–38.

Brown, M.J. (2019). Teacher perceptions of factors influencing classroom management practices: A comparative case study of two public high schools in the Western Cape.

Chaplain, R. (2016). *Teaching Without Disruption in the Primary School: A Practical Approach to Managing Pupil Behaviour*. Routledge.

Cheng, Y.-H. & Chen, Y.-C. (2018). Enhancing classroom management through parental involvement by using social networking apps. *South African Journal of Education, 38*(Supplement 2), 1–14. https://doi.org/10.15700/saje.v38ns2a1427.

Cho, V., Mansfield, K.C., & Claughton, J. (2020). The past and future technology in classroom management and school discipline: A systematic review. *Teaching and Teacher Education, 90*, 103037. https://doi.org/10.1016/j.tate.2020.103037.

Chuang, C.C., Reinke, W.M., & Herman, K.C. (2020). Effects of a universal classroom management teacher training program on elementary children with aggressive behaviors. *School Psychology, 35*(2), 128–136. https://doi.org/10.1037/spq0000351.

Collier-Meek, M. A., Gage, N. A., & Sugai, G. (2020). Classroom management strategies and their effects on academic engagement. *Journal of Educational Psychology, 112*(4), 867–879. https://doi.org/10.1037/edu0000403

Collier-Meek, M. A., Sanetti, L. M. H., & Horner, R. H. (2020). Classroom management as a core practice for fostering academic competence and engagement. *Educational Psychology Review, 32*(4), 739–757.

Cook, C.R., Coco, S., Zhang, Y., Fiat, A.E., Duong, M.T., Renshaw, T.L., Long, A.C., & Frank, S. (2018). Cultivating positive teacher–student relationships: Preliminary evaluation of the establish–maintain–restore (EMR) method. *School Psychology Review, 47*(3), 226–243.

Cooper, J.T. & Scott, T.M. (2017). The keys to managing instruction and behavior: Considering high probability practices. *Teacher Education and Special Education*, *40*(2), 102–113.

Cooper, J.T., Gage, N.A., Alter, P.J., LaPolla, S., MacSuga-Gage, A.S., & Scott, T.M. (2018). Educators' self-reported training, use, and perceived effectiveness of evidence-based classroom management practices. *Preventing School Failure: Alternative Education for Children and Youth*, *62*(1), 13–24.

de Oliveira Lima, C.L. & Kuusisto, E. (2019). Parental engagement in children's learning: A holistic approach to teacher-parents' partnerships. *Pedagogy in Basic and Higher Education-Current Developments and Challenges*, 973–983.

Díaz, C., González, G., Jara-Ramírez, L.I., & Muñoz-Parra, J.A. (2018). Validation of a classroom management questionnaire for pre and Inservice teachers of English. *Revista Colombiana de Educación*, *75*, 263–286.

Donnelly, J. & Berry, L. (2019). Considering the environment: An expanded framework for teacher knowledge. *Journal of Learning Spaces*, *8*(1), 42–49.

Dwyer, J. (2013). The impact of classroom management strategies on student learning. *Journal of Educational Research and Practice*, *12*(3), 45–58.

Englund, M.M., Luckner, A.E., Whaley, G.J.L., & Egeland, B. (2004). Children's achievement in early elementary school: Longitudinal effects of parental involvement, expectations, and quality of assistance. *Journal of Educational Psychology*, *96*(4), 723–730. https://doi.org/10.1037/0022-0663.96.4.723.

Evertson, C.M. & Weinstein, C.S. (2006). Classroom management as a field of inquiry. *Handbook of Classroom Management: Research, Practice, and Contemporary Issues*, *3*(1), 16.

Franklin, H. & Harrington, I. (2019). A review into effective classroom management and strategies for student engagement: Teacher and student roles in today's classrooms. *Journal of Education and Training Studies*, *7*(12). https://doi.org/10.11114/jets.v7i12.4491.

Fredricks, J.A., Blumenfeld, P.C., & Paris, A.H. (2004). School engagement: Potential of the concept, state of the evidence. *Review of Educational Research*, *74*(1), 59–109.

Froiland, J.M., Worrell, F.C., & Oh, H. (2019). Teacher–student relationships, psychological need satisfaction, and happiness among diverse students. *Psychology in the Schools*, *56*(5), 856–870. https://doi.org/10.1002/pits.22245.

Gage, N. A., MacSuga-Gage, A. S., & Lewis, T. J. (2018). Discrete classroom management strategies and their impact on primary school student behavior. *Behavioral Disorders*, *43*(2), 137–149.

Gaias, L.M., Johnson, S.L., Bottiani, J.H., Debnam, K.J., & Bradshaw, C.P. (2019). Examining teachers' classroom management profiles: Incorporating a focus on culturally responsive practice. *Journal of School Psychology*, *76*, 124–139.

Girardet, C. & Jean-Louis, B. (2018). Factors influencing the evolution of vocational teachers' beliefs and practices related to classroom management during teacher education. *Australian Journal of Teacher Education (Online)*, *43*(4), 138–158.

Gisewhite, R.A., Jeanfreau, M.M., & Holden, C.L. (2019). A call for ecologically-based teacher-parent communication skills training in pre-service teacher education programmes. *Educational Review*, *73*(5), 597–616. https://doi.org/10.1080/00131911.2019.1666794.

Grace, M. & Gerdes, A.C. (2019). Parent-teacher relationships and parental involvement in education in Latino families. *Contemporary School Psychology*, *23*, 444–454.

Hằng, N., Nguyen, D., & Le, T. (2022). Effective classroom management strategies for promoting student learning. *Journal of Educational Leadership and Teaching*, *48*(3), 215–228. https://doi.org/10.1080/XXXX

Haydn, T. (2012). *Managing Pupil Behaviour: Improving the Classroom Atmosphere* (2nd edn.). Routledge. https://doi.org/10.4324/9780203134078.

Hepburn, L., Beamish, W., & Alston-Knox, C.L. (2020). Classroom management practices commonly used by secondary school teachers: Results from a Queensland survey. *The Australian Educational Researcher*, *48*(3), 485–505. https://doi.org/10.1007/s13384-020-00402-y.

Herman, J., Liu, X., & Wang, P. (2022). Exploring the link between classroom management and student academic achievement. *Educational Psychology Quarterly*, *38*(1), 15–30.

Hirsch, S.E., Randall, K., Bradshaw, C., & Lloyd, J.W. (2021). Professional learning and development in classroom management for novice teachers: A systematic review. *Education and Treatment of Children*, *44*(4), 291–307. https://doi.org/10.1007/s43494-021-00042-6.

Jeynes, W.H. (2005). A meta-analysis of the relation of parental involvement to urban elementary school student academic achievement. *Urban Education*, *40*(3), 237–269. https://doi.org/10.1177/0042085905274540.

Kalu-Mba, F. (2019). The impact of classroom management on students' learning outcomes. *International Journal of Education and Practice*, *7*(4), 123–135.

Kontor Owusu, M., Yusuf Dramanu, B., & Owusu Amponsah, M. (2021). Classroom management strategies and academic performance of junior high school students. *International Journal of Education and Management Engineering*, *11*(6), 29–38. https://doi.org/10.5815/ijeme.2021.06.04.

Korpershoek, H., Harms, T., & de Boer, H. (2016). The role of teacher–student relationships in promoting effective classroom management. *Educational Psychology Review*, *28*(3), 635–653.

Kowalski, M.J. & Froiland, J.M. (2020). Parent perceptions of elementary classroom management systems and their children's motivational and emotional responses. *Social Psychology of Education*, *23*(2), 433–448. https://doi.org/10.1007/s11218-020-09543-5.

Krane, D., & Klevan, T. (2019). The impact of teacher–student relationships on student learning. *Journal of Educational Psychology*, *111*(3), 505–517.

Kyriacou, C. (2018). *Essential Teaching Skills* (5th edn., Ebook). Oxford University Press-Children.

Lei, H., Cui, Y., & Chiu, M.M. (2016). Affective teacher-student relationships and students' externalizing behavior problems: A meta-analysis. *Frontiers in Psychology*, *7*, 1311. https://doi.org/10.3389/fpsyg.2016.01311.

Lei, H., Wang, X., Chiu, M.M., Du, M., & Xie, T. (2022). Teacher-student relationship and academic achievement in China: Evidence from a three-level meta-analysis. *School Psychology International*, *44*(1), 68–101. https://doi.org/10.1177/01430343221122453.

Lettink, J. (2020). The role of classroom management in fostering effective learning environments. *Teaching and Teacher Education Review*, *37*(4), 40–52.

Manangan, R. D. (2022). Classroom management and its relationship with student performance: A meta-analytic approach. *Journal of Education and Development*, *48*(2), 200–215.

Martin, A.J. & Collie, R.J. (2019). Teacher–student relationships and students' engagement in high school: Does the number of negative and positive relationships with teachers matter? *Journal of Educational Psychology*, *111*(5), 861.

Martin, L.D. (2021). Reconceptualizing classroom management in the ensemble: Considering culture, communication, and community. *Music Educators Journal*, *107*(4), 21–27. https://doi.org/10.1177/00274321211015180.

Martin, N.K. & Sass, D.A. (2010). Construct validation of the behavior and instructional management scale. *Teaching and Teacher Education*, *26*(5), 1124–1135.

Marzano, R.J., Marzano, J.S., & Pickering, D. (2003). *Classroom Management that Works: Research-Based Strategies for Every Teacher*. ASCD.

Maxwell, L. (2010). Chaos outside the home: The school environment. In *Chaos and Its Influence on Children's Development: An Ecological Perspective*. https://doi.org/10.1037/12057-006.

Mitchell, B.S., Hirn, R.G., & Lewis, T.J. (2017). Enhancing effective classroom management in schools: Structures for changing teacher behavior. *Teacher Education and Special Education*, *40*(2), 140–153.

Myende, P.E. & Nhlumayo, B.S. (2022). Enhancing parent–teacher collaboration in rural schools: Parents' voices and implications for schools. *International Journal of Leadership in Education*, *25*(3), 490–514.

Nisar, M., Khan, I.A., & Khan, F. (2022). Relationship between classroom management and students academic achievement. *Pakistan Journal of Distance and Online Learning*, *5*(1), 209–220.

Nwankwo, I.N., Matthew, M.O., & Christiana, M.A. (2019). Extent of teachers' classroom management practices for quality teaching and learning in secondary schools in ebonyi state. *International Journal of Humanities and Social Science, 9*(1), 106–113.

Nyabando, T. & Evanshen, P. (2022). Second grade students' perspectives of their classrooms' physical learning environment: A multiple case study. *Early Childhood Education Journal, 50*(5), 709–720.

Oliver, R.M., Wehby, J.H., & Reschly, D.J. (2011). Teacher classroom management practices: Effects on disruptive or aggressive student behavior. *Campbell Systematic Reviews, 7*(1), 1–55.

Oppong-Sekyere, D., Asante, K., & Nketiah, S. (2013). Enhancing student performance through supportive classroom environments. *International Journal of Education and Psychology, 9*(4), 120–135.

Roorda, D.L., Jak, S., Zee, M., Oort, F.J., Koomen, H.M.Y., & Dowdy, E. (2019). Affective teacher–student relationships and students' engagement and achievement: A meta-analytic update and test of the mediating role of engagement. *School Psychology Review, 46*(3), 239–261. https://doi.org/10.17105/spr-2017-0035.V46-3.

Sabol, T.J. & Pianta, R.C. (2012). Recent trends in research on teacher-child relationships. *Attachment & Human Development, 14*(3), 213–231. https://doi.org/10.1080/14616734.2012.672262.

Sailor, W., Dunlap, G., Sugai, G., & Horner, R. (2009). *Handbook of Positive Behavior Support*. Springer.

Santos, D. & Miguel, L. (2019). The relationship between teachers' beliefs, teachers' behaviors, and teachers' professional development: A literature review. *International Journal of Education and Practice, 7*(1), 10–18.

Sebastian, J., Herman, K.C., & Reinke, W.M. (2019). Do organizational conditions influence teacher implementation of effective classroom management practices: Findings from a randomized trial. *Journal of School Psychology, 72*, 134–149.

Sengul, S., Yalcin, S., & Bektas, O. (2019). Teacher-student relationships and their effect on students' academic success. *Educational Psychology International, 39*(5), 509–522.

Shakespeare, S., Peterkin, V.M., & Bourne, P.A. (2018). A token economy: An approach used for behavior modifications among disruptive primary school children. *MOJ Public Health, 7*(3), 89–99.

Sieberer-Nagler, K. (2015). Effective classroom-management & positive teaching. *English Language Teaching, 9*(1). https://doi.org/10.5539/elt.v9n1p163.

Storey, A. (2023). The physical classroom environment: A key to inclusion and student engagement. Retrieved from https://viurrspace.ca/handle/10613/26901.

Thornberg, R., Forsberg, C., Hammar Chiriac, E., & Bjereld, Y. (2022). Teacher–student relationship quality and student engagement: A sequential explanatory mixed-methods study. *Research Papers in Education, 37*(6), 840–859.

Vairamidou, A. & Stravakou, P. (2019). Classroom management in primary and secondary education literature review. *Journal of Education and Human Development, 8*(2). https://doi.org/10.15640/jehd.v8n2a7.

Valente, S., Monteiro, A.P., & Lourenço, A.A. (2019). The relationship between teachers' emotional intelligence and classroom discipline management. *Psychology in the Schools, 56*(5), 741–750.

Vandenbroucke, L., Spilt, J., Verschueren, K., Piccinin, C., & Baeyens, D. (2017). The classroom as a developmental context for cognitive development: A meta-analysis on the importance of teacher–student interactions for children's executive functions. *Review of Educational Research, 88*(1), 125–164. https://doi.org/10.3102/0034654317743200.

Wills, H.P., Caldarella, P., Mason, B.A., Lappin, A., & Anderson, D.H. (2019). Improving student behavior in middle schools: Results of a classroom management intervention. *Journal of Positive Behavior Interventions, 21*(4), 213–227.

Wiseman, D. & Hunt, G. (2008). *Best Practice in Motivation and Management in the Classroom.* Springfield, IL: Charles C. In: Thomas Publisher Ltd.

Xu, X., & Qi, X. (2019). The impact of teacher-student relationships and self-efficacy on mathematics achievement among Year 8 students in mainland China. *Asia Pacific Education Review, 20*(3), 415–424.

Yagyaeva, E. & Zokirov, A. (2019). The role of a teacher in teaching-learning process. *Scientific Bulletin of Namangan State University, 1*(3), 276–278.

Zakaria, F., Ismail, S., & Rahman, N. A. (2013). The importance of classroom management in achieving student success. *Journal of Educational Research and Practice, 14*(2), 30–40.

Chapter 11

Homework and Teachers' Responsibilities

Yang Yang Zhao[*], Muhammad Faizal Bin A. Ghani[†], and Kazi Enamul Hoque[‡]

Faculty of Education, University of Malaya, Kuala Lumpur, Malaysia

[*]adainmalaysia@gmail.com
[†]mdfaizal@um.edu.my
[‡]keh2009@um.edu.my

Abstract

Homework which is a part of students' daily school life plays a key role in teaching and learning. In this chapter, the definition and elements of homework and homework effectiveness and the factors that influence homework effectiveness are explored. Homework is generally considered to be a task assigned by the teacher outside the class. In practice, it is frequently necessary to consider the goal, type, number, and tactics of homework that prompt complementarity. Given that studies have shown inconsistent results relating to homework effectiveness, the factors that influence it have been analyzed in terms of homework characteristics, homework assignment by teacher, parental involvement, individual student, and cultural factors.

Keywords: Homework, homework practice, homework effectiveness, assignment, cultural factor.

1. Introduction

Homework is an important extension of classroom teaching and learning, which is essential to improving student performance. Many studies have verified that one of the most common and contentious instructional methods is homework, which has been shown to improve students' performance (Fan *et al.*, 2017; Núñez *et al.*, 2015; Valle *et al.*, 2019). Some scholars have reported that another component of formal education is homework, which means what is learned in school should be reinforced at home because this is the only way to help kids develop the abilities they need to study on a consistent basis. Thus, teachers should keep encouraging students to do their homework. Buyukalan & Altinay (2018) also mentioned that teachers' methods of encouraging homework outside of classrooms are tied to students' performance, which ultimately determines how well they learn. Because school is not the only place where education takes place, education is a lifelong process that can occur in many contexts. Chen (2022) acknowledged the significance of homework in terms of managing instruction and enhancing student learning. In China, most parents and teachers believe that homework is essential to the learning process (Jiang, 2018); meanwhile, the assignment of homework is common in Chinese primary and secondary schools. Moreover, according to a study, homework's purpose (Medwell & Wray, 2018), homework types (Medwell & Wray, 2018), homework frequency (Trautwein *et al.*, 2009), the amount of homework (Dolean & Lervag, 2021), and homework time (Songsirisak & Jitpranee, 2019) all impact students' performance. Thus, it is necessary and meaningful to take homework into account as a prediction factor to measure students' performance.

2. Definition and Elements of Homework

Cooper (1989) described homework in general terms as a task assigned by the teacher that needs to be completed outside of school. However, Cooper (2015) later amended the term "non-school time" to "non-instructional time." Corno (1996) considered homework as written/oral individual or group tasks that are assigned by educators to students to complete after school hours to prepare new learning materials or to reinforce, extend, practice, or complete new learning materials. Haq *et al.* (2020) and Chaya (2021) stated that homework is a task that children do beyond the regular school day, which is supposed to help them understand the learning material. Hafezi & Etemadinia (2022) also reported that "Homework is an activity that the student does outside of school hours." Hu (2019) agreed that homework is an output-bearing, dedicated learning activity for students, an activity in which they self-construct a good view of knowledge, competence, character, and learning, and a cultural process by which they identify with their role as learners. When it comes to homework practice, Hu (2019) argued that when it comes to homework practice, assignments should cover the following essential topics: the activity's basic goals, a variety of topics covered, time and place specificity, flexibility, a diversity of teachers, and the subjectivity of the students involved.

Despite being universally accepted as an important part of a student's everyday life, homework has changed and grown more complicated over time (Hernandez, 2020). Homework assignments also vary depending on the teacher, subject, and school. However, there are some basic elements of homework that need to be considered in practice generally. Salend & Schliff (1988) provided guidelines for the practice of homework in eight dimensions based on the purpose and value of homework:

- **Amount of homework:** Teachers should give an appropriate amount of homework according to the age and educational background of the student.
- **Content of homework assignments:** Homework topic will undoubtedly be the emphasis of high-quality assignments. The content of the assignment should take into account the diversity of the students and should contribute to the mastery of the content previously taught in class.
- **Homework type:** The type of homework should be chosen based on the purpose of the homework. Teachers assign drill assignments to provide chances to practice material learned in class. If the homework aims to prepare the student for the next class session, the assignment framework should include the information required for good class performance.
- **Clear explanations of homework:** When giving homework, teachers should explain the assignment clearly to ensure that students understand what the homework assignment is.

- **Teachers' support for homework assignments:** Teachers should conduct a useful analysis of homework assignments to determine the areas in which students require assistance, such as organizing materials and using instruments.
- **Encourage students to do their homework well:** Some students need to be inspired to complete their homework. Teachers can motivate these students by making homework creative and fun. Students can also be motivated to complete their homework through praise, rewards, etc.
- **Assessment of homework:** Teachers' evaluations, comments, and grading will motivate students to complete assignments; meanwhile, immediate feedback on homework assignments is also significant.
- **Parental involvement:** Parents have an important role in monitoring and helping with homework. Teachers and parents should exchange homework information regularly.

Nowadays, the following factors are important in terms of the discussion on homework:

Homework's purpose: Bas *et al.* (2017) concluded two purposes of homework: instructional purpose and non-instructional purpose. Instructional purpose includes skill exercises, teaching new materials, and creating opportunities for students to apply and integrate new concepts and skills to build projects and use new resources. The non-instructional goals of homework include improving home–school connections; improving communication among parents, teachers, and students; encouraging learning skills and time management; and fostering accountability in children. Keane & Heinz (2019) argued that homework should have a clear objective and provide opportunities for review, continuation, and extension of learning.

Homework quantity: Assigning a reasonable amount of homework to elementary school students is at the center of the homework debate (Hoeke, 2017). Homework quantity is defined as the frequency of assignments and the amount of time it takes students to complete the assignments, in other words, how long it will likely take to complete the homework (Bedford, 2014). According to Cooper *et al.* (2006), when families and students are assigned an excessive amount of homework, the stress they feel leads to counterproductive homework. Besides, the researchers observed a negative association between the time spent on homework and outcomes.

Homework type: Jones (2021) and Rosário *et al*. (2015) argued that there were four main types of homework: practice, preparation, extension, and creativity. According to Jiang (2018), there are six general types of assignments that teachers typically use in their classrooms: homework for students to make up or revise what they missed in class; homework on a richer basis to assess, grade, and read; homework for repetition or exercise; homework preparation for the next lesson; authentic homework (i.e. interviews, participation in off-campus activities).

Strategies for homework implementation: In order to increase the effectiveness of homework or improve homework performance, previous researchers mentioned homework implementation strategies involved in all stages of the homework process. Cooper (1989) proposed that teachers should consider a particular day to give homework to prevent overload. Teachers also ought to be mindful of the time it takes to finish the homework and should ensure that students know how to do it. Also, timely feedback from the teacher is key to completing the homework. Brookhart (2008) argued that it was essential for teachers to check, comment on, and return homework to the student in a timely for homework effectiveness. Also, parents are expected to help students with homework assignments. Some teachers send parents a resource list to help them better support their students with homework, which includes explanations of math topics and how to solve problems. Some teachers also encouraged students to seek parental help when they were having difficulty with the homework (Bedford, 2014).

3. Effectiveness of Homework

There has been ongoing discussion for more than a century regarding the value of homework and how it affects academic performance (Dolean & Lervag, 2021). Previous studies have shown that students can get benefits from homework assignments. It is widely recognized that students' performance is strongly related to homework assignments. Homework can be used to assess students' academic progress, foster autonomous study habits, accelerate classroom learning, and increase students' enthusiasm to learn (Muijs & Reynolds, 2017). Dolean & Lervag (2021) mentioned that homework allows students to extend their learning time outside of the classroom, thereby improving their performance. Ramdass & Zimmerman (2011) pointed out that students' motivation, cognition, and metacognitive abilities in language acquisition are all enhanced by homework. Students' motivation for studying, self-control, and academic achievement can all be predicted by teachers based on their homework (Núñez et al., 2014). Furthermore, a study conducted in Thailand by Songsirisak & Jitpranee (2019) showed that homework has an impact on students' achievement, emotions, motivation, and free time management, as well as their capacity for managing homework. Epstein & Van Voorhis (2010) reported that homework can foster attitudes that promote positive learning behaviors, self-reliance, and self-discipline.

Numerous previous studies have shown the positive impact of homework on student performance and achievement. Studies comparing students who were given homework with those who were not have shown that completing homework benefited academic performance (Cooper, 2015; Fan et al., 2017). Rosário et al. (2018) conducted research which showed that students' commitment to homework was positively related to their academic performance. Homework gave students the chance to enhance their skills and performance and the goal of improving their academic achievements (Songsirisak & Jitpranee, 2019). Buyukalan & Altinay (2018) reviewed that homework reinforced what was learned in the school, helped students develop good study habits, made students lifelong learners, increased learner responsibility, and improved students' social, emotional, and academic skills. And it has been confirmed that those students who do homework regularly have better study skills, a more positive attitude, and better habits. According to Ramdass & Zimmerman (2011), improving students' self-regulation through homework can increase their motivation, cognition, and thinking abilities in language learning. Also, homework helps kids become more motivated and responsible for their education based on Songsirisak & Jitpranee's (2019) study.

However, there is controversy about the effectiveness of homework despite the many benefits of homework. Additionally, it appears that scientific study after scientific study is consistently proving the doubts around the effectiveness of homework. According to Sullivan & Sequeira (1996), the important issue is the manner in which teachers assign assignments. Maloney et al. (2015) recognized that the quantity of homework, which is a major cause of stress for students, is a significant factor as, in addition to taking away from their free time and lowering the quality of other activities, homework has a detrimental impact on how kids and their parents engage with school. This notion is exactly what China's ever-increasing strategy of repeatedly lowering loads has ingrained in the homework component in recent years. In China, homework is a topic that has been addressed in all the basic education policies launched since the turn of the century, including 2021 new double reduction policy, which focused on the issue of homework. Meanwhile, the research on homework has also increasingly attracted the attention of Chinese scholars, and a new round of heated debate on homework has been sparked, especially after the new homework reduction policies released in 2018 and 2021. In an ongoing 11-year study on homework, 2,433 university students were asked to rate the effectiveness of homework in 12 courses. The findings revealed that the percentage of students who said they did not benefit from homework rose from 14% in 2008 to 55% in 2017 (Glass & Kang, 2022). Chaya (2021) agreed that in most instances, the data gathered did not support the claim that assigning homework helps students' academic performance. An empirical study in the USA recently suggested that homework had little impact on raising academic achievement (Stevenson, 2021). Students' academic performance and some previous studies have shown that homework has a negligible effect on children's well-being in grades 3–6 in terms of sleep, emotional health, and parent–child relationships (Holland *et al.*, 2021). Other studies have shown that homework can cause tension in families and is also a source of frustration and conflict in families (Clarke, 2022). In the same study, Clarke (2022) also found that few kids showed interest or enthusiasm for their assignments. Homework is also frequently viewed as a source of stress by both students and parents (Moè *et al.*, 2020).

4. Factors Influencing Homework Effectiveness

According to Cooper (1989), the completion of homework and the impact of homework on students are influenced by the following main factors: the characteristics of the assignment itself such as frequency and length of homework; initial classroom factors such as the way homework is proposed; classroom follow-up such as feedback on homework; home community factors such as parental help; and other external factors such as student gender and parental education. These influences were later expanded by Trautwein *et al.* (2006), with the main factors being the quality of homework, the classroom learning environment, student motivation, and student behavior such as personal effort. It has also been shown that the strength of the relationship between homework and student learning outcomes is influenced by the following factors: student age, time spent on homework, time management, motivation, cognitive engagement, quality of parental involvement, and the quality of homework set by the teacher (Rodríguez *et al.*, 2019). A study conducted by Xu & Corno (2022) in China showed that homework frequency, time, interest, and homework complication positively predicted students' mathematics achievement.

The effectiveness of the homework depends on the assignment. Homework qualities, including duration, frequency, quality, interest, and favorability, are a group of variables that have so far earned the greatest attention in the field (Fan *et al.*, 2017; Rosário *et al.*, 2018; Xu, 2022). In Cooper's model, the amount of homework or time spent on homework is considered an important factor in homework completion and academic achievement (Xu, 2022). The amount of homework considerably affected writing skills in a comparative study, but only the group that received the proper quantity of assignments for writing practice continued to have this impact after 4 months (Dolean & Lervag, 2021).

Trautwein *et al.* (2006) noted that the quality of homework is also an important influencing factor, and recent studies have confirmed this view. The study concluded that there was a significant correlation between the quality of homework, students' homework performance, and further academic achievement (Rosário *et al.*, 2018; Xu, 2016). In addition to the influence of the above-mentioned homework characteristics, research has also shown that homework interests and preferences or attitudes have a significant impact on academic performance and academic achievement (Rosário *et al.*, 2018; Suárez *et al.*, 2019; Xu, 2022). Dikmen & Bahadir (2021) reported that an effective homework assignment should be feasible, relevant to the course content, planned, interpretive, and tailored to the student's ability. Recent research has shown that the way homework is assigned also has a direct impact on students' attitudes to homework and the effectiveness of homework. Wiggins & van der Hoff (2021) conducted a survey of university students on online homework systems and the results showed that the vast majority of students agreed that online homework was worth doing, with less than 2% saying it was a waste of time. The survey also revealed that most mainstream students found online homework to be very beneficial to their studies. Songsirisak & Jitpranee (2019) confirmed that one of the most effective resources for knowledge about homework and student learning is the Internet. Magalhães *et al.* (2020) systematically reviewed the literature to compare online homework and traditional homework, aiming to understand which homework format contributed most to student performance. The review revealed comprehensive findings, with half of the studies showing no correlation between student performance and the format of homework delivery, eight of the nine studies supporting the advantages of online homework delivery over traditional homework delivery, and one study confirming the superiority of traditional homework delivery.

In addition to the impact of the above-mentioned characteristics of homework and the way it is assigned, differentiated homework has recently been a hot topic of discussion. In China, for example, tiered homework has been a focus of research in practice and in the field of education, driven by the continuous policy of reducing the burden and the reform toward student-centered classroom teaching. Keane & Heinz (2019) conducted a study to investigate the impact of differentiated homework on student engagement. In their study, in order to give students a better balance between out-of-school activities and homework, teachers only assigned homework once a week and students were given a choice of three tasks ranging from low to high difficulty, but the difficulty of the task was not directly indicated to the students. The results of the study showed that not only did the students' attitudes toward homework change significantly but the completion rate of homework increased to almost 100%.

Furthermore, teachers' implementation strategy has a direct impact on the completion of assignments, including timely corrections and feedback. According to Keane & Heinz (2019), timely correction and meaningful feedback on assignments lead to better engagement in learning, and students' motivation to complete assignments is better reinforced when the teacher emphasizes the value and importance of the assignment. Additionally, the type of homework, how it is graded, and whether or not the assignment's subject matter corresponds with what is taught in class all have an impact on how well students perform on their homework (Zhou *et al.*, 2020). In short, the factors that influence the effectiveness of homework include the teacher's design of the assignment (frequency, length, type, quality), the homework follow-up strategies (evaluation, feedback), individual student factors (gender, age, effort, attitude), parental involvement, and the objective environment (classroom learning environment, home learning environment).

The importance and necessity of parental involvement in student learning are widely recognized, but research shows inconsistent effects of parental involvement on student learning outcomes. Núñez et al. (2015) suggested that parental help with homework is effective in shaping students' study habits, developing positive attitudes toward learning, and reinforcing what they have learned in class, and that parental support makes students feel loved and cared for, especially when they are struggling. Parental involvement in homework is more likely to be necessary and important for low-achieving students and students who are socioeconomically disadvantaged according to a study by Li & Hamlin (2019), which demonstrates a significant and positive correlation between parental support for homework and student achievement. The study also showed that parents' daily help and support with homework had a small compensatory effect on students in grades 1–3. A Chinese study also demonstrated that parental involvement in homework had a small effect on kids' performance in mathematics and did not cause them to be dissatisfied with their assignments (Zhou et al., 2020). However, a recent study in the US investigating the impact of parental involvement in homework in primary schools showed that parents' affective involvement in homework was negative compared to involvement in activities, especially among parents with low self-efficacy. This study further showed that the more negative the parents' affective involvement in homework, the lower the students' motivation and achievement in mathematics (Wu et al., 2022).

Individual student factors are also an important aspect of the effectiveness of homework. According to Rodríguez et al. (2019), students' prior academic performance has a direct impact on students' engagement in homework, and students' intrinsic motivation has a mediator effect on engagement performance. Another study of Chinese students also showed that compared to low academic achievers, high academic achievers are better at organizing their environment, managing time, dealing with distractions, focusing on motivation, and controlling their emotions when it comes to homework behavior (Yang & Tu, 2020). Additionally, gender is one of the influencing factors, although the research field has shown mixed results on this idea. Some studies have revealed that girls are more active and positive in their homework behaviors compared to boys (Xu, 2006). However, Oubrayrie-Roussel & Safont-Mottay (2011) reported the absence of any association between gender and the performance of homework self-regulatory behaviors.

Besides the above-mentioned influence factors, culture should also be considered when discussing students' homework. Despite having more homework than American students, previous research comparing Chinese and American students revealed that Chinese students are more motivated and have a more positive attitude toward homework (Chen & Stevenson, 1989). The analysis concluded that teachers consider homework to be very important in the context of traditional Chinese culture and the real social pressure to progress to higher education (Chen & Stevenson, 1989), and parents also want to adopt more learning strategies to improve their child's academic performance (Hong et al., 2011), which include homework. As a result, teachers and parents' expectations have a significant influence on students' attitudes toward homework, and students are more likely to spend more time on and put more effort into homework.

5. Conclusion

In order to improve student performance, homework is typically considered a critical addition to classroom teaching and learning. In practice, some important factors including homework purpose, homework type, quantity of homework, and strategies to facilitate students' competition are necessary to consider. However, the effectiveness of homework is controversial. Some studies support the positive effect on students' learning, while many other results reveal some negative influence. The differences in the results may be caused by factors including teachers, parents, individual students, and even culture.

Reference

Bas, G., Senturk, C., & Cigerci, F.M. (2017). Homework and academic achievement: A meta-analytic review of research. *Issues in Educational Research*, 27(1), 31–50.

Bedford, P.D. (2014). *Teachers' Beliefs and Practices Regarding Homework: An Examination of the Cognitive Domain Embedded in Third Grade Mathematics Homework*. The University of Wisconsin-Milwaukee.

Brookhart, S.M. (2008). Feedback that fits. In M. Scherer (ed.), *Engaging the Whole Child: Reflections on Best Practices in Learning, Teaching, and Leadership* (Vol. 65, No. 4, pp. 54–59), ASCD.

Buyukalan, S.F. & Altinay, Y.B. (2018). Views of primary teachers about homework (a qualitative analysis). *Journal of Education and Training Studies*, *6*(9). https://doi.org/10.11114/jets.v6i9.3382.

Chaya, H. (2021). Effects of homework on student academic achievement: A descriptive study. *Journal of Advances in Education and Philosophy*, *5*(9), 294–301.

Chen, C. & Stevenson, H.W. (1989). Homework: A cross-cultural examination. *Child Development*, *60*(3), 551–561.

Chen, J. (2022). The reform of school education and teaching under the "double reduction" policy. *Scientific and Social Research*, *4*(2), 42–45.

Clarke, C. (2022). Investigating homework as a family practice in Canada: The capital needed. *Education 3–13*, *50*(6), 789–802.

Cooper, H. (1989). Synthesis of research on homework. *Educational Leadership*, *47*(3), 85–91.

Cooper, H., Robinson, J.C., & Patall, E.A. (2006). Does homework improve academic achievement? A synthesis of research, 1987–2003. *Review of Educational Research*, *76*(1), 1–62.

Cooper, H.M. (2015). *The Battle Over Homework: Common Ground for Administrators, Teachers, and Parents*. Simon and Schuster.

Corno, L. (1996). Homework is a complicated thing. *Educational Researcher*, *25*(8), 27–30.

Dikmen, M. & Bahadir, F. (2021). University students' views on the effectiveness of learning through homework. *International Online Journal of Educational Sciences*, *13*(3), 689–704.

Dolean, D.D. & Lervag, A. (2021). Variations of homework amount assigned in elementary school can impact academic achievement. *The Journal of Experimental Education*, *90*(2), 280–296. https://doi.org/10.1080/00220973.2020.1861422.

Epstein, J.L. & Van Voorhis, F.L. (2010). More than minutes: Teachers' roles in designing homework. *Educational Psychologist*, *36*(3), 181–193. https://doi.org/10.1207/s15326985ep3603_4.

Fan, H., Xu, J., Cai, Z., He, J., & Fan, X. (2017). Homework and students' achievement in math and science: A 30-year meta-analysis, 1986–2015. *Educational Research Review*, *20*, 35–54. https://doi.org/10.1016/j.edurev.2016.11.003.

Glass, A.L. & Kang, M. (2022). Fewer students are benefiting from doing their homework: An eleven-year study. *Educational Psychology*, *42*(2), 185–199.

Hafezi, A. & Etemadinia, S. (2022). Investigating the relationship between homework and academic achievement in elementary students. *Journal of Social, Humanity, and Education*, *2*(3), 185–195.

Haq, M., Shakil, A., & Din, M. (2020). Impact of homework on the student academic performance at secondary school level. *Global Social Sciences Review*, *1*, 586–595.

Hernandez, M. (2020). *Homework Implications Across Diverse Student Populations* Sacramento: California State University.

Hoeke, C. (2017). *Homework Practices: Teacher and Parent Perceptions of Efficacy and Purpose.* East Tennessee State University.

Holland, M., Courtney, M., Vergara, J., McIntyre, D., Nix, S., Marion, A., & Shergill, G. (2021). Homework and children in grades 3–6: Purpose, policy and non-academic impact. *Child & Youth Care Forum, 50*(2), 21. https://doi.org/10.1007/s10566-021-09602-8.

Hong, E., Wan, M., & Peng, Y. (2011). Discrepancies between students' and teachers' perceptions of homework. *Journal of Advanced Academics, 22*(2), 280–308.

Hu, Y. (2019). Outline discussions on the reconstruction of the concept of "student work" in basic education. *Educational Science Research,* (10), 47–52. https://doi.org/CNKI:SUN:JYKY.0.2019-10-011.

Jiang, Z. (2018). Homework! What, Why, How?: Primary school English teachers' attitudes towards and use of homework in China. Stockholms: Department of Language Education, Stockholms Universitet.

Keane, G. & Heinz, M. (2019). Differentiated homework: Impact on student engagement. *Journal of Practitioner Research, 4*(2), 1.

Li, A. & Hamlin, D. (2019). Is daily parental help with homework helpful? Reanalyzing national data using a propensity score–based approach. *Sociology of Education, 92*(4), 367–385.

Magalhães, P., Ferreira, D., Cunha, J., & Rosário, P. (2020). Online vs traditional homework: A systematic review on the benefits to students' performance. *Computers & Education, 152.* https://doi.org/10.1016/j.compedu.2020.103869.

Maloney, E.A., Ramirez, G., Gunderson, E.A., Levine, S.C., & Beilock, S.L. (2015). Intergenerational effects of parents' math anxiety on children's math achievement and anxiety. *Psychological Science, 26*(9), 1480–1488. https://doi.org/10.1177/0956797615592630.

Medwell, J. & Wray, D. (2018). Primary homework in England: The beliefs and practices of teachers in primary schools. *Education 3–13, 47*(2), 191–204. https://doi.org/10.1080/03004279.2017.1421999.

Moè, A., Katz, I., Cohen, R., & Alesi, M. (2020). Reducing homework stress by increasing adoption of need-supportive practices: Effects of an intervention with parents. *Learning and Individual Differences, 82,* 101921.

Muijs, D. & Reynolds, D. (2017). *Effective Teaching: Evidence and Practice.* Sage.

Núñez, J.C., Suárez, N., Rosário, P., Vallejo, G., Cerezo, R., & Valle, A. (2014). Teachers' feedback on homework, homework-related behaviors, and academic achievement. *The Journal of Educational Research, 108*(3), 204–216. https://doi.org/10.1080/00220671.2013.878298.

Núñez, J.C., Suárez, N., Rosário, P., Vallejo, G., Valle, A., & Epstein, J.L. (2015). Relationships between perceived parental involvement in homework, student homework behaviors, and academic achievement: Differences among elementary, junior high, and high school students. *Metacognition and Learning, 10*(3), 375–406. https://doi.org/10.1007/s11409-015-9135-5.

Oubrayrie-Roussel, N. & Safont-Mottay, C. (2011). Adolescent homework management strategies and perceptions of parental involvement. *International Journal About Parents in Education, 5*(2), 78–85.

Ramdass, D. & Zimmerman, B.J. (2011). Developing self-regulation skills: The important role of homework. *Journal of Advanced Academics, 22*(2), 194–218.

Rodríguez, S., Núñez, J.C., Valle, A., Freire, C., Ferradás, M.D.M., & Rodríguez-Llorente, C. (2019). Relationship between students' prior academic achievement and homework behavioral engagement: The mediating/moderating role of learning motivation. *Frontiers in Psychology, 10*, 1047.

Rosário, P., Carlos Núñez, J., Vallejo, G., Nunes, T., Cunha, J., Fuentes, S., & Valle, A. (2018). Homework purposes, homework behaviors, and academic achievement. Examining the mediating role of students' perceived homework quality. *Contemporary Educational Psychology, 53*, 168–180. https://doi.org/10.1016/j.cedpsych.2018.04.001.

Rosário, P., Núñez, J.C., Vallejo, G., Cunha, J., Nunes, T., Mourão, R., & Pinto, R. (2015). Does homework design matter? The role of homework's purpose in student mathematics achievement. *Contemporary Educational Psychology, 43*, 10–24.

Salend, S.J. & Schliff, J. (1988). The many dimensions of homework. *Academic Therapy, 23*(4), 397–403.

Songsirisak, P. & Jitpranee, J. (2019). Impact of homework assignment on students' learning. *Journal of Education Naresuan University, 21*(2), 1–19.

Stevenson, M.N. (2021). *Homework and Academic Achievement: A Meta-analysis Examining Impact*. University of Dayton.

Suárez, N., Regueiro, B., Estévez, I., del Mar Ferradás, M., Guisande, M.A., & Rodríguez, S. (2019). Individual precursors of student homework behavioral engagement: The role of intrinsic motivation, perceived homework utility and homework attitude. *Frontiers in Psychology, 10*, 941.

Sullivan, M.H. & Sequeira, P.V. (1996). The impact of purposeful homework on learning. *The Clearing House, 69*(6), 346–348.

Trautwein, U., Schnyder, I., Niggli, A., Neumann, M., & Lüdtke, O. (2009). Chameleon effects in homework research: The homework–achievement association depends on the measures used and the level of analysis chosen. *Contemporary Educational Psychology, 34*(1), 77–88.

Valle, A., Pineiro, I., Rodriguez, S., Regueiro, B., Freire, C., & Rosario, P. (2019). Time spent and time management in homework in elementary school students: A person-centered approach. *Psicothema, 31*(4), 422–428. https://doi.org/10.7334/psicothema2019.191.

Wiggins, H. & van der Hoff, Q. (2021). Using an online homework system for fostering self-directed learning. *International Journal of Technology in Education and Science*, *5*(3), 323–335.

Wu, J., Barger, M.M., Oh, D., & Pomerantz, E.M. (2022). Parents' daily involvement in children's math homework and activities during early elementary school. *Child Development*, *93*(5), 1347–1364.

Xu, J. (2006). Gender and homework management reported by high school students. *Educational Psychology*, *26*(1), 73–91.

Xu, J. (2016). A study of the validity and reliability of the teacher homework involvement scale: A psychometric evaluation. *Measurement*, *93*, 102–107. https://doi.org/10.1016/j.measurement.2016.07.012.

Xu, J. (2023). A latent profile analysis of homework time, frequency, quality, interest, and favorability: Implications for homework effort, completion, and math achievement. *European Journal of Psychology of Education*, *38*, 751–775. https://doi.org/10.1007/s10212-022-00627-8.

Xu, J. & Corno, L. (2022). Extending a model of homework: A multilevel analysis with Chinese middle school students. *Metacognition and Learning*, *17*(2), 531–563.

Yang, F. & Tu, M. (2020). Self-regulation of homework behaviour: Relating grade, gender, and achievement to homework management. *Educational Psychology*, *40*(4), 392–408.

Zhou, S., Zhou, W., & Traynor, A. (2020). Parent and teacher homework involvement and their associations with students' homework disaffection and mathematics achievement. *Learning and Individual Differences*, *77*, 101780.

Index

B
behavior management, 156

C
classroom climate, 106
classroom follow-up, 179
classroom management, 152
cognitive and non-cognitive development, 165
collective bargaining, 21, 27
collective bargaining agreement, 24
collective bargaining process, 27
communication channels, 12
competency-based assessment, 50
competitive environment, 119
constructivist theory, 39
continuous learning, 124
continuous professional development, 48
counterproductive homework, 176
critical race theory, 86
cultural process, 175
curiosity theory, 119
curriculum decision-making, 68
curriculum management, 62

D
differentiated homework, 181
distributive justice, 86
dual education system, 48
dynamic leadership, 68

E
education 2030 framework, 36
educational equity, 86
emotional agility, 131
emotional intelligence, 128
emotional stability, 128
empirical research, 2
employability skills, 36, 46
employee evaluation, 100
equality and fairness, 26
equity and inclusivity, 93
extrinsic motivation, 116

F
flexibility for employees, 130
formative assessment, 42
Fourth Industrial Revolution, 50
fundamental framework, 38
future-focused curriculum, 39

G
goal setting, 105

H
human capital development, 44

I
inclusive management, 85
industrial relations principles, 21
innovation and efficiency, 27
institutional context, 39
instructional management, 162
interactive learning, 41
intrinsic motivation, 116

J
job performance, 116

L
labor union, 20
leadership succession, 2
legal recognition, 29

M
Maslow's hierarchy of needs, 117
metacognitive abilities, 178
moral leadership, 89
motivation theory, 107
multicultural education, 88
multiculturalism, 87

N
non-instructional goals, 176
non-monetary incentives, 144

O
organizational stability, 13

P
paid leave, 144
parental involvement, 176, 180
parents' affective involvement, 182
performance appraisal, 108
performance feedback, 103
personal growth, 118
power relationships, 5
principal burnout, 9
principal rotation, 3
principal succession, 2
principal turnover, 3
PRISMA method, 135
professional development, 9, 120

Q
qualitative data analysis, 5

R
resistance to change, 63
responsible leadership, 129
revolving door principalship, 2
right-to-work laws, 25

S
school community, 90
school culture, 5
school development, 2
school effectiveness, 10
school management, 144
school sustainability, 2
self-determination theory, 118
social inclusion, 47
social justice, 84
social learning theory, 41
societal context, 39
sociocultural learning theory, 41
socioeconomic status, 14
standardized accountability, 2
student achievement, 5
student motivation, 180
student performance, 174
students' self-regulation, 178
summative assessment, 42
supportive learning environment, 153
Sustainable Development Goals, 36

T
teacher attrition, 136
teacher competency, 40
teacher development, 109
teacher effectiveness, 108
teacher morale, 5
teacher retention, 12
teacher trust, 5
teacher turnover, 5, 136
transformational leadership, 89
trust and recognition, 135

U
unionization in education, 27
unionized teachers, 20

V
visionary leadership, 68

W
work–life balance, 123

www.ingramcontent.com/pod-product-compliance
Lightning Source LLC
Chambersburg PA
CBHW050447020625
27513CB00004B/172